Internet Through the Year

Primary

Editor
Sara Connolly

Editorial Project Manager
Elizabeth Morris, Ph.D.

Editor-in-Chief
Sharon Coan, M.S. Ed.

Illustrator
Howard Chaney

Cover Artist
Denise Bauer

Art Coordinator
Kevin Barnes

Imaging
Alfred Lau
Rosa C. See

Product Manager
Phil Garcia

Publishers
Rachelle Cracchiolo, M.S. Ed.
Mary Dupuy Smith, M.S. Ed.

Author
Mary Zinn-Beiting, M.Ed.

Teacher Created Materials, Inc.
6421 Industry Way
Westminster, CA 92683
www.teachercreated.com
ISBN-0-7439-3823-2
©2002 Teacher Created Materials, Inc.
Made in U.S.A.

The classroom teacher may reproduce copies of materials in this book for classroom use only. The reproduction of any part for an entire school or school system is strictly prohibited. No part of this publication may be transmitted, stored, or recorded in any form without written permission from the publisher.

Table of Contents

Introduction 3
Apple Theme 4
Banana Theme 19
Bat Theme 33
Bubble Theme 46
Chameleon Theme 57
Cloud Theme 73
Dolphin Theme. 88
Earth Theme 99
Egg Theme 112
Flag Theme 123
Frog Theme 133
Gingerbread Theme 147
Hat Theme 164
Heart Theme 176
Kite Theme 189
Moon Theme 203
Pancake Theme 212
Penguin Theme. 223
Pig Theme 237
Pizza Theme 252
Polar Bear Theme 263
Popcorn Theme. 274
Potato Theme 287
Pumpkin Theme 299
Rain Theme 311
Rainbow Theme 321
Rock Theme 330
Snow Theme. 343
Spider Theme 352
Star Theme 362
Tooth Theme 371
Turkey Theme 391

Introduction

Take the day off from planning! With *Internet Activities Through the Year*, an entire day's lessons are at your fingertips. The thirty-two themes included in this book can be used during holidays, incorporated into existing units, or simply be one-day mini units. Have a "Kite Theme" day in the fall or spring when students can go outside and fly their own creations. Incorporate "Moon Theme" ideas into a longer unit on Space. Introduce the activities presented in the "Heart Theme" during the excitement that builds around February 14th.

You'll find that all of the themes start off with a list of related Web sites. At the primary level, the Internet is most effectively used as a stimulus or motivating tool to spark enthusiasm for the study of a particular theme. Project the site from a central computer onto a large monitor or gather around the computers so the entire class can view relevant sites together. Brainstorm the ideas presented at these grade-appropriate Web sites. This "virtual visit" serves as the exciting kick-off for the many related activities that follow. Each theme consists of lesson plans for Language Arts, Math, Science, Social Studies, Art, and Movement, a list of related literature, and reproducible worksheets.

Because the Internet is always changing, and many Web sites may even disappear over the course of time, Teacher Created Materials maintains an active table of the sites in this book and updates them regularly. This table can be found at the following URL:

http://www.teachercreated.com/books/3823

Type this into your browser locator bar, and then bookmark it or include it in your Favorites list for easy access later on. Once at this main index site, you can easily link to the sites related to each theme in the book without having to even type in an address. Simply note the page number in this book for the theme or activity you would like to use. Find that page number on the site index page (**http://www.teachercreated.com/books/3823**) and click on the name of the site you wish to visit. The link will take you right there!

The CD-ROM in the back of this book has a direct link to our index page. You may want to simply insert the CD in your CD-ROM drive, click on the index page, and access the Teacher Created Materials site from the direct link. Note: your computer must already have a live connection to the Internet before the CD will link to that page within your browser (*Microsoft Internet Explorer* or *Netscape Navigator*).

To prepare for a theme day, read over the lesson plans, visit, view, and familiarize yourself with the related Web sites, and gather any related literature you would like to use from the list provided. You may want to send a note home to parents letting them know of any items the children should bring to school, or a special color or outfit the students might wear for the planned day of activities.

Many teachers and students have successfully used and enjoyed these activities. They are the perfect lesson plans to leave for substitute teachers, and also great activities to share with parents when they ask for ideas to try out at home. Enjoy!

Apple Theme

Related Web Sites

Apples and More
This is a fantastic site loaded with information. It includes history and legends, apple facts and recipes, a section on education, and links to other great sites.

Apples
This site has a lot of information on how apples are grown, their nutritional value, and their history. Learn about apples and related fruits and diseases and pests that affect apples. This site even answers the question "Why is New York City known as the Big Apple?"

Michigan Apples
Learn about Michigan's number one fruit, apple festivals and facts, and new apple varieties. Find out which apples make the best pie, and explore trivia, health benefits, and recipes.

The Story of Johnny Appleseed
Read a detailed story about Johnny Appleseed at this site. Learn about the man who explored new territory as he planted his apple seeds, and made friends with the people and animals he encountered. Lesson plans for this folk tale and other folk tales and tall tales are included.

Related Literature

An Apple A Day—Over 20 Apple Projects for Kids by Jennifer Story Gillis
Filled with activities!

The Apple Pie Tree by Zoe Hall
In this story, two young sisters observe an apple tree throughout the year and in the autumn make a pie!

An Apple Tree Through the Year by Claudia Schnieper
This book has good information on apple trees, emphasizing their changes through the seasons.

Apple Trees by Dorothy Hinshaw Patent
This is a true book about apple trees.

Apples by Elaine Landau
Apples is filled with good information on all aspects of the apple, including the history.

Applesauce by Shirley Kurtz
This is the story of a family making enough applesauce to last through the winter.

How Do Apples Grow? (A Read and Find Out Book) by Betsy Maestro
This book provides a straightforward look at how a fruit comes from a flower.

How to Make an Apple Pie and See the World by Marjorie Priceman
What to do if you want to bake an apple pie and the market is closed? Go on a trip around the world to collect the freshest ingredients. This book is great for a Social Studies Lesson!

Johnny Appleseed (All Aboard Reading, Level 1) by Patricia Demuth
This book retells the story of Johnny Appleseed in simple language.

The Life and Times of the Apple by Charles Micucci
This book has information on the life cycle, growing practices, and history of the apple.

Picking Apples and Pumpkins by Amy Hutchings
Beautiful photographs compliment this story of a family's outing to pick apples and pumpkins.

The Seasons of Arnold's Apple Tree by Gail Gibbons
This is a fun look at a changing apple tree.

The Story of Johnny Appleseed by Aliki
This is a retelling of the legend.

Apple Theme

Apple Language Arts

Objective

The students will explore the concept of analogy and form connections between vocabulary words.

Materials

- *A House is a House For Me* by Mary Ann Hoberman, if available
- an apple—to be cut in half
- "A House is a House for…" Activity Sheet (most appropriate for younger students)
- plain paper for older students

Procedure

1. Read the story *A House is a House for Me*. Brainstorm with the students what an apple is a house for. (Examples: seeds, apple juice, a worm, a star, etc.) If the book is not available, facilitate a discussion on how different objects can be houses for one another. For example, a box is a house for crackers, a glove is a house for a hand, etc.

2. If desired, share the riddle "What is red, has no doors or windows, and has a star inside?" (The answer is an apple. Show the students that when an apple is cut in half, there is a star shape inside which houses the seeds.)

3. Pass out the "A House is a House for…" Activity sheet and have the students match up the objects with their houses. For older students, have them get in pairs and list as many different items and houses they can think of. Give them a time limit and then allow the students to share their lists with the rest of the class.

Extension Ideas

- Discuss popular phrases which include the word "apple." For example, "He's the apple of my eye," "An apple a day keeps the doctor away," "One bad apple spoils the whole bunch," etc.
- Do a phonics lesson on short "a."
- Have a discussion on what a legend is in relation to the story of Johnny Appleseed. Research as a class what is fact and what is fiction in the stories. Relate Johnny Appleseed to other tall tales, such as the story of Paul Bunyon.
- Write simple apple recipes.

Apple Theme

A House is a House for...

Name: _____

Draw a line from the item to its house.

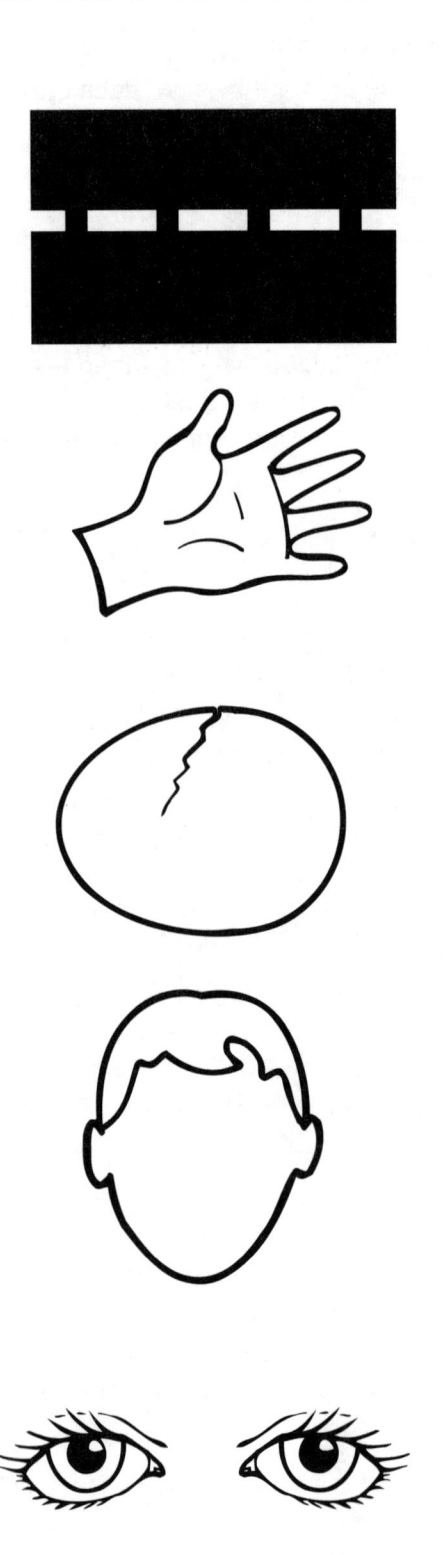

Apple Theme

Apple Math

Objective

The students will make patterns and graphs, and count by fives.

Materials:

- large piece of butcher paper marked off in three columns to make a graph
- cutouts of red, yellow, and green apples (or the students may use red, yellow, and green crayons)
- long strips of paper (about 12" long)
- "Counting by 5s with Apples" Activity Sheet, if desired
- "Same Shapes" Activity Sheet, if desired

Procedure:

(You may choose to only do parts of this lesson, depending on the age of the students and any time constraints.)

1. Tell the students they are going to do a variety of math activities with apples. They will graph, pattern, and count by fives.

2. Graph—Make a whole-class graph of the students' favorite types of apples: red, green, or yellow. Each student can choose an apple cutout, or make his or her own with their crayons. Have the students place their apple shapes in the correct color columns. Ask the students questions such as; "Which color apple do the most students like?" "How many more children like red apples than green apples?" "How many children like red and green apples added together?"

3. Pattern—Give each student a long strip (about 12" long) on which to make apple patterns. Using their red, yellow, and green crayons (or cut outs, if available), students create a pattern of colored apples. Depending on the age of the students, and how much they have been exposed to the concept of patterning, their patterns may be as simple or as complex as appropriate. If desired, use the Same Shapes activity sheet to practice identifying patterns.

4. Count by Fives—Discuss with the students how many aspects of apples happen in fives.
    - There are five petals on an apple blossom.
    - Apple blossoms grow in clusters of fives.
    - When an apple is cut in half, there is a "star" inside with five points.
      Given these facts, give the students some math problems to compute the answers. If desired, you may want to use the "Counting by 5s with Apples" activity sheet.

Extension Ideas

- Make apple prints and have the students count the star points by fives, as well as stamp the apples to make a pattern with red, yellow, and green paint.

- Read the book *Ten Apples Up on Top* by Theodore LeSieg. Have the students create math problems equaling ten. For example, 4 red apples plus 6 green apples = 10 apples. They can depict their math problems with red, yellow, and green crayons.

- For more math practice, have students complete the "Apple Word Problems" activity sheet and the "I Wonder . . ." activity sheet.

Apple Theme

Name: _____

Counting by 5s with Apples

1. If John picks 2 apple blossoms, how many petals will there be?

2. If Susan makes 3 apple prints, how many star points will there be?

3. If 5 clusters of apple blossoms grow, how many flowers will there be?

4. If there are 4 baskets and they each have 5 apples in them, how many apples are there altogether?

5. If 2 children each have 5 apples, how many apples are there altogether?

Apple Theme

Same Shapes

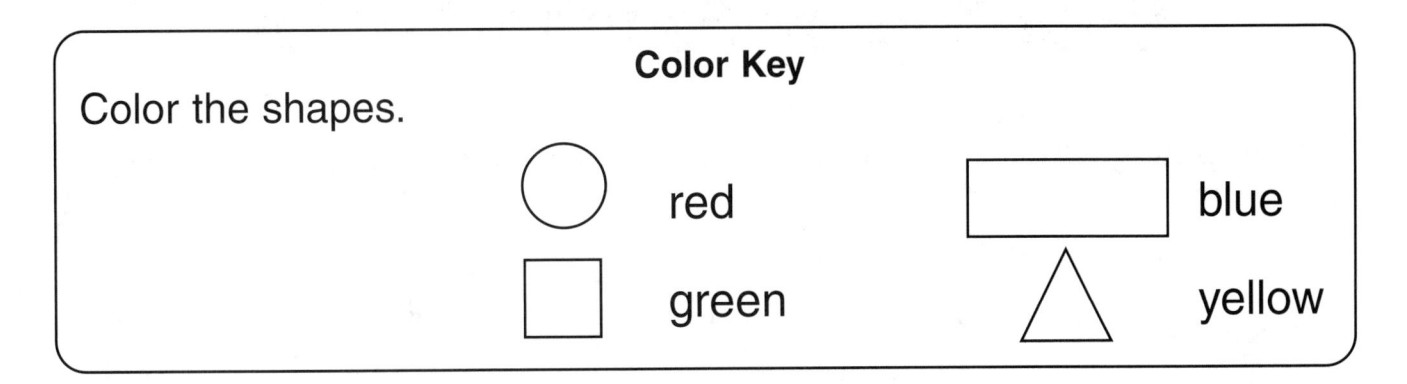

Color the shapes.

Color Key

○ red ▭ blue

□ green △ yellow

Color the shapes below that are the same as the first one in each row. Use the Color Key.

©Teacher Created Materials, Inc.   9   #3823 Internet Activities Through the Year

Apple Theme

Apple Word Problems

Teacher: These problems may be cut out and glued to index cards or to an apple for an *Apple Time* Bulletin Board. Students can solve problems with a partner.

---

1. Which apple is cut in fourths? a b c ☐

2. 12 🍎s. José ate 4. How many are left? ☐

3. 6 🍎s, 4 🍎s, 3 🍎s. How many altogether? ☐

4. 10 🍎s on a 🌳. 3 🍎s fell. How many 🍎s left on the 🌳? ☐

5. 3 🌳s. 3 🍎s on each 🌳. How many 🍎s altogether? ☐

6. Which apple is cut in half? a b c ☐

7. 7 🍎s. 4 more 🍎s. How many 🍎s altogether? ☐

8. 15 🍎s. Only 5 🍎s have 🐛s. How many 🍎s do not have 🐛s? ☐

#3823 Internet Activities Through the Year ©Teacher Created Materials, Inc.

Apple Theme

I Wonder...?

1. Cut an apple in half around its middle. What pattern do you see? Draw a picture.

2. Get an apple. Guess how many seeds are in the apple. Write your guess in the box.

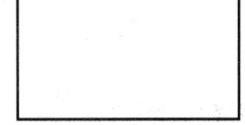

   Now, cut your apple in half the long way. Count the seeds. Write the number in the box.

   Did you make a good guess? _____

3. This apple has been cut into two equal pieces. Each piece is one half. Color one half.

   Here is another way to write one half. Trace the fractions.

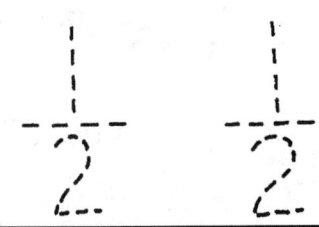

   $\frac{1}{2}$ $\frac{1}{2}$

4. This apple has been cut into four equal pieces. Each piece is one fourth. Color one fourth.

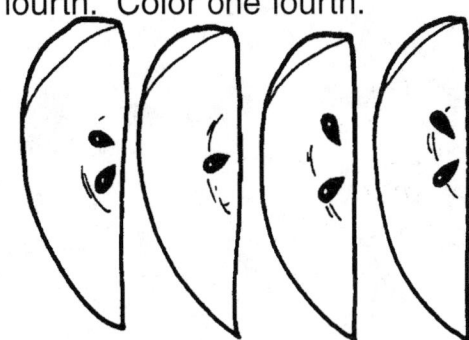

   Here is another way to write one-fourth. Trace the fractions.

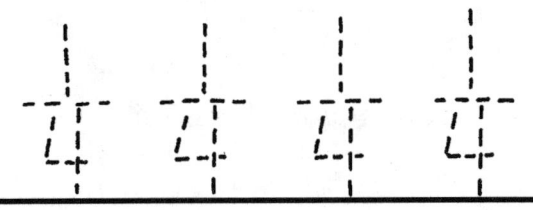

   $\frac{1}{4}$ $\frac{1}{4}$ $\frac{1}{4}$ $\frac{1}{4}$

Apple Theme

Apple Science

Objective

The students will observe, compare, and contrast dried apple pieces and fresh apple pieces.

Materials

- a dried apple piece and a fresh apple piece for each student or pair of students.
- "Apple Observations" activity sheets

Procedure

1. Give each student, or pair of students, a dried apple and a fresh apple piece.

2. Depending on the age of the students, either discuss the similarities and differences within the pair or as a whole class. Have them record their observations on the activity sheet.

3. Once the observations have been made, question the students as to why the two pieces are different. What does the fresh piece contain that the dried piece does not?

Extension Ideas

- Examine apple seeds and read a book on how apple seeds grow into apple trees.
- Plant an apple seed and watch what happens in the coming weeks.
- Make applesauce.
- Have students complete the "From Seed to Apple" Flap Book to show the life cycle of an apple tree.

Apple Theme

Name: _____

Apple Observations

The fresh apple looks like this:	The dried apple looks like this:

Three words to describe the fresh apple are:

_____

_____

_____

Three words to describe the dried apple are:

_____

_____

_____

The fresh apple and the dried apple are different because

_____

_____

©Teacher Created Materials, Inc.

Apple Theme

"From Seed to Apple" Flap Book

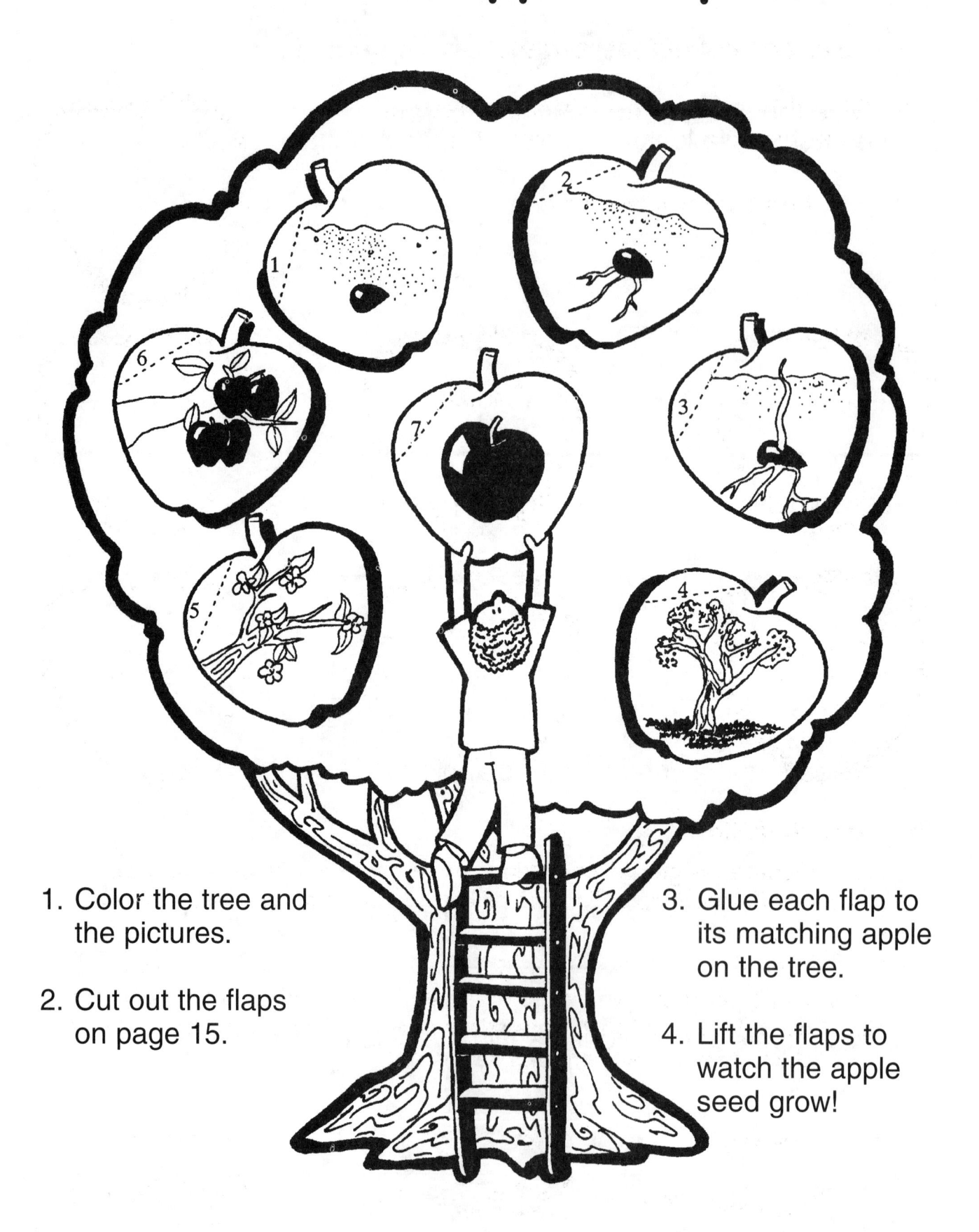

1. Color the tree and the pictures.

2. Cut out the flaps on page 15.

3. Glue each flap to its matching apple on the tree.

4. Lift the flaps to watch the apple seed grow!

Apple Theme

"From Seed to Apple" Flap Book *(cont.)*

1. Color and cut out the apples.

2. Glue the flaps to the matching spaces on the tree.

3. Bend back at the dotted line.

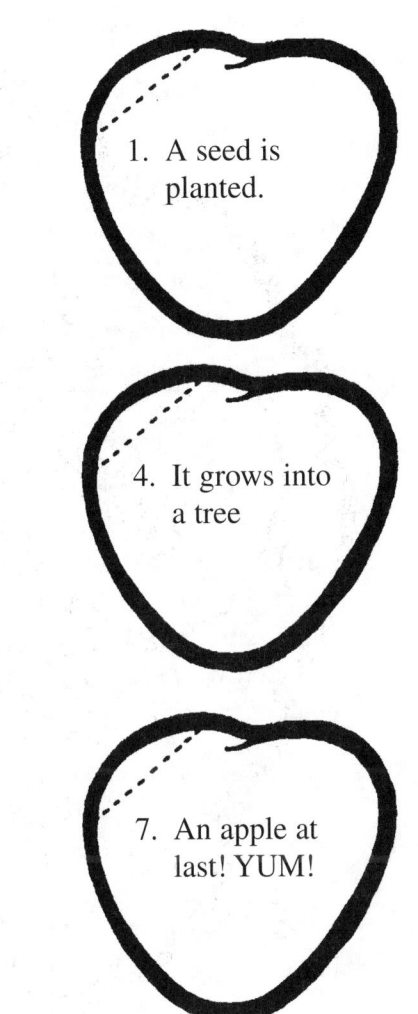

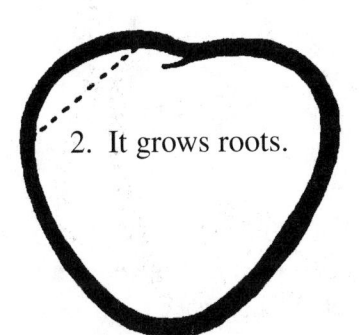

1. A seed is planted.

Flaps

2. It grows roots.

3. The seed sprouts.

4. It grows into a tree

5. Flowers begin to blossom.

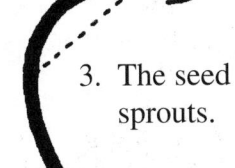

6. Apples are growing.

7. An apple at last! YUM!

Extension Activities:

- Have cooperative groups of children write their own "seed-to-full-grown plant" story. Topics could include different kinds of seeds: beans, wheat, water lilies.
- Draw a germinating seed; label the seed skin, root, and seed leaves.
- Grow seeds between two pieces of moist blotting paper. Remove the top piece just long enough to observe daily growth. Keep paper moist. Have the students log the daily progress with words and pictures.

Day 1   Day 3   Day 5

©Teacher Created Materials, Inc.   #3823 Internet Activities Through the Year

Apple Theme

Apple Social Studies

Objective

The students will listen to the story of Johnny Appleseed and locate the region he traveled through on a map.

Materials

- A book or Web site containing information on Johnny Appleseed
  Suggested Web Sites:
  Johnny Appleseed Homepage
  Encarta Online Encyclopedia on Johnny Appleseed
  The Story of Johnny Appleseed

- United States maps

Procedure

1. Read a selected story about Johnny Appleseed. Have a discussion on what the word "legend" means. Point out that this story is based in truth. For example, we know that his name was John Chapman but people referred to him as Johnny Appleseed. Certain aspects of his story may have changed with subsequent tellings. For example, do we really know that he wore a pot on his head?

2. Have the students look at a map of the United States and locate the states Johnny traveled through and in which he planted apple seeds. Where are those states in relation to the state of your students?

Extension Ideas

- Have a lesson on how apples get from orchards to the supermarkets.

- Create a time line beginning with the birth of Johnny Appleseed (1774) in relation to more current events.

- Have an apple farmer come to your classroom and discuss his/her job (or make a trip to an orchard).

- Locate the states which are the biggest apple producers—Washington, New York, and Michigan.

Apple Theme

Apple Art

Objective

The students will create apple trees using a variety of art mediums.

Materials

- brown and green tempera paint
- red tissue paper
- large pieces of white paper
- apples cut in half

Procedure

1. Help the students paint the palms of their hands and their forearms (almost to their elbows).
2. Have them then make prints of their painted arms onto a large piece of paper. This will create the trunk and the branches of their trees.
3. Have the students dip the apples, cut in half (or quarters), in green paint and stamp them onto the branches of their trees to form the leaves.
4. The students can then roll up small pieces of red tissue paper to form apples to glue on their trees.

Extension Ideas

- Create designs from apple prints. Have the students notice the star shape in the center of the apples.
- Make a large, whole-class apple tree. This can be a large mural of an apple tree filled with apples. The students can help paint a large tree and then design individual apples to hang on the tree.

Apple Theme

Apple Movement

Objective
The students will act out picking apples and putting them in baskets.

Materials
- music, if desired
- an open area for movement

Procedure
1. Discuss with the students the steps required in reaching to pick apples and bending over to place them in a bushel basket.
2. Play music, if desired, and have the students reach and pick the apples, then place them in the basket.

Extension Ideas
- Play "Toss the Apples in the Baskets." However, use balls instead of real apples. This could be made into a type of relay race.
- Have the students imitate apple seeds growing—starting out small, sprouting, and moving upward.
- Have an "apple hunt." Hide apples (real or paper) around the classroom or outside and have the students hunt for apples.
- Work as a class to make up an apple song to a familiar tune, such as "Twinkle, Twinkle, Little Star." For example, "Shiny, Shiny, Little Apple."

Banana Theme

Setting the Stage
If possible, have each student bring a banana to school on banana day, or have them wear yellow to school. If this is not possible, then you may want to bring in a bunch of bananas yourself for activities and discussions.

Related Web Sites

Chiquita Kids
Kids can play Shockwave games, write crazy stories, learn facts and information, and even journey through Central America. Banana recipes are included.

Dole.com
This site has information, games, and classroom activities pertaining to the "5-a-Day" program. The funhouse has lots of games for kids to play and recipes for them to try.

Turbana.com
This site is sponsored by a cooperative of banana growers in Columbia and has good information on banana plants as well as the banana journey from plantation to supermarket.

Related Literature

Anna Banana: 101 Jump-Rope Rhymes by Joanna Cole
This book is referred to in the Movement Lesson for a jumping rope activity.

Bananas! by Jacqueline Farmer
This is a fun nonfiction book with lots of information, recipes, jokes, and songs.

Bananas by Elaine Landau
This nonfiction book has factual information on bananas, how they are grown, and how they get to market.

Bitter Bananas by Isaac Olaleye
An African boy sets a trap to try and stop baboons from stealing his palm sap. The trap includes lacing bananas with wormwood.

The Day the Teacher Went Bananas by James Howe
What happens when your substitute teacher is a gorilla?

I Want My Banana! Quiero Mi Platano! by Mary Risk and Rosa Martin
This I Can Read Spanish book has a simple story about a monkey and his desire for a banana.

The Turtle and the Monkey by Paul Galdone
This is a story about a greedy monkey and his struggle with a wise turtle over a banana plant.

What's For Lunch?... Banana by Pam Robson
Good information and real-life pictures of banana plantations can be found in this nonfiction book.

Banana Theme

Banana Language Arts

Objective

The students will write a recipe (either individually or as a class) for a banana split.

Materials

- "My Banana Split Recipe" activity sheet (one for each student, if done individually)
- a sample of a recipe showing the list of ingredients and the steps

Procedure

1. Discuss the elements needed for writing a recipe. Read an example of a simple recipe, including the ingredients and the steps for completing the dish.

2. Either working as a class, or individually, have the students write a recipe for a banana split. Allow them to be as creative as they would like to be.

3. If time allows, have the students draw an illustration of their banana split and share their recipes with the class (see Art Lesson).

Extension Ideas

- Have the students write a "B" Story by filling in the blanks with words beginning with the letter "B." Use the "B Story" activity sheet.
- Give a story prompt of "One morning I awoke to discover I was a hungry little monkey…."
- Discuss homophones starting with the example of "peel" and "peal."

Banana Theme

Name: _____

My Banana Split Recipe

Ingredients:

_____ _____

_____ _____

_____ _____

Steps:

1. _____

2. _____

3. _____

4. _____

5. _____

Banana Theme

Name: _____

A "B" Story

Directions: Fill in the blanks with words beginning with the letter "B."

One beautiful day a _____ named _____ woke up and decided to go to the zoo. He got out of his _____. First he needed to eat his _____. He ate _____ and _____. When he was done, he had to _____ his teeth. He then put on his favorite _____ shirt and his _____ pants.

He went outside and got on a _____ to ride to the zoo. It was a bumpy ride! When he got to the zoo he saw a man selling _____. He bought a _____ one. He then went to see the _____ and the _____. They were his favorite things to see at the zoo!

#3823 Internet Activities Through the Year ©Teacher Created Materials, Inc.

Banana Theme

Banana Math

Objective

The students will measure the curved length of bananas.

Materials

- cloth measuring tapes (or pieces of string and hard rulers)
- bananas (or cutout shapes of bananas) numbered 1–12 (or with the numbers you need so that each pair of students has a banana)
- "Banana Measurement" activity sheets for results

Procedure

1. Show the students a banana and brainstorm how to measure it. Discuss how a hard ruler would not be able to account for the curve in the banana. You may demonstrate this by holding up your index finger and asking if when you curve your finger, the length is changed. Show how to measure a curved banana either using a measuring tape or a piece of string marked off and held up to a hard ruler.

2. Put the students in pairs. Give each pair a banana (or banana cutout), a measuring tape (or a piece of string and a hard ruler), and an activity sheet.

3. Have the students measure their banana and record their results. They will then want to exchange their banana with at least two other pairs, so they measure a total of three bananas.

4. Have the students measure at least three other items in the classroom, either straight or curved, of their choice.

Wrap Up

Have the students think of other larger items that are curved which people may measure, i.e., roads, a race track, playground slides, a monkey's tail.

Extension Ideas

- Weigh bananas on a scale.
- Make up lists of items in the classroom that are bigger or smaller than bananas.
- Using the basis of the "Five a Day for Better Health" slogan, practice counting by fives to see how many servings of fruits and vegetables should be eaten for any given number of days.
- Add the number of bananas in different bunches to get a total.

Banana Theme

Name: _____

Banana Measurement

Write the length of your bananas:

Banana # _____ is _____ long.

Banana # _____ is _____long.

Banana # _____ is _____long.

Find 3 other items in the classroom to measure:

The _____ is _____ long.

The _____ is _____ long.

The _____ is _____ long.

#3823 Internet Activities Through the Year ©Teacher Created Materials, Inc.

Banana Theme

Banana Science

Objective

The students will explore banana seeds and learn how bananas grow in comparison to other fruits.

Materials

- a slice of banana for each pair, or small group of students
- a magnifying glass for each group
- a computer with the *How Bananas Are Grown* site displayed or information from the site (If available, a book which has pictures of banana plants in it would also work. One suggestion would be *Bananas* by Elaine Landau.)
- "Where Fruits Grow" activity sheet, one for each student

Procedure

1. Give each pair of students a slice of banana and a magnifying glass. Have them look at the seeds in the bananas. Talk about other kinds of fruit seeds, where they are on the fruits, and what they look like. Explain that banana plants do not grow from these seeds. Actual banana plants grow from "suckers" which are small plants that grow around the base of a banana plant. Banana farmers cultivate the suckers to grow into new banana plants.

2. Show the students pictures of banana plants and explain how they are not trees, but actually very large plants. They do not have a woody stem like trees. Banana plants grow clusters of flowers, which then turn into bananas. Each cluster of bananas is called a hand and the individual bananas are called fingers.

3. Give each student an activity sheet and as a class brainstorm different fruits and where they should be placed on the sheet.

Extension Ideas

- Bring a variety of fruit seeds (apple, orange, grape, peach, watermelon, etc.) in to school and have the students try and determine from what fruit each seed came. This can be set up in separate centers around the room. The students can travel from center to center, fill out an observation journal about each seed and from what fruit they believe it came. The class can then reconvene and the teacher can give the answers regarding each seed. See the "Fruit Seed Observations" journal sheet to reproduce for the students to record their data.

- Inform students of the "Five a Day for Better Health" campaign which promotes eating five servings of fruits and vegetables every day. Have them write a list of five fruits and vegetables they like to eat to fill this nutrition requirement. The **Dole.com** site (see page 19) has a variety of Five a Day information for teachers and students.

Banana Theme

Name: _____

Where Fruits Grow

On Trees	On Vines
On Bushes	On Big Plants

Banana Theme

Name: _____

Fruit Seed Observations

Seed # _____

This seed looks like this:

Two words to describe this seed are: _____

_____

I believe this seed is from a _____.

Seed # _____

This seed looks like this:

Two words to describe this seed are: _____

_____

I believe this seed is from a _____.

Seed # _____

This seed looks like this:

Two words to describe this seed are: _____

_____

I believe this seed is from a _____.

©Teacher Created Materials, Inc.   #3823 Internet Activities Through the Year

Banana Theme

Banana Social Studies

Objective

The students will sequence how a banana gets from a banana plantation to a supermarket.

Materials

- a world map or globe

- information from the following Web site which tells where bananas are grown: **Where Your Bananas Are Grown**.

- a printout or a computer displaying one of the following sites which tell how bananas are transported: **How Bananas Are Packaged And Transported** or **The Banana Journey**.

- "A Banana's Journey" activity sheet.

Procedure

1. Show the class on the map where bananas are grown. Have them find where their hometown is on the same map.

2. Discuss what types of transportation the bananas need to go on to arrive at local supermarkets.

3. Read, or discuss the printout of how bananas are transported.

4. Using a real or pretend bunch of bananas, have the students act out the banana journey from farm to market through assigned roles. (They can come up with prop ideas, or it can be done in mime form.) The following steps need to be portrayed:

    - Green bananas are picked.

    - The bananas are washed and inspected.

    - Bananas are put in boxes.

    - Bananas are loaded on refrigerated ships for their journey over sea.

    - Bananas are unloaded from ships and placed on refrigerated trucks.

    - Bananas are taken to a large warehouse to ripen.

    - Bananas are reloaded on trucks to be taken to supermarkets.

    - Distribute the "A Banana's Journey" activity sheet for students to review the process of bananas going from farm to market. This can be done individually, or as a group for nonreaders.

Extension Ideas

- Share some history facts regarding bananas which can be found in the book *Bananas* by Jacqueline Farmer or at the following site: **Banana History**.

- Since the students probably know that monkeys are fond of bananas, have them do some research on where monkeys can be found.

Banana Theme

Name: _____

A Banana's Journey

Number the following steps in order to correctly show the journey of a banana from farm to supermarket.

_____ The bananas are unloaded from the ships and put on refrigerated trucks.

_____ The green bananas are picked.

_____ The bananas are taken to a warehouse to ripen.

_____ The bananas are taken to supermarkets.

_____ The bananas are put on refrigerated ships.

_____ The bananas are washed.

_____ The bananas are put in boxes.

Banana Theme

Banana Art

Objective

The students will create a "banana split" using various art supplies. (This banana split will be based on the recipe they wrote in their language arts lesson.)

Materials

- various art supplies such as construction paper, cotton balls, yarn, scraps of fabric, paints, craft sticks, markers, crayons, etc.

Procedure

1. Have the students review their banana split recipes.

2. Give them the art supplies and allow them to create their banana splits using these items.

Extension Ideas

- Use real bananas or pictures of bananas to facilitate a discussion on shades of green and yellow. Have the students mix yellow and green paints with white to achieve various shades. They can use their paint colors to paint cutout banana shapes. They may also want to create shades of brown for any spots or bruises on the bananas.

- Try making caged banana animals. See the activity sheet on page 31.

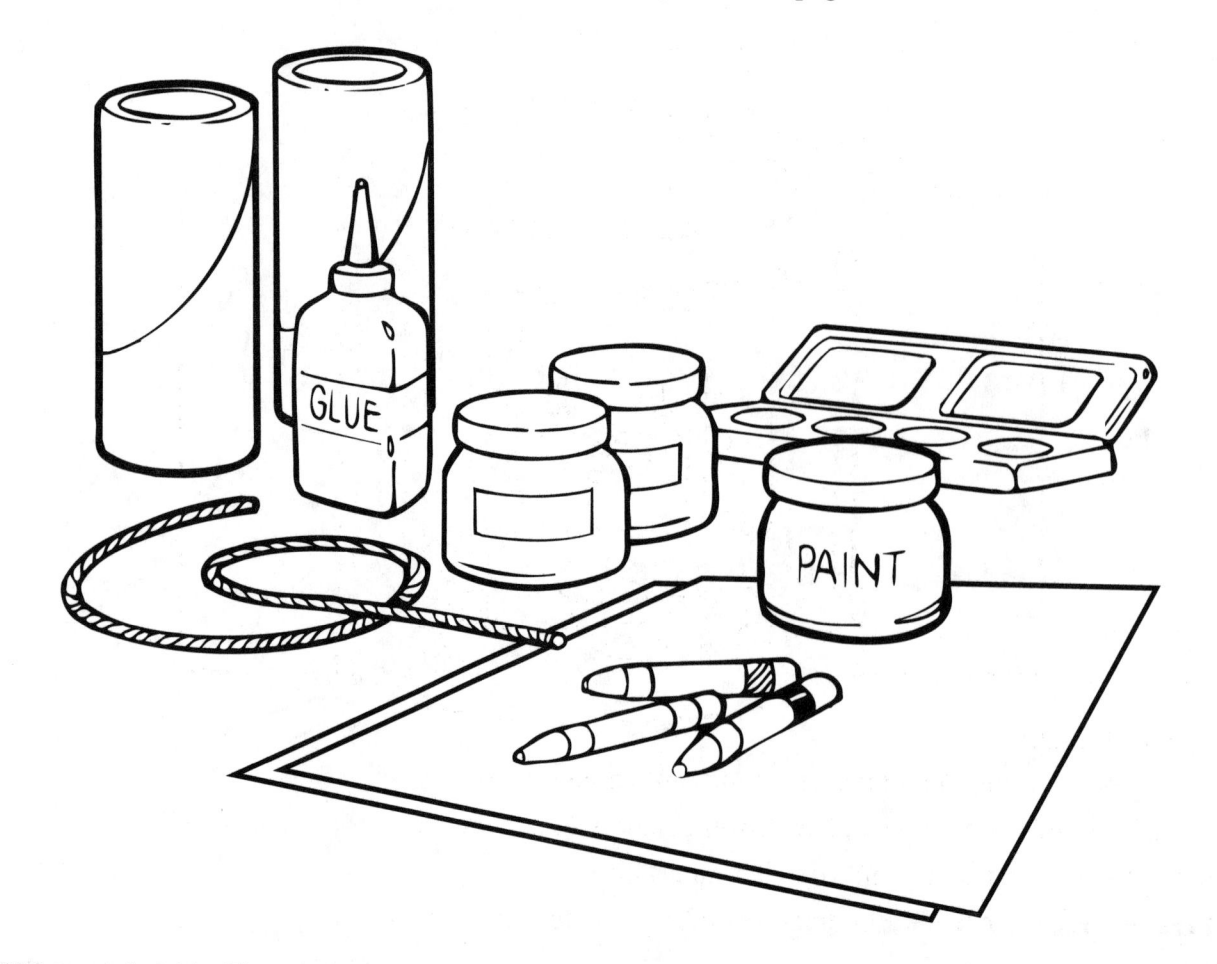

Banana Theme

Caged Banana Animals

Encourage students to use their imaginations to create edible animals. The wild creatures they make can be captured in cages for classroom display until snack time.

"Caged banana animals" can be assembled without kitchen facilities. The animals can be made using only fruits, vegetables, cereal products, nuts, and cream cheese. Although the nutritional value would be decreased, creative options could be increased by adding various types of candy as decorations.

Supplies: Cutting board, sharp knife, table knives, pastry brush, shredder, plastic bags, food coloring, plates, wooden picks.

Ingredients: Oranges, parsley, bananas, cream cheese (whipped or soft-style), lemon juice, coconut flakes, crackers, carrots, raisins, maraschino cherries, dry cereal, pretzel sticks, chow mein noodles, and whole, sliced, and chopped nuts.

Directions for animal:

- Cut a 1½" piece of banana.
- Use a pastry brush to coat it with lemon juice.
  OR
  Use a table knife to cover it with cream cheese and roll it in one of the following:
  Cracker crumbs
  Shredded carrots
  Colored coconut flakes (To color coconut, put coconut in a plastic bag, add a drop or two of food coloring, and shake.)
- Use cream cheese to attach eyes, nose, mouth, ears, hair, whiskers, etc.

Directions for cage:

- Cut a large orange into thick slices, discarding end slices.
- Place an orange slice on a plate. Cover center with parsley. Place "banana animal" on top.
- Poke wooden picks around edge of orange slice.
- Put another orange slice on top of wooden picks for roof of cage.

Banana Theme

Banana Movement

Objective

The students will jump rope to jump-rope rhymes.

Materials

- the book *Anna Banana: 101 Jump-Rope Rhymes* by Joanna Cole
- jump ropes

Procedures

1. Share some of the jump rope rhymes out of the book and have the children jump rope to ones they select.

2. If the book is not available to you, work as a class to make up a jump rope rhyme using the word "banana."

Extension Ideas

- Have the students play "hot banana," similar to "hot potato."
- Have relay races using a banana as the baton.
- Pretend you are monkeys and act out climbing trees and eating bananas.

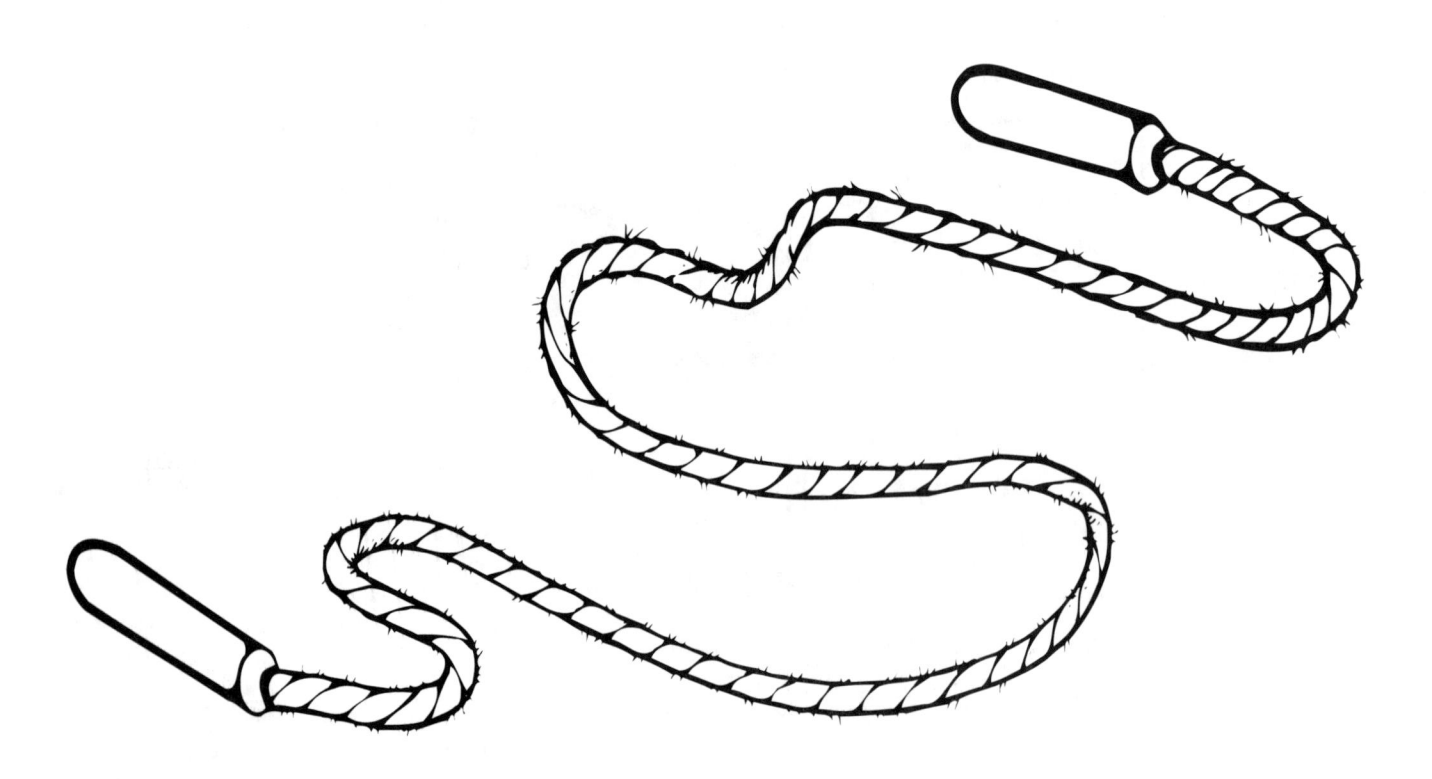

Bat Theme

Related Web Sites

Bats, Bats, Everywhere
A site specifically designed for children containing lots of good information on bats. Kids can learn about where bats live, what they eat, what they look like, myths about bats, and how they help humans. A bat quiz allows kids to show what they have learned.

Bat Conservation International
This organization was formed to "protect and restore bats and their habitats worldwide." Read about different projects sponsored by Bat Conservation International, view different types of bats, adopt a bat or get involved, and hear actual audio tape of bat calls.

Bat World Sanctuary
Bat World is a sanctuary for bats that cannot survive in the wild. Information on bats, including a good page on the myths and facts of bats, can be found here. The Kid's Page has activity pages that kids can cut out and complete.

Bats—A Thematic Resource for Students and Teachers
This site has facts, resources, projects, and leads to other great links about bats. Kids can test their knowledge with a true/false bat quiz and explore a collection of bat illustrations.

University of Michigan's Zoology Information on Bats
This site is written for adults, however, there are great photographs of different species of bats.

Related Literature

Bats! Strange and Wonderful by Laurence Pringle
This book has wonderful illustrations and information on bats.

Bats by Gail Gibbons
Another great informational book on bats.

Shadows of Night: The Hidden World of the Little Brown Bat by Barbara Bash
Engaging illustrations enhance this factual story of the little brown bats.

Screech! A Book About Bats by Melvin and Gilda Berger
Lots of information and amazing photographs can be found in this "Hello Reader" book.

Bats: Shadows in the Night by Diane Ackerman
The photographs are the highlight of this book, as the text is for older children.

Stellaluna by Janell Cannon
This is the touching story of a baby bat who gets separated from her mother and befriends a nest full of baby birds. It's a wonderful lesson on differences.

Amazing Bats by Frank Greenaway
More great information and photographs can be found in this book.

The Magic School Bus Going Batty: A Book About Bats (Magic School Bus) by Nancy E. Krulik
In Magic School Bus style, Ms. Frizzle and her class have a nocturnal adventure and learn about bats.

Zipping, Zapping, Zooming Bats (Let's-Read-And-Find-Out Science, Stage 2) by Anne Earle
This book contains good information on the brown bat.

Beautiful Bats by Linda Glaser
Wonderful watercolors help to share the facts about bats.

Bat Jamboree, Bats Around the Clock, and Bats on Parade by Kathi Appelt
These fun books have lessons on counting, telling time, and, for older children, multiplication.

Bat Theme

Bat Language Arts

Objective

The students will determine the difference between fact and myth.

Materials

- a nonfiction book about bats, such as *Bats* by Gail Gibbons, or a link to the **Myths—Don't You Believe It** Web site
- chart paper or chalkboard
- the "Myth or Fact?" activity sheet

Procedure

1. Ask the students what they know about bats. List their responses on a chalkboard or chart paper.
2. Read the book or share the Web link about bats. Ask the students what they know about bats. Add their answers to the list.
3. Discuss whether any facts they originally gave ended up being myths. Discuss the terms *fact* and *myth*.
4. Pass out the "Myth or Fact?" activity sheet.
5. Have the students complete the activity sheets individually, or as a group, depending on the grade level.
6. As an alternative, have the students work in pairs to write a true and false bat quiz to take home to their families.

Extension Ideas

- Use the bat clip art on pages 36 and 37 to make Big Books about bats.
- Do a phonics lesson on 'at' family words.
- Make "Bat Vocabulary" books. Have the students enter words such as: mammal, roost, echolocation, nocturnal, etc., as well as their definitions.
- Explain to students that bats are a sign of luck in China. Have the students write a story about a bat being a sign of luck to them. "One evening I saw a bat flying in the sky. The next day I had one of my luckiest days ever. This is what happened…"

Name: _____

Myth or Fact?

A fact is true/not true (circle one).

Here are 3 bat myths:

1. _____
2. _____
3. _____

Here are 3 bat facts:

1. _____
2. _____
3. _____

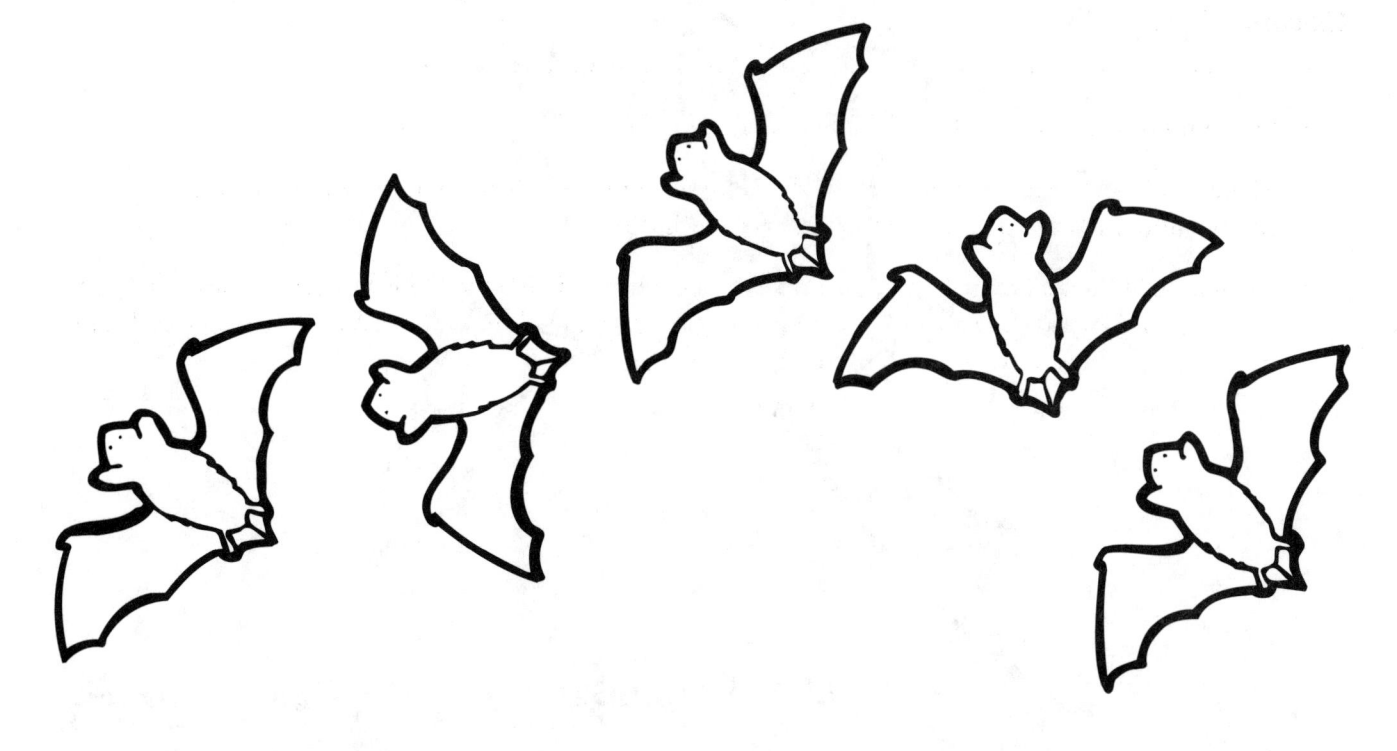

Bat Theme

Bat Clip Art

Hog-nosed Bat

Little Brown Bat

Bat Theme

Bat Clip Art *(cont.)*

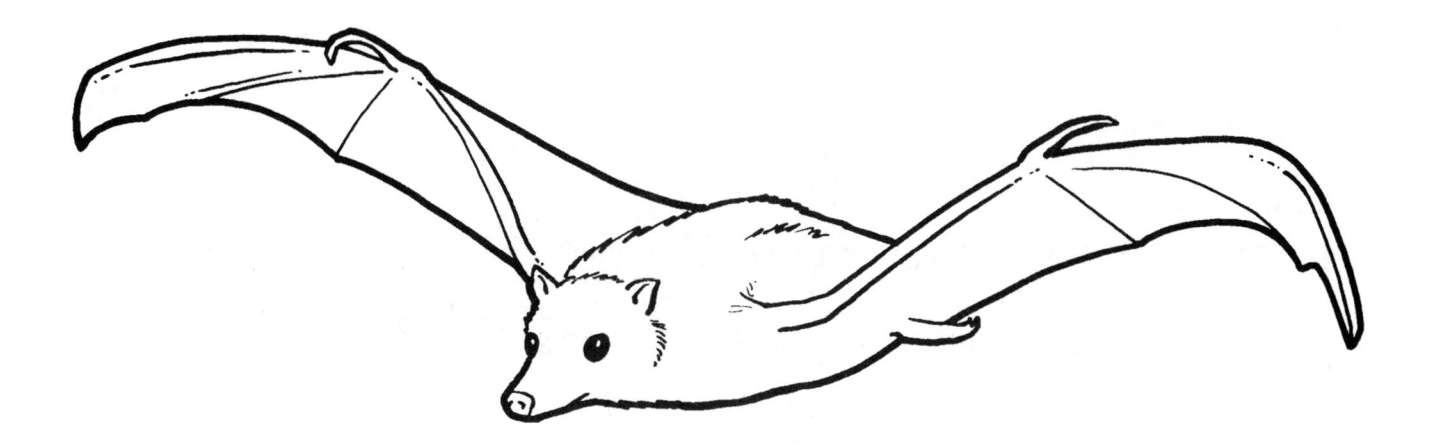

Flying Fox

Long-eared Bat

Bat Theme

Bat Math

Objective
The students will measure objects in their environment to compare to given lengths.

Materials
- two pieces of string for each pair of students—one piece cut to five feet and one string cut to five inches
- "Measuring with Bat Wings" activity sheet.

Procedure
1. Put the students in pairs and give each pair a string cut to 5 feet and a string cut to 5 inches.
2. Discuss with the students that the long piece of string is similar to the length of some megabat wingspans and the short string is similar to some types of microbat wingspans.
3. Pass out the "Measuring with Bat Wings" activity sheet.
4. Have the students complete the activity sheets by moving about the room and measuring classroom items in comparison to their strings.

Extension Ideas
- Count by fives with questions such as "What would the wingspan be of three megabats tip to tip?" (With their wingspans being five feet.)
- Research and find out the average wingspan of different kinds of bats. Cut strips of paper, or string, to those lengths, label them and display them in the classroom or hallway.
- Measure how many inches are in five feet. Ask how much longer a megabat's wingspan is than a microbat's.

Bat Theme

Name: _____

Measuring With Bat Wings

1. The long string is _____ long. This is similar to the wingspan of some types of megabats.

2. The short string is _____ long. This is similar to the wingspan of some types of microbats.

3. Here are some items in the classroom that are about the same length as the long string:

   _____
   _____
   _____

4. Here are some items in the classroom that are about the same length as the short string:

   _____
   _____
   _____

©Teacher Created Materials, Inc. #3823 Internet Activities Through the Year

Bat Theme

Bat Science

Objective

The students will explore echolocation as a mechanism used by bats for locating food.

Materials

- a nonfiction bat book which explains echolocation or a link to one of the following Web sites: **Echolocation And How it Works** or **Bat Conservation International** (this site contains actual audio clips of bat calls)
- tuning forks, musical triangles or drums (or any other object available to demonstrate sound vibrations)
- a space, such as the school gym or auditorium which allows for hearing echoes

Procedure

1. Introduce the term echolocation. You may want to do this through a book or at an aforementioned Web site.
2. If possible, play the audio clips of the bat calls.
3. Pass out the tuning forks (or other object) and have the students explore "feeling" the sound waves in the vibration.
4. Discuss how sound waves actually travel through the object and the air.
5. Go to the space which was selected for the students to test making their own echoes. Discuss how they actually hear their own voices (or other noises made) by the sound waves of their voices bouncing off the objects (such as the walls) of the room.

Extension Ideas

- Introduce to the students that bats are the only flying mammal. Have the students classify animals using the "Animal Classification" activity sheet.
- Do a Venn Diagram comparing a bat wing and a human hand.
- As also listed in the language arts lesson, make Bat Vocabulary books. These books can include words such as roost, mammal, echolocation, and nocturnal.
- Compare the varied diets of different types of bats.
- Compare and contrast two types of bats.

Name: _____

Animal Classification

Mammals	Birds
Reptiles	Fish

Bat Theme

Bat Social Studies

Objective

The students will explore the different measures bat preservationists are taking to save bats from becoming extinct.

Materials

- a book (*Bats! Strange and Wonderful* by Laurence Pringle, for example) or Web sites which discuss bat preservation. A good site for information is **Bat Conservation International** (The information is presented at an adult level, but there are good photographs to show the students.)
- large pieces of paper
- writing utensils, such as crayons, markers, and colored pencils
- "Protect the Bats" activity sheet (optional)

Procedure

1. Read the book or paraphrase the information given at the web site.
2. The main points to discuss are:
   - Some people are building bat houses.
   - Some people are making bridges, which are good roosting places for bats.
   - Some people are putting grill work on old mines and caves to keep people out, but still provide a safe place for bats.
   - some people have set up nature preserves to protect large groups of bats.
   - In addition, mention the things people should not do which can harm bats, i.e. hurting them, driving them from their homes, polluting, etc.
3. Allow the students to create posters with a "Save the Bats" message.
4. As an alternative, have the students complete the "Protect the Bats" activity sheet.

Extension Ideas

- Visit the **Bat Species** Web site to view photographs of different species of bats, and locate their homes on maps.
- Have a lesson on the continents. (Bats live on every continent, except Antarctica.)

Bat Theme

Name: _____

Protect the Bats!

Here are 4 things people can do to help protect bats:

1. _____

2. _____

3. _____

4. _____

©Teacher Created Materials, Inc. #3823 Internet Activities Through the Year

Bat Theme

Bat Art

Objective

The students will explore perspective using their art work.

Materials

- paper
- art mediums such as crayons, markers, or paint
- wall space to display the students' "Art for Bats"

Procedure

1. Discuss with students how bats hang upside down when at rest.
2. Tell them you are going to create an art museum for bats.
3. Allow the students to create pictures of any scenes they would like. Younger students may need some guidance, such as "Draw your favorite place to play, draw a picture of your family," etc.
4. Once the art pieces are complete, turn them upside down and display them in the classroom or hallway. Discuss with students how their pictures are from the correct perspective when viewed by hanging bats. Entitle your art exhibition "Art for Bats."
5. See if visitors can determine why your exhibit is for bats.
6. For older students, you may want to have them try to create their pictures from an upside-down perspective, instead of simply turning their picture around once they are done.

Extension Ideas

- Create a whole-class mural of a bat cave or night sky on butcher paper. Have the students create hanging or flying bats to be placed on the mural.
- Have the students create "Save the Bats" posters emphasizing the facts about bats and what humans can do to protect them. (Refer to the social studies lesson for further ideas.)

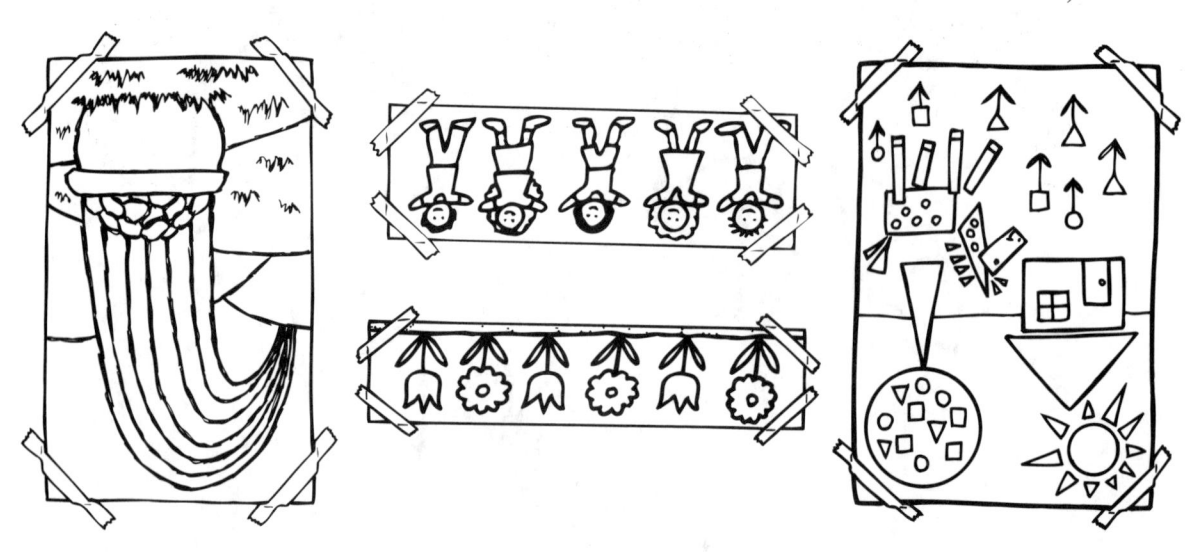

Bat Theme

Bat Movement

Objective

The students will imitate the flight of bats.

Materials

- A large open space.
- Music which sounds like flying and gliding through the air (classical may be best).

Procedure

1. Play the music and have the students pretend they are bats flying through the air. If possible, play music with both a fast and a slow tempo to allow for different types of movement.

Extension Ideas

- Go to the **Education Place** Web site for a fun game on echolocation.
- Play a game in which some of the students are bats and the others are insects and the bats try to tag the insects.
- Have the students hang their heads upside down and observe the world from a hanging bat's perspective.

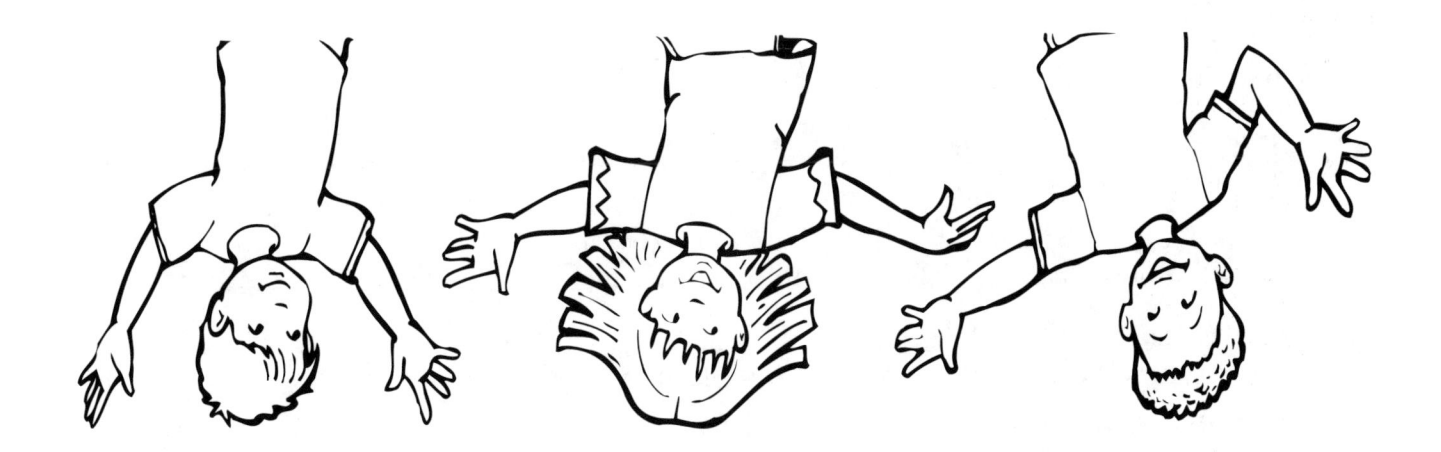

©Teacher Created Materials, Inc. #3823 Internet Activities Through the Year

Bubble Theme

Related Web Sites

Bubble Town
This is a site filled with bubble activities, recipes, games, and more! Build a bubble-blowing tube, mix special bubble solutions, and play games.

BubbleSphere
Another great site with solution recipes, activities, and links to other bubble sites. Included is a history of bubbles, bubble inventions, and the adventures of Professor Bubbles, who created and owns the site.

Exploratorium
This is a good site with sophisticated information on bubbles. Descriptions of the molecular properties of bubbles, the colors found in bubbles, and different formulas for making bubbles are included.

Bubble Geometry—Science Museum of Minnesota
Find the answers to questions such as "Have you ever seen a square bubble?" and "How can you catch a bubble?" Bubble questions are answered through experiments and activities.

Bubble-Mania
This is a site used to promote the services of a bubble program that can be brought to your school. However, there is also good information as well, including bubble formulas, amazing photos, and frequently asked questions.

The Art and Science of Bubbles
This is a section of the Soap and Detergent Association site created especially for kids. It is filled with fun activities perfect for younger children! Try the tips on creating "Bigger, Better Bubbles," print out pages to play games, learn about magic tricks and bubble art, try some experiments, and read the "Ode to a Bubble."

Related Literature

Benny's Big Bubble (Picture Readers) by Jane O'Connor
A little boy blows a huge bubble and it takes off on an airborne trip around his neighborhood.

Bubble Trouble (Rooke Reader) by Joy N. Hulme
This is a rhyming easy reader.

Bubble Trouble (My Hello First Reader With Flash Cards) by Mary Packard
The rhyming text of this book describes a day filled with bubbles!

The Magic Bubble Trip by Ingrid Schubert
A boy goes on a trip inside a bubble and ends up in a land of frogs.

Soap Science by J.L. Bell
This is a science book of experiments all involving soap and/or bubbles.

Strega Nona Takes a Vacation by Tomie dePaola
When Strega Nona takes a much-needed vacation, Big Anthony accidentally floods the town with bubbles!

The Unbelievable Bubble Book by John Cassidy
Included in this book is a toy to create huge bubbles. The book also has history, science and information on bubbles.

Bubble Theme

Bubble Language Arts

Objective
The students will write a story about a bubble trip.

Materials
- "Story Map for My Bubble Trip" activity sheet
- paper
- writing utensils
- *The Magic Bubble Trip* by Ingrid Schubert, if available

Procedure
1. Read *The Magic Bubble Trip* or have a discussion on what it would be like to be inside a bubble and go on a special trip. Where would the students want to end up? What would they see along the way? Who would they meet?
2. Pass out the Story Maps for the students to fill out their initial ideas.
3. Based on the Story Maps, have them write a story about their trip.
4. Younger students may complete a simple sentence such as "On my magic bubble trip I would go to…."
5. If time allows, have them illustrate their stories.

Extension Ideas
- As a variation on the above lesson, have the entire class create a story on chart paper. Each student may add a sentence to what happens on the trip to complete the entire story. Give each student a piece of paper and have him/her write the sentence he/she contributed. They may then illustrate their sentences and put the final pages together to create a class book.
- Have a phonics lesson on short "u."
- Have a phonics lesson on double consonants and short vowels, i.e., bubble, pepper, happy, puppy, middle, etc.
- Write poems describing a bubble.

Bubble Theme

Name: _____

Story Map for My Bubble Trip

1. Where will my bubble trip start? _____
   _____

2. Where will my bubble trip take me? _____
   _____

3. What will I see along the way? _____
   _____

4. Who or what will I meet? _____
   _____

5. What will I do at the end of my trip? _____
   _____

Bubble Theme

Bubble Math

Objective

The students will identify the geometric three dimensional shapes of sphere, cone, cube, and cylinder.

Materials

- a collection of items representing a sphere, cone, cube, and cylinder. (For example, a ball, a party hat, a block, and a paper towel tube.)
- bubble solution and bubble blower
- chart paper or blackboard
- clay or Play Dough™ (just a small amount for each student)
- "How Long Until They Pop?" activity sheet

Procedure

1. Blow a bubble and ask the students to name its shape. Many may say round, ball, circle, etc. Introduce the term "sphere." Write the word on the chart paper, or blackboard, and have the students brainstorm other items which are spheres.

2. Go on to discuss the other three-dimensional shapes of cone, cube, and cylinder and continue the same process of making lists.

3. Pass out the clay, or Play Dough™, and have the students form each shape.

Extension Ideas

- Have the students make predictions on how many seconds a bubble will stay afloat before it pops. (Either use the second hand on a clock, or have them count slowly.) Then blow the actual bubble and have the students record the actual amount of time it stayed afloat. Use the Bubble Prediction Activity sheet. They may then figure by how many seconds their prediction and the actual number differed. This activity can be done as a whole class with just the teacher blowing while the students make the predictions.

- Write addition and subtraction story problems using blowing bubbles as the addition factor and popping bubbles as subtraction.

- Have the students predict how many bubbles can be blown from one bubble wand of solution. Blow the wand and count the actual number.

- Blow bubbles and have a lesson on size words, *big*, *bigger*, *small*, *smaller*, etc.

Bubble Theme

Name: _____

How Long Until They Pop?

Predict how many seconds the bubble will stay afloat. Blow a bubble and record the actual amount of time it can stay afloat. Figure the difference between the two numbers.

1. Prediction _____

    Actual _____

    Difference _____

2. Prediction _____

    Actual _____

    Difference _____

3. Prediction _____

    Actual _____

    Difference _____

4. Prediction _____

    Actual _____

    Difference _____

5. Prediction _____

    Actual _____

    Difference _____

6. Prediction _____

    Actual _____

    Difference _____

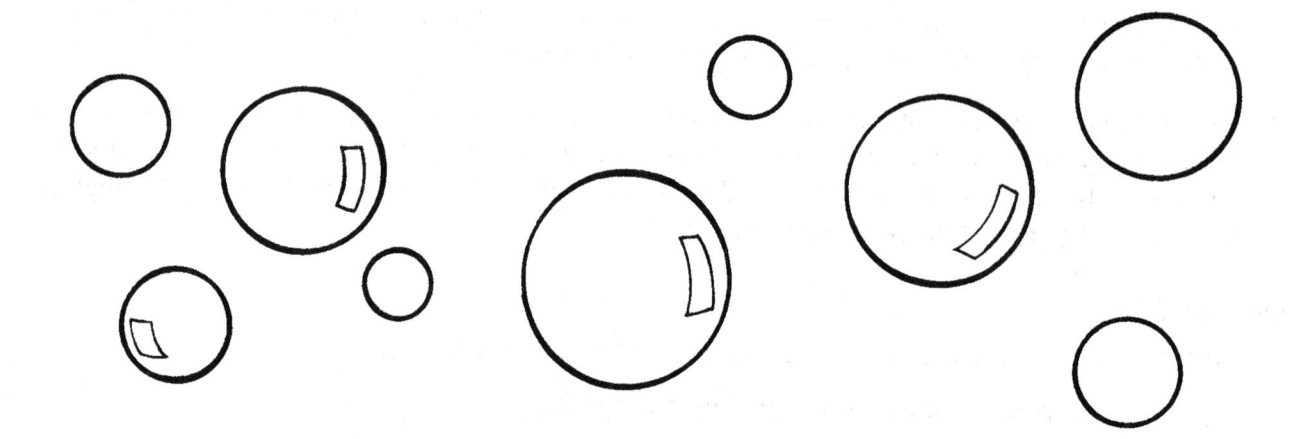

Bubble Theme

Bubble Science

Objective

The students will follow a recipe to create their own bubble mixture and create their own structure for a bubble wand.

Materials

- Use the following recipe and ingredients: ¼ c. of dishwashing soap (Dawn™ or Joy™ appears to work the best), 4 c. of water, and 1 T. of glycerin (optional). (There are other recipes on the internet sites listed on the Bubble Theme page. You may want to experiment ahead of time to see what works best for you.) The recipe may be modified to make more or less solution, depending on the size of the class. Also, decide ahead of time whether the students will be working together as a whole class, in small groups, or individually to make the solution. Have the recipe written on chart paper or the blackboard for all the students to view.

- measuring cups

- measuring tablespoon

- a large container (a bucket or large bowl, for example) to mix the solution

- smaller containers (paper cups, for example) for each student to have some of their own bubble solution.

- Visit the following Web Sites for ideas on materials to make bubble wands: **Bubble Geometry** or **Bubble Town**. Collect some items for the students to create their own bubble wands, as discussed in the Web Sites: straws, two pieces of regular white paper rolled into a cone shape, pipe cleaners, toilet paper rolls, etc.

Procedure

1. Discuss with the students how part of science is mixing ingredients to create end products. Explain to them that they are going to make their own bubble solution.

2. Pass out the materials to individual students, groups of students, or work as a whole class to follow the recipe and make the final bubble solution.

3. Once the solution is complete, tell the students they will be creating their own bubble wands to blow the bubbles. Share with them the materials which have been gathered. Depending on the age of the students, either allow them to pick their own material and create their own design, or have younger children follow specific steps to create a bubble wand.

4. Go outside and test the solution and the wands! Have a discussion on which wands work the best. Why do they think that is? Discuss how wands that are not circular in shape still create bubbles. An answer for this can be found at the Web site **Why are bubbles round?** (This may be slightly advanced for young children to understand.)

Extension Ideas

- Test whether it's easier to catch a bubble on a wet finger or a dry finger.
- Try the "King Size Bubble Blower" activity on page 52.

Bubble Theme

King Size Bubble Blower

Materials:

- 2-liter plastic soda bottles, 1 for each child
- shallow baking dish
- liquid dish detergent (Joy™ or Dawn™ are preferred brands, as they make the most bubbles.)
- water
- scissors
- weather stickers

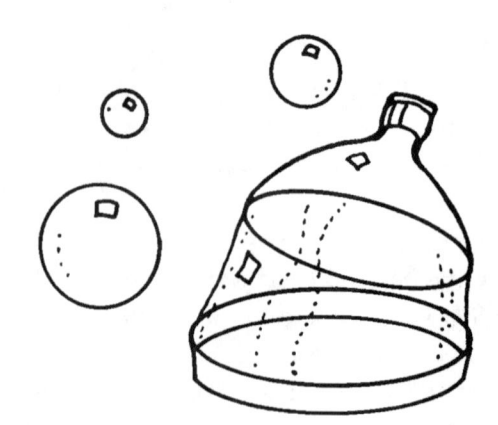

Directions:

1. Use scissors to remove the sides and bottom from each plastic bottle, leaving each child with a horn-shaped blowing instrument. Be sure the cut edge is smooth. Recycle the bottom sections of the bottles.

2. Let the children decorate these blowers with weather stickers.

3. To make the bubble solution, combine 1 part detergent with 12 parts water. Pour the solution into the baking dish to measure about a half-inch (1 cm).

4. Let the children place their blowers into the solution, then pick them up, and gently blow through the bottle top to make king size bubbles.

Additional Activities:

- Provide bubble wands, berry baskets, and fly swatters for the children to make bubbles in various sizes. Note how colorful bubbles are in the sunlight. Catch some, chase some, and watch them float through the air.

- Make three pipe cleaner wands. Shape the first one round, the second one square or triangular, and third one with an unfastened loop. What shape bubbles can you make with the round wand? Will the square and triangular wands make bubble squares and triangles? Does the unfastened loop make bubbles?

- Use the blowers to make wind sounds, as funnels at a water or sand table, and as trumpets in a rhythm band.

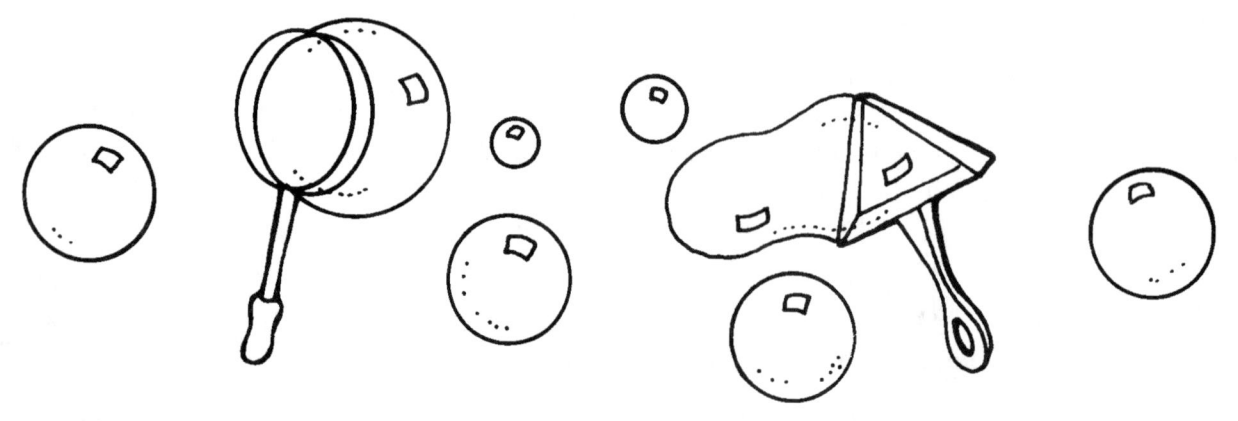

#3823 Internet Activities Through the Year

©Teacher Created Materials, Inc.

Bubble Theme

Bubble Social Studies

Objective

The students will construct a map of a bubble's journey.

Materials

- examples of maps either on posters, out of books, or from a Web site such as **Maps.com**
- "A Bubble's Journey" activity sheet or a very large piece of butcher paper (if the lesson is going to be done as a whole-class activity)
- crayons, markers, or colored pencils

Procedure

1. Discuss what a map is and how its people get to where they're going. Show the students examples of maps. Discuss how they are drawn in a view from up above.

2. Have the students imagine a bubble taking a journey from their classroom to somewhere else in their school building. For younger children, actually take the walk and observe what they pass on the way. When returning to the classroom, either have them work individually, or as a whole class to create a map which includes the starting point (their classroom) and the ending point (the library, school office, etc.). The teacher may draw this on the butcher paper under the "direction of the students." The student may add to it by cutting items such as drinking fountains, doors, tables, etc. out of construction paper to be glued on the final map. As a finishing touch, draw the path of the bubble on the map from it's starting to its ending point.

3. Older students may make their own maps on the "A Bubble's Journey" activity sheet or some other larger piece of paper. If desired, they may map their bubble journey somewhere other than school. Perhaps somewhere in their house or on the school grounds. As an extension, have the older students write directions to accompany their maps. For example, "walk out the classroom door and turn left..." This may be tied in with a Language Arts Lesson on writing directions.

Extension Ideas

- Learn to say "Pop!" in other languages. Use the **Free Translation.com** Web site for help. Locate the corresponding countries on a map.
- Read about the history of soap at the **Soap History** Web site.

Bubble Theme

Name: _____

A Bubble's Journey

Bubble Theme

Bubble Theme

Bubble Art

Objective
The students will create bubble prints.

Materials
- bubble solution (recipe can be found in the science lesson)
- small amounts of powder tempera paint or food coloring
- a number of bowls or containers in which to mix the colored bubble solution (Decide ahead of time whether the student will do this activity individually, in pairs, or supervised one at a time. This will determine how many containers of bubble mixture should be made.)
- white paper
- straws or egg beater

Procedure
1. Mix the bubble solution and tempera paint or food coloring in a bowl. Have the students observe how the bubble solution changes color. Try mixing two food colors or paints together to experiment with color mixing.
2. Have the students blow through straws or use the egg beater to mix up a mound of bubbles that reaches above the rim of the containers.
3. Have the students place their white paper on top of the mound, causing them to burst. This will create a "bubble print" on the paper. They may want to try layering different colors on top of one another.

Extension Ideas
- Have the students create fancy bubble wands. Ideas for materials are listed in the science lesson.
- Have the students draw pictures which accompany their "bubble journey" in the language arts lesson.

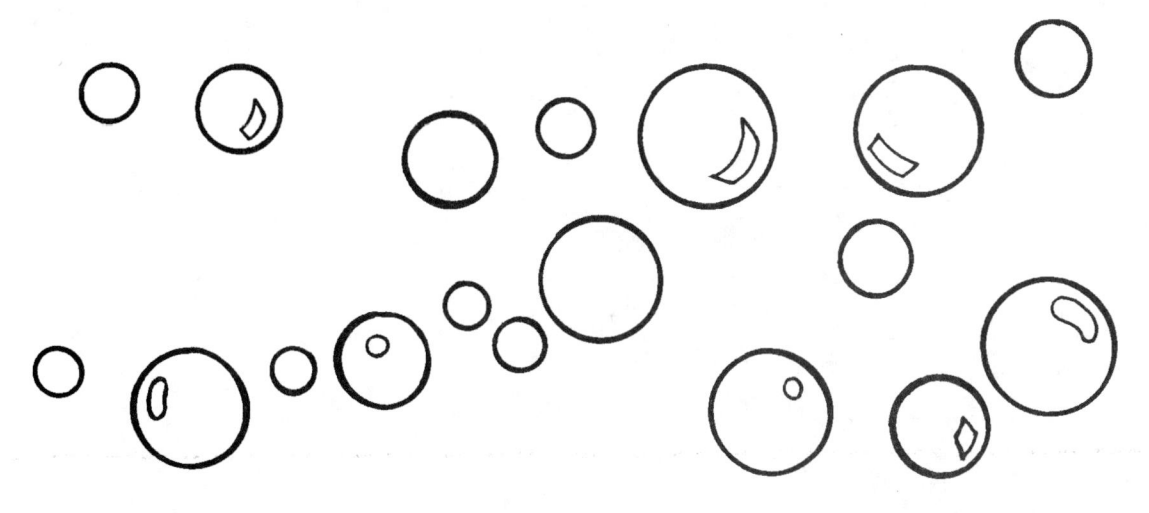

Bubble Movement

Objective

The students will move to music.

Materials

- soft music
- a wide open space

Procedure

1. Discuss the floating movement of bubbles. Compare the movement of a bubble to soft, flowing music.

2. Play music and have the students imitate floating bubbles. Abruptly stop the music and have them "Pop" by crouching down quickly on the floor.

Extension Idea

- Go outside and blow bubbles. Challenge the students to run through them or try to catch and/or pop them. To make lots of bubbles, have half of the class blowing bubbles while the other half is running through them.

Chameleon Theme

Related Web Sites

The Chameleon Information Network
The content of this site mainly consists of information for chameleon owners. However, there is also information on conservation and a number of photographs available for free download.

Chameleon—Encarta Encyclopedia
This site has good basic information on the chameleon, in particular on the unique body features of the chameleon.

Jackson's Chameleon
This section of the A1 Reptiles Web site features photographs of a specific type of chameleon—the Jackson Chameleon. Included are photos of the male, female, and hatchling.

Disappearing Act
This site is a demonstration of camouflage. Move a shape across a background of identical pattern.

The Tech Museum of Innovation
This site shows a drawing of a robotic chameleon and describes its features, including an extendable tongue, protective backbone and spine, camouflage patterns, prehensile tail, eyes, brain, and nose. Also included is basic information on chameleons.

Lizards!
This interactive Web site shows a variety of lizards from around the world, including some chameleons. Click on the different areas of the map to learn about the lizards that live there.

WebShots!—Chameleons
This site has some good photographs of different types of chameleons.

Related Literature

Changing Colors (Animal Clues) by Neecy Twinem
A chameleon appears piece by piece to reveal his entire body at the end.

Chameleons Are Cool by Martin Jenkins
This is a basic introduction to chameleons.

A Color of His Own by Leo Lionni
A little chameleon wants his own color like all the other animals.

Colorful Chameleons (Step into Reading Library) by Michelle Knudsen
There are lots of facts to be found here about chameleons.

Hard to See Animals (Rookie Read-About Science) by Allan Fowler.
This is a good introduction to camouflage

Konte Chameleon Fine, Fine, Fine! A West African Folktale by Cristina Kessler
A chameleon thinks he's sick when his body changes color!

Leon the Chameleon by Melanie Watt
In this story, a little chameleon feels different due to his bright color changes.

The Mixed-Up Chameleon by Eric Carle
The mixed-up chameleon envies and acquires attributes of some of the other animals.

They Thought They Saw Him by Jose Aruego
Here a chameleon hides himself from various animals and a boy by changing his colors.

Chameleon Theme

Chameleon Language Arts

Objective

The students will compare and contrast two pieces of literature.

Materials

- *A Color of His Own* by Leo Lionni and *The Mixed-Up Chameleon* by Eric Carle.
- chart paper or the "Chameleon Books" activity sheet.

Procedure

1. Read each of the books to the students.

2. For younger students have a whole-class discussion on how the books are similar and how they are different. Record their answers on chart paper in list form or on a Venn Diagram. For older students, have them fill out the "Chameleon Books" activity sheet on their own. Following this activity, reconvene as a class and discuss their responses.

Extension Ideas

- See the main social studies lesson which has been combined with a language arts lesson.

- Read the book *The Mixed-Up Chameleon* by Eric Carle. Have the students create and write about their own silly animals.

- Use "*The Mixed-Up Chameleon* Flannel Board Patterns" on pages 60 and 61 to explore the story further.

- Discuss how words can easily be changed, just as chameleons change. Adding silent *e* on the ends of words can make the vowel long. Initial consonants are changed to create entire word families. Endings (-ing, -ed, -s, etc.) are placed on words to change their meaning or tense.

Chameleon Theme

Name: _____

Chameleon Books

After reading *The Mixed-Up Chameleon* by Eric Carle and *A Color of His Own* by Leo Lionni, answer the following questions.

1. How were the books alike? _____

   _____

   _____

   _____

   _____

   _____

2. How were the books different? _____

   _____

   _____

   _____

   _____

   _____

Chameleon Theme

The Mixed-Up Chameleon Flannel Board Patterns

Cut out the patterns here and on the following page. Trace onto felt the appropriate number of times. Draw in any desired details with a permanent marker. Or you may simply copy the patterns twice on heavy paper, color, cut out, and laminate, attaching Velcro™ to the back or gluing them to felt.

chameleon

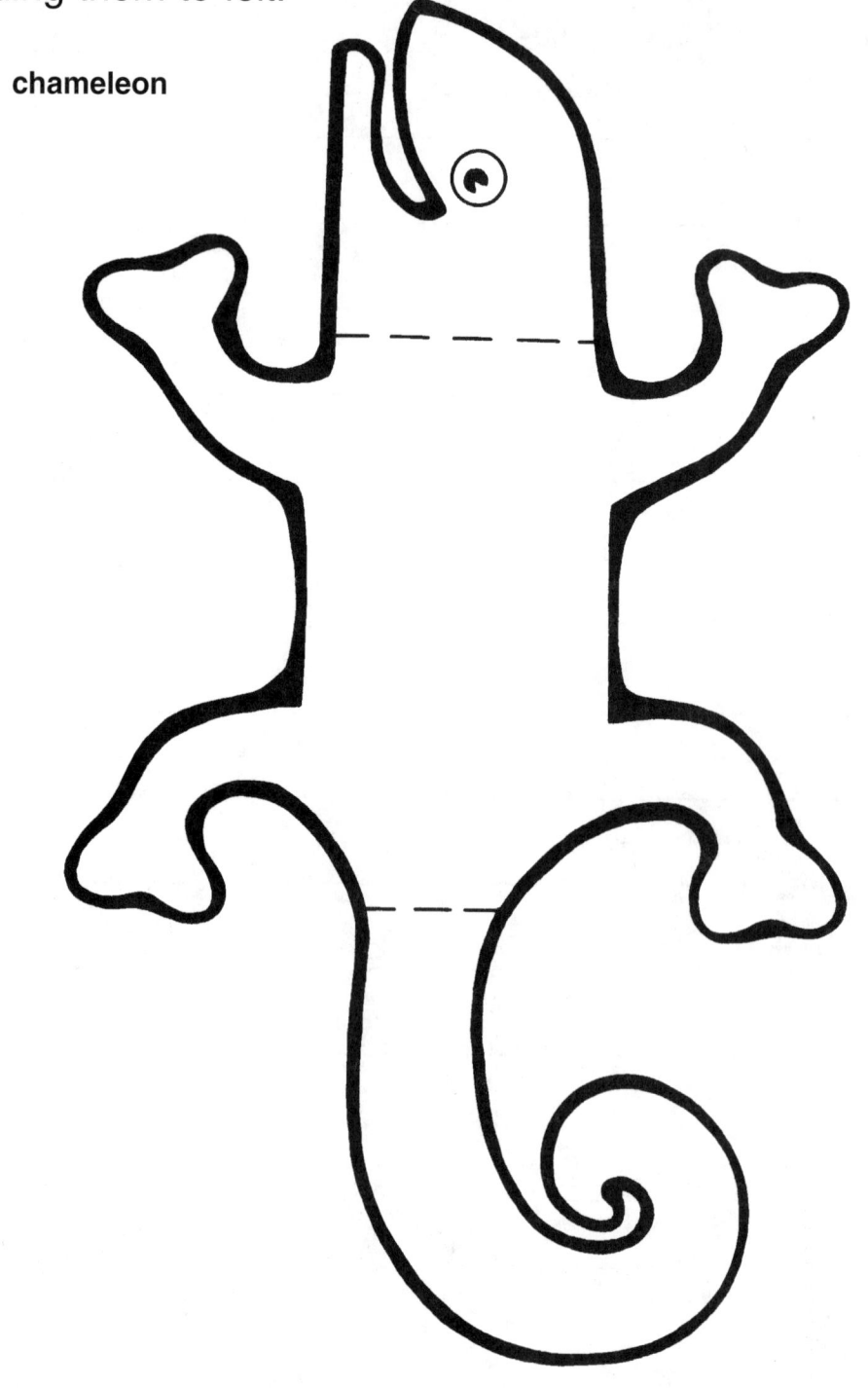

Chameleon Theme

The Mixed-Up Chameleon Flannel Board Patterns *(cont.)*

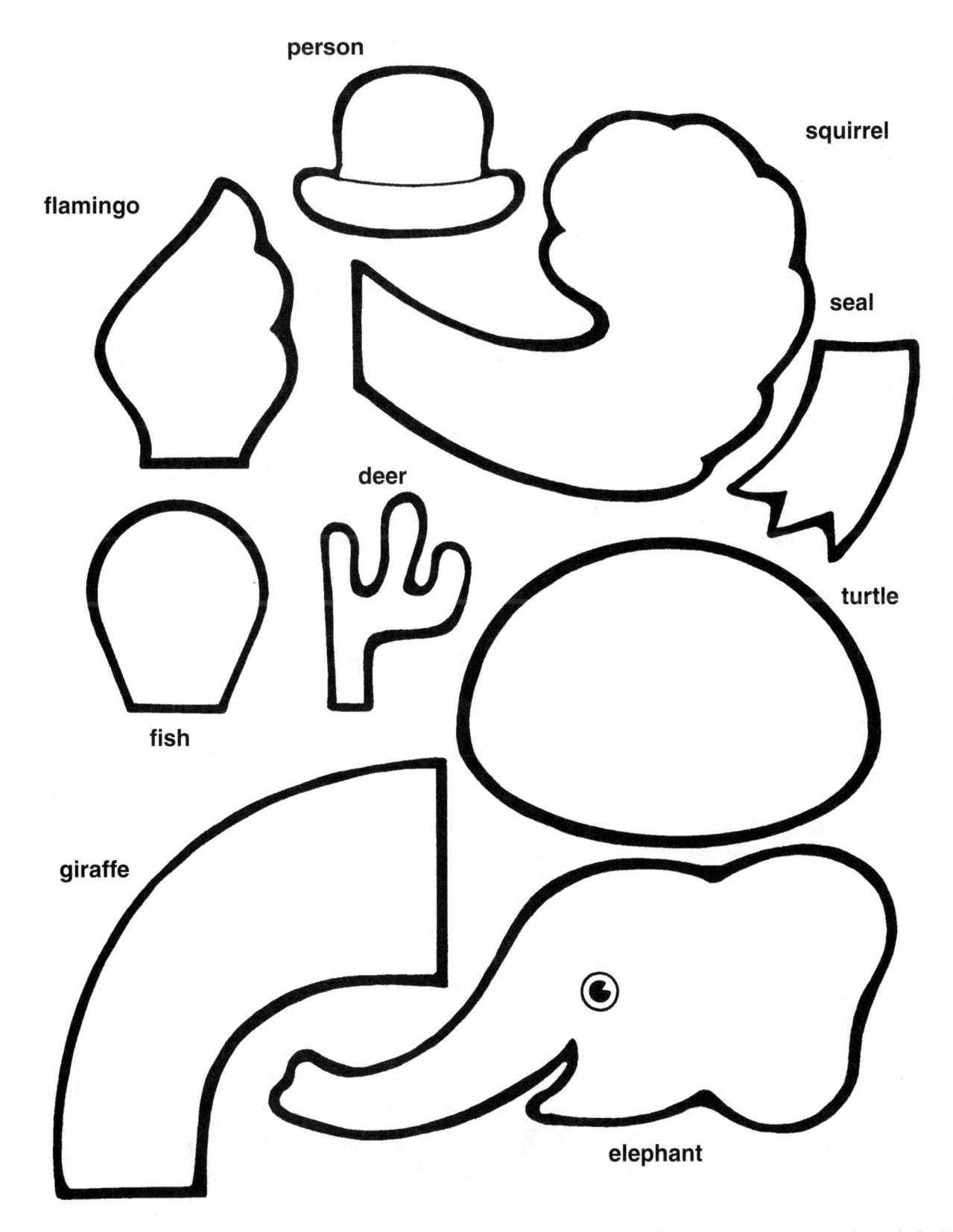

person

squirrel

flamingo

seal

deer

fish

turtle

giraffe

elephant

©Teacher Created Materials, Inc.   #3823 Internet Activities Through the Year

Chameleon Theme

Chameleon Math

Materials
- "Chameleon Cutouts" on page 63
- crayons
- scissors
- glue
- long strips of paper (the size of sentence strips)

Procedure
1. Discuss patterns with the students.
2. Give each student a chameleon cutout. For smaller classes, give the students two chameleons. Direct the students to color their chameleon one of the following colors—red, yellow, green or blue. Have them do this individually trying to keep a secret of the color they have chosen.
3. Have the students convene in an area where they may lay their chameleons on the floor and create patterns as a whole class. Discuss how patterns are formed and how they repeat. Label the patterns with letters, A-D, if appropriate.
4. As a follow up, give each student an entire sheet of "Chameleon Cutouts." Have them color, cut, and glue them onto long pieces of paper to create their own patterns.

Extension Ideas
- For older students, have a lesson on probability. Give each student a chameleon printout. Have them secretly color it one of the four above mentioned colors. Once they are done, graph the number of colors chosen. Then discuss the probability of drawing each of the colors if they were all placed in a container together.
- Discuss how numbers can change, just as chameleons do. Numbers change by having other numbers added or taken away. Have a lesson on subtraction and addition.
- For additional practice of math skills, use the Hands-On Reptiles activity found on page 64.

Chameleon Theme

Chameleon Cutouts

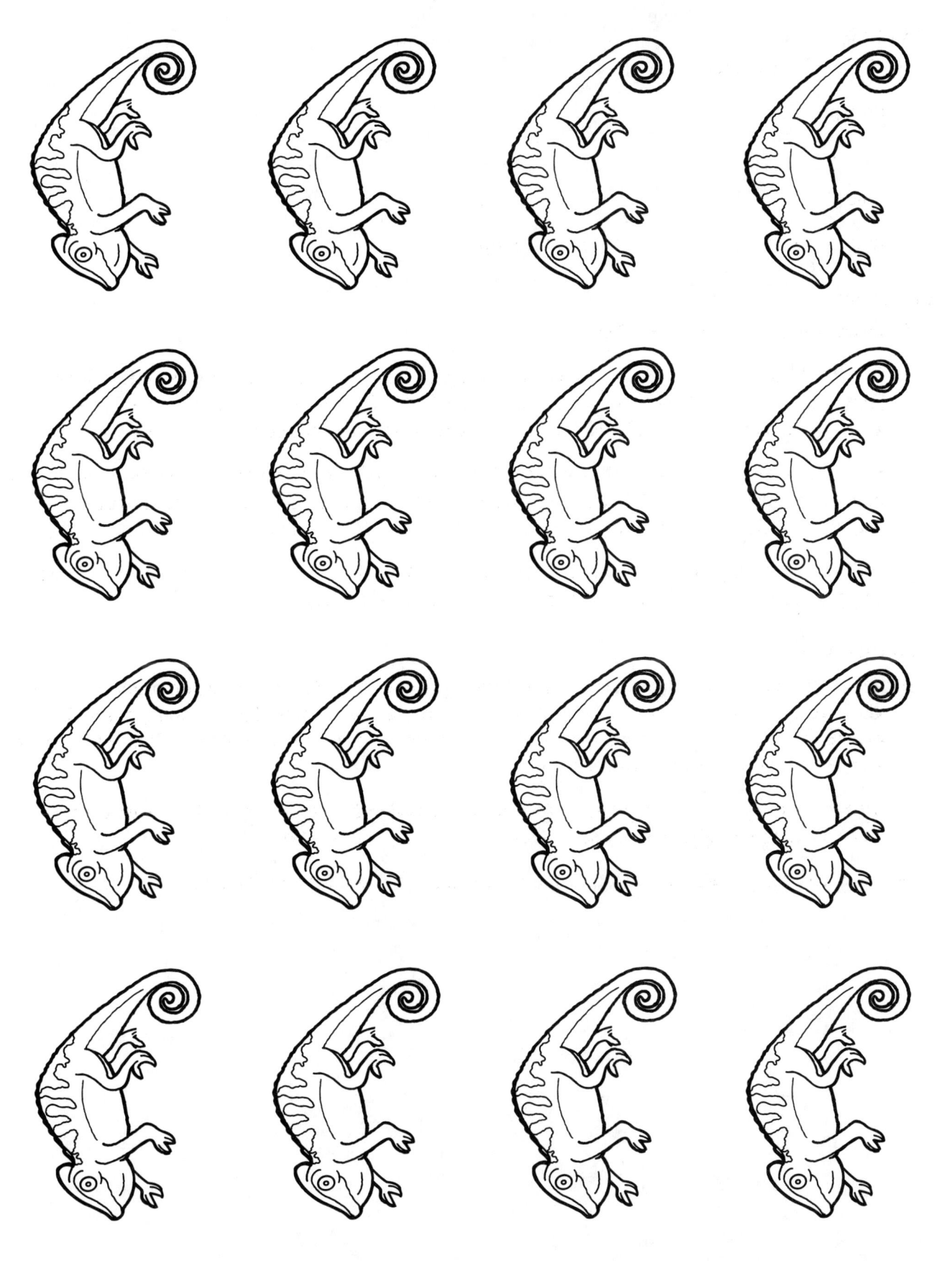

Chameleon Theme

Hands-On Reptiles!

Looking for a creative new manipulative to use for learning and practicing math skills? Here's your answer. Follow these tips to create exciting, thematic manipulatives that your students will love.

1. Duplicate the pieces on pages 65 and 66 as many times as you would like or until each child has a set.
2. Everyone can color and cut out his or her own manipulatives as desired. Or, have each child color one of each creature red, one blue, one yellow, and one green (or any other four colors you would like or upon which the class decides). Duplicate more and use more colors if you have the need.
3. You might enlarge some sheets so you have reptiles of various sizes for sorting and comparisons.
4. To preserve the manipulatives, color and laminate them. Then cut out the individual pieces. You might also duplicate them onto index or some other heavy paper.

Here are some hands-on activity ideas.

- Sort by color.
- Sort by reptile.
- Sort by size.
- Create patterns to follow. Have students challenge one another.
- Practice addition and subtraction.
- Practice color knowledge.
- Drill reptile name identification.
- Practice sets.
- Brainstorm as a class other possible ways to sort and classify the reptiles.

Finally, here are some other uses for the reptiles.

- Use for art projects.
- Use as writing springboards.
- Use for identification research.
- Sing "Old MacDonald," replacing the traditional animals with these and holding them up when their names are called.
- Make up a board game using these as playing cards.
- Play the "Concentration" card game by turning two of each card upside-down, then turning them over two by two, looking for matches. This is great practice for memory skills.

Chameleon Theme

Hands-On Reptiles! *(cont.)*

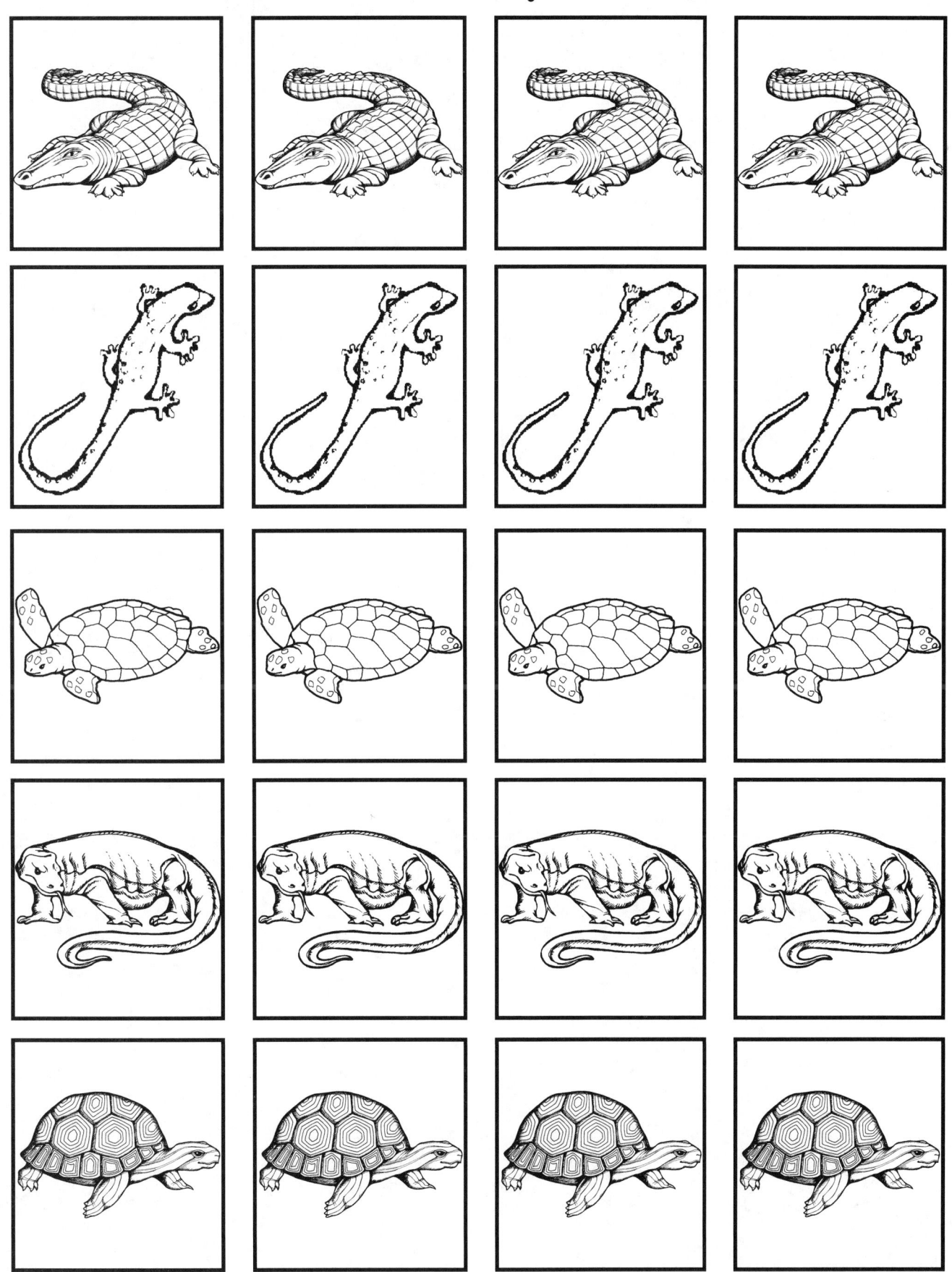

©Teacher Created Materials, Inc.   65   #3823 *Internet Activities Through the Year*

Chameleon Theme

Hands-On Reptiles! *(cont.)*

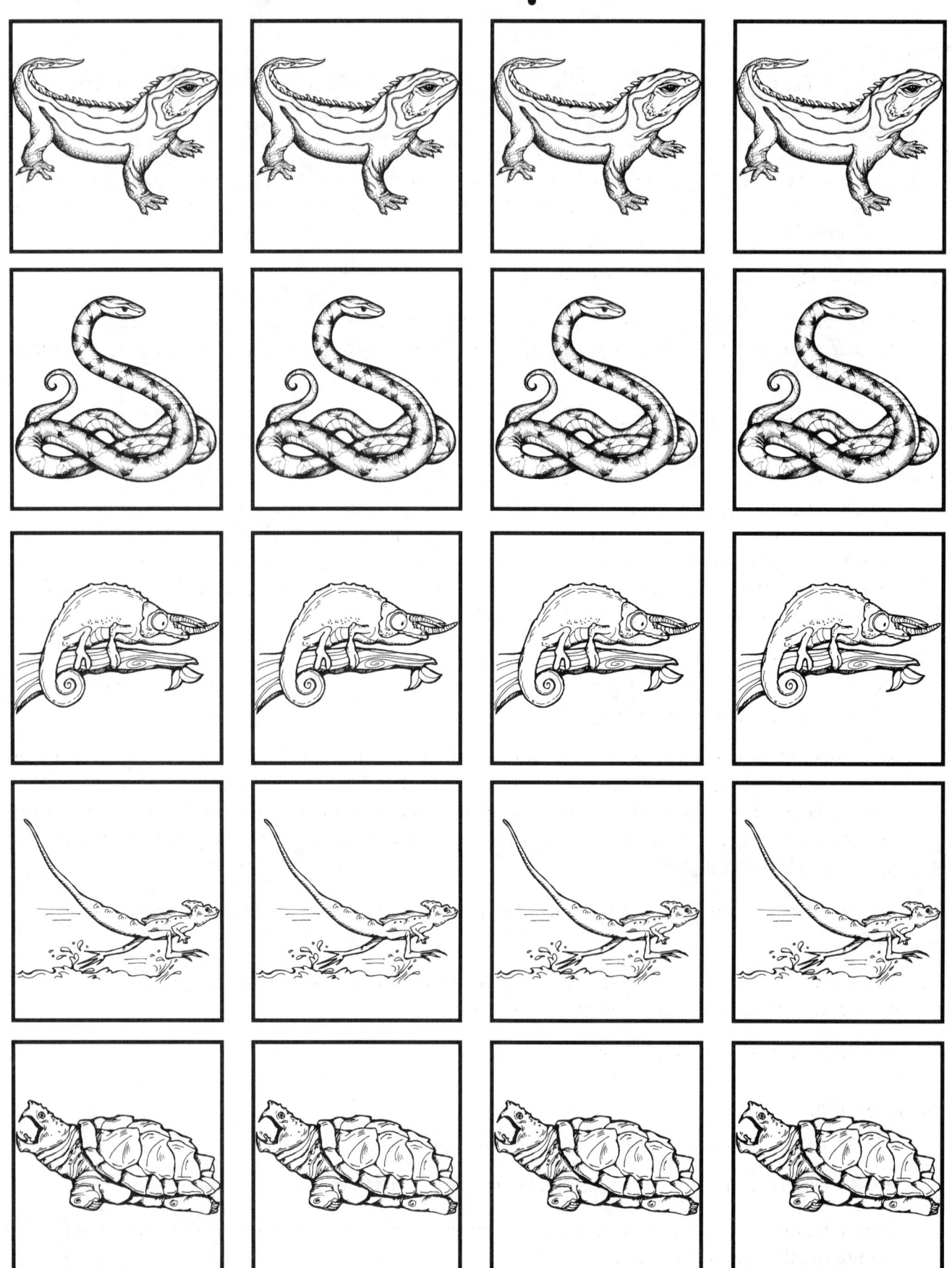

#3823 Internet Activities Through the Year 66 ©Teacher Created Materials, Inc.

Chameleon Theme

Chameleon Science

Objective

The students will experiment with camouflage and relate it to chameleons in their natural environment.

Materials

- manipulatives which are handy in the classroom, such as blocks, counting bears, scrap pieces of construction paper, marbles, cotton balls, etc. (See step 1 below to help determine the materials to be gathered.)

- "Camouflage" activity sheet (for older students)

- a book about camouflage, such as *Hard to See Animals* (Rookie Read-About Science) by Allan Fowler, *Disguises and Surprises* by Claire Llewellyn, or any of the *How to Hide . . .* a series by Ruth Heller

- the **Disappearing Act** Web site, if available

Procedure

1. Create a camouflage demonstration by gathering a collection of any of the above mentioned manipulatives. For example, put red and yellow counting bears in a see-through container or in an open box. Then add some red and yellow scraps of paper along with some green and blue scraps. Mix the contents up. Discuss with the students how much easier it is to see and find the green and blue scraps rather than the orange and yellow ones.

2. Relate this activity to the process of chameleons camouflaging themselves. Point out that chameleons are not always trying to hide themselves. Sometimes they change color in response to temperature, moods, and whether they are sick.

3. Show the link to the above mentioned Web site and how movement affects camouflage in addition to color and markings. (If the link is not available on your computer, it demonstrates how a moving object against a similarly colored background is easier to see than a still object. This can be shown by moving a small piece of colored paper across a bigger piece of the same color as opposed to keeping it still.)

4. Pass out the "Camouflage" activity sheet and have the students complete it individually or in pairs.

5. Older students may work in groups to create their own collection of items and present a camouflage demonstration to the rest of the class.

6. Read the chosen book on camouflage.

Extension Ideas

- Have the class research animals with prehensile tails and how they use them.

- Read a variety of nonfiction chameleon books. Make fact lists about chameleons.

- Have a lesson on how chameleons capture their prey with long, sticky tongues. Compare this feature to other animal tongues.

Chameleon Theme

Name: _____

Camouflage

After the teacher demonstrates the camouflage experiment, answer the following questions:

1. Draw a picture of the items in the container.

   [ ]

2. Which items were the hardest to find? _____
   _____

3. Which items were the easiest to find? _____
   _____

4. Why? _____
   _____

5. Is it easier to see an object that is moving or one that is still?
   _____

6. Why do chameleons and other animals blend in to their surroundings?
   _____
   _____

#3823 Internet Activities Through the Year ©Teacher Created Materials, Inc.

Chameleon Theme

Chameleon Social Studies

Objective

The students will identify, write about, and illustrate personal feelings.

Materials

- *My Many Colored Themes* by Dr. Seuss
- paper and writing utensils
- art materials to illustrate their writings (paint, colored chalk, colored pencils, crayons, etc.)

Procedure

1. The following procedure may be combined to meet the required Language Arts Objective and the Art Objective for the day.
2. Read *My Many Colored Themes* by Dr. Seuss.
3. Brainstorm and list on chart paper as many feelings as the students are able to identify.
4. Have the students make suggestions for what feelings different colors can represent. For example, "On a pink day I feel excited."
5. Pass out the paper and writing materials. Have the students complete the thought "On a (Theme) I feel _____." Older students may expand further on what contributed to their feeling a certain way. Younger students may need adult assistance in completing the sentence.
6. Pass out the art materials and have the students illustrate their writings. This step of the process may be combined to complete the daily art lesson as well.

Extension Ideas

- Identify on a map where chameleons live: Africa, Madagascar, Spain, southern Europe, Arabia, India, Sri Lanka, and the Seychelles Islands.
- Have a specific lesson on Madagascar since it is home to many species of chameleons. The following Web Sites will be helpful:

    Madagascar: Up Close and Personal, **Explore Madagascar**, and **Animals of Madagascar**

- Since Chameleons can change their colors in response to temperature and light, conduct a lesson on how people dress to fit their environment.

Chameleon Theme

Chameleon Art

Objective

The students will use paper to create a chameleon.

Materials

- torn pieces of tissue paper (if not available, use construction paper scraps)
- glue
- plain white paper
- crayons, paint, or colored pencils
- "Chameleon Printout" activity sheet (if desired) copied onto white construction paper

Procedure

1. Demonstrate using torn pieces of tissue paper to fill in a space.
2. Pass out the white paper or the "Chameleon Printout."
3. Have the students create their own chameleon by using torn pieces of tissue paper.
4. Have the students use the medium of their choice (paint, crayons, etc.) to create a background for the chameleon. Discuss how they can camouflage the chameleon by creating a background similar to the chameleon colors they have chosen.

Extension Ideas

- See the social studies lesson, which has an art component in it.
- Have the students paint a chameleon of their own and experiment with color mixing.

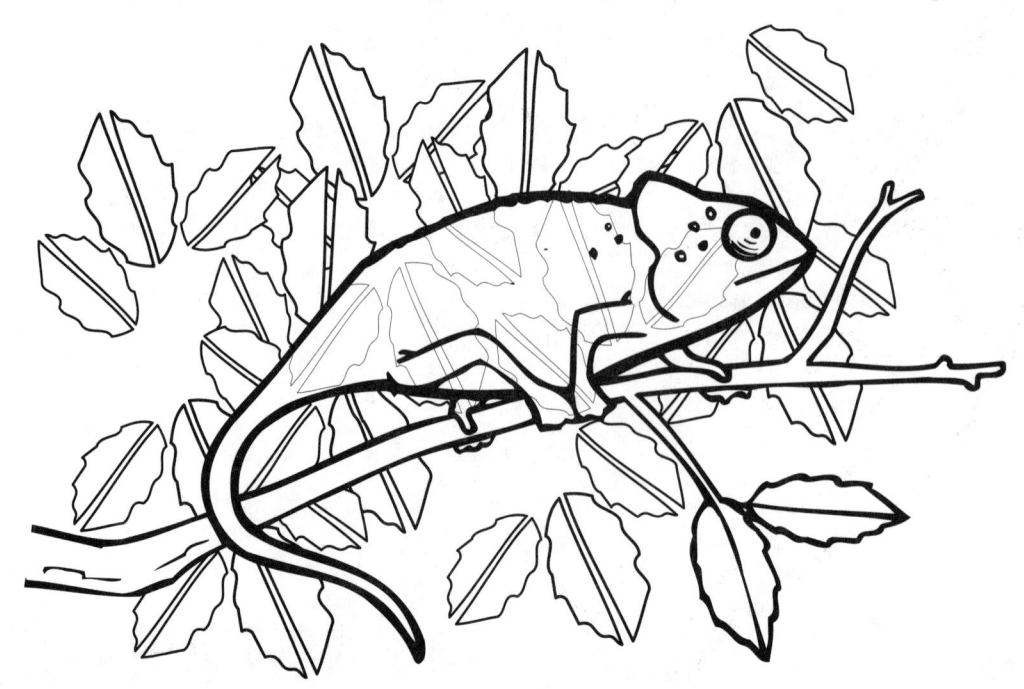

Chameleon Theme

Chameleon Printout

©*Teacher Created Materials, Inc.* #3823 *Internet Activities Through the Year*

Chameleon Theme

Chameleon Movement

Objective

The students will act out feelings.

Materials

- different colors of construction paper
- a wide open space

Procedure

1. Similar to the social studies lesson, discuss how colors can represent feelings.
2. Brainstorm together as a class at least five different feelings and a color to match each feeling.
3. Have the students spread out in an open area.
4. Hide the pieces of paper behind your back. As a piece is held up, have the students act out that feeling.

Extension Ideas

- As a variation on the above game, play a game of charades in which a student acts out a feeling and the other students have to guess the feeling by holding up a colored piece of paper that matches the feeling.
- Go outside and have the students get into small groups. Give each group a small collection of items. Have the groups find places in their surroundings which would best camouflage those items. For example, a group may choose to place a brown item in an area of mulch and a yellow pencil on a yellow piece of playground equipment.

Cloud Theme

Related Web Sites

Cloud Boutique
This site has photographs and definitions of different types of clouds. Clouds are classified by their characteristics, such as high clouds, middle clouds, low clouds, fog, multi-level clouds, and orographic clouds.

Weather.Com Education Index
This is a good resource for lesson plans and information related to weather. Included are links to newsletters and activity guides, a weather dictionary, and the Weather Classroom series.

WW2010—Clouds and Precipitation
This site from the University of Illinois has sophisticated information on clouds and cloud types. Photographs of different cloud types are included.

Clouds
This site is filled with more good photographs. Images can be downloaded royalty-free for educational use. A Cloud Glossary is also included.

Related Literature

Cloudy With a Chance of Meatballs by Judi Barrett
This is a fun, fanciful story of what would happen if food, rather than water, fell from the sky.

The Cloud Book by Tomie dePaola
This is a factual book, with humorous illustrations, regarding the science of clouds. It also includes some myths and folklore regarding cloud formations.

Clouds by Gail Saunders-Smith
This is a nonfiction book of clouds.

Cloudland by John Burningham
In this story, a little boy falls into the clouds and spends some time with the "cloud children."

Little Cloud by Eric Carle
This is the story of a little cloud who drifts away from his friends and changes his form into a lot of different shapes.

It Looked Like Spilt Milk by Charles G. Shaw
This book encourages children to use their imagination and see different shapes in cloud formations. It leads in nicely to an art lesson or to a trip outside to do some cloud gazing.

Cloud Theme

Cloud Language Arts

Objective

The students will write and present a fictitious weather report after listening to *Cloudy with a Chance of Meatballs* by Judi Barrett.

Materials

- *Cloudy with a Chance of Meatballs* by Judi Barrett
- "My Weather Report" activity sheet (or plain paper)
- writing utensils

Procedure

1. Read the story *Cloudy with a Chance of Meatballs* by Judi Barrett. If it is not available, have a discussion on what it would be like if items other than water fell from clouds.

2. Working in pairs, have the students write their weather reports using the "My Weather Report" activity sheet or plain paper. Tell them to include the temperature, what the clouds look like, what type of items are falling from the sky, and any other weather-related "facts." For younger children, the whole class can work together to write a report. The teacher can record their work on large chart paper.

3. Have the pairs of students present their weather report to the rest of the class.

Extension Ideas

- Do a phonics lesson on the "cl" or "ou" sound.

- Discuss the terms "his head is in the clouds," "he's in a fog," "he's on cloud nine," "every cloud has a silver lining." Have the students write about any of these topics. For example, a time they were so happy they felt they were on cloud nine, or a time something bad happened but something good came out of it.

- Have the students write stories about what it would be like to be able to play on the clouds.

- Have a lesson on describing words for clouds—fluffy, white, etc.

- Go outside and observe the clouds. Have the students identify clouds that look like certain objects. Have them write a story about what they see.

- Complete the "Cloudy Words" activity on page 76 in which students make new words out of the letters in "cumulonimbus."

Cloud Theme

Name: _____

My Weather Report

Tomorrow it will be cloudy with a chance of _____.

The temperature will be _____. The wind will

be _____. The sun will _____.

People should wear _____, because of

the _____ which may fall from the clouds.

People should also watch for _____.

Cloud Theme

Cloudy Words

How many words can you make using the letters from the cloud word **cumulonimbus**? Print one word in each cloud.

Cloud Theme

Cloud Math

Objective

The students will discover different combinations for arriving at the number 9.

Materials

- cotton balls
- "How Many Ways Can I Get to Cloud 9?" activity sheet

Procedure

1. Depending on the age and math ability of the students, they may either work individually, in pairs, or as a whole class.

2. Discuss how being on Cloud 9 means being happy. Tell them they need to find out how many different combinations of numbers there are for getting to Cloud 9.

3. Depending on how the class is grouped, give each child, or group of children, nine cotton balls (to serve as clouds).

4. Pass out the "How Many Ways Can I Get to Cloud 9?" activity sheet and have them use the manipulatives for assistance in discovering ways for arriving at the number nine. They may either write addition problems using just two numbers, or more, if appropriate.

Extension Ideas

- Have the students play "The Cloud 9 Game." Give each pair of students a pair of dice. Have them take turns rolling the dice. Whoever rolls closer to nine, without going over, is the winner of that roll. This can also be played as the whole class vs. the teacher. The students just take turns rolling the dice.

- Have the students estimate how many clouds (cotton balls) you have placed in a see-through container.

Cloud Theme

Name: _____

How Many Ways Can I Get to Cloud 9?

Write addition problems for reaching the number 9.

Cloud Theme

Cloud Science

Objective

The students will observe a demonstration of how clouds form.

Materials

- a clear plastic bottle
- black construction paper
- water
- a match
- ice
- a nonfiction book about clouds (if available)

Procedure

1. Read the book, if available.

2. Do a cloud-making demonstration by putting warm water in the bottom ⅓ of the clear plastic bottle.

3. Light the match, drop it in the bottle and immediately place the ice on top of the opening of the bottle.

4. Have the students observe what happens. Black construction paper taped to the back of the bottle will help them see the bottle fog up with your "classroom cloud."

5. Explain that any evaporating water droplets in the bottle attach to the dust particles from the lit match forming the cloud. The ice is like the cold atmosphere and the water represents any water on earth. (Be sure to warn the children of the dangers of playing with matches.)

Extension Ideas

- Read a nonfiction book about clouds, such as Tomie dePaola's *The Cloud Book* which talks about the different types of clouds. Information and pictures of different cloud types can also be found at the **Cloud Boutique** Web site. Pass out the "Cloud Types" activity sheet on page 80 or the "New Cloud Words" activity sheet on page 81 and have the students draw pictures of or name the different types of clouds.

- Go outside and identify what types of clouds are in the sky on that particular day. Have students draw observations of the clouds in the sky and then discuss what types they are.

Cloud Theme

Name: _____

Cloud Types

Draw a picture and write 2 describing words for each type of cloud.

Cumulus

1. _____

2. _____

Stratus

1. _____

2. _____

Cirrus

1. _____

2. _____

Cloud Theme

Name: _____

New Cloud Words

A. **Directions:** Make new words by joining one word part from column 1 with one word part from column 2.

Column 1	Column 2	
Alto	cumulus	_____
Cirro	stratus	_____
Cumulo	nimbus	_____
Strato	cumulus	_____

B. **Directions:** Using *The Cloud Book* or any other books on clouds, list the names of other clouds.

_____   _____

_____   _____

_____   _____

_____   _____

©Teacher Created Materials, Inc.

Cloud Theme

Cloud Social Studies

Objective
The students will make maps of a familiar room.

Materials
- "Here's a Cloud's View of My . . ." activity sheet or blank paper
- writing utensils (crayons, pencils, colored pencils, etc.)
- examples of maps (some can be found at **Maps.com** if needed)

Procedure
1. Show examples of maps to the students. Discuss how map markers draw things from a "cloud's-eye view." Some good aerial photos can be found at **City Scenes.com**.
2. Pass out the paper or activity sheet and writing utensils.
3. Have the students draw a map of their bedrooms, the classroom, or some other familiar place.
4. As an alternative for younger children or as a bigger whole-class project, a classroom map can be made together on a large piece of butcher paper. The children can make cutouts of their desks, tables, bookshelves, etc., and then work as a class to glue them in the correct place.

Extension Ideas
- Use newspaper weather maps to locate cities with hotter and colder temperatures than the students' city.
- Have a meteorologist come in and give a presentation on what his/her job entails. This could also tie into a science lesson on using cloud types for predicting the weather.

Cloud Theme

Name: _____

Here's a Cloud's View of My _____

©*Teacher Created Materials, Inc.* 83 *#3823 Internet Activities Through the Year*

Cloud Theme

Cloud Art

Objective
The students will create cloud pictures.

Materials
- blue construction paper
- cotton balls
- glue
- markers, crayons, and/or paint

Procedure
1. Look at the clouds outside, or pictures of clouds and discuss how some look full and puffy, while others can be thin and wispy.
2. Ask the students how they could turn a puffy cotton ball into a thin wispy cloud shape.
3. Pass out the art supplies and have the students create skies full of clouds. They may also add in other items, such as birds, rainbows, etc. using the other art materials.

Extension Ideas
- Read the book *It Looked Like Spilt Milk* by Charles G. Shaw. Pass out blue construction paper. Have the students fold it in half. They should then open it up and drop white paint along the middle crease and on one side of the fold line. They can then refold it, press down hard and smooth the paint around. Once they open the paper back up they can inspect the "cloud" and see what image it looks like.
- Have younger students complete the "Clouds" activity sheet on page 85. Have older students complete the "Painting Clouds" activity on page 86.
- Make fog pictures. Discuss how fog is really low clouds. The students can then do a crayon drawing (pressing down hard with their crayon) and then make a wash with gray watercolor paint and water. They should do this wash over their entire picture to create a fog scene.
- Make clouds with torn white paper glued on blue paper.

Clouds

Draw the sky. Stretch and glue cotton balls over the sky to make the clouds look fluffy.

Clouds are pretty.
Clouds are not soft and fluffy.
Clouds are wet and cold.

Cloud Theme

Painting Clouds!

Materials

watercolors; paintbrushes; jars of water; 2 or 3 plastic drop sheets or old shower curtains; large sheets of white construction paper; pictures of storms, sunsets, sunrises.

Preparation

1. Spread out the drop sheets and set out the materials.
2. Show the children pictures of storms, sunsets, sunrises.
3. Challenge them to be inventive—to get away from stereotypical blue sky and white clouds.
4. Divide them into 2 or 3 groups.

Directions

Wet Brush: A Daytime Sky

1. Paint your paper with water first.
2. Paint clouds. Use lots of water.
3. Add some daytime colors on top.
4. Let your painting dry flat.

Wet Brush: A Sunrise or Sunset Sky

1. Paint your paper with water.
2. Paint clouds colored by a sunset, sunrise, or a storm.
3. Let your painting dry flat.

Dry Brush: On Top of Your Paintings

After your painting is dry, add finishing touches with a small paintbrush and a small paintbox of paints. This time use lots of paint and very little water! Your paintbrush will leave textured bristle marks. This technique is called Dry Brush.

Choose your best painting. Mount it on construction paper. Display it on the bulletin board.

Cloud Theme

Cloud Movement

Objective
The students will imitate cloud movement.

Materials
- An open space allowing for movement
- Slow music
- Fast music

Procedure
1. Discuss how clouds can either move slowly across the sky or more quickly, depending on the amount of wind.
2. Play the soft music and have the students imitate slow-moving clouds.
3. As a contrast, play the fast music and have the students imitate faster-moving clouds.

Extension Ideas
- Using sidewalk chalk, have the students draw large clouds on an open outdoor space. They can then jump from cloud to cloud.
- Have the students jump as high as they can and try and "touch the clouds."

Dolphin Theme

Related Web Sites

David's Whale and Dolphin Watch
This site has information, great photographs, and dolphin sounds!

Enchanted Learning
Great site for activities, printouts, and lesson plan ideas all relating to dolphins.

Scholastic —Dolphins
This site is a must-see for lots of good information, activities, and links.

The National Marine Mammal Laboratory's Education Web Site
This site contains information on cetaceans, which includes whales, dolphins and porpoises.

Cetacea
Filled with information on all different species of dolphins.

Time for Kids
An article about dolphins being able to recognize themselves in mirrors.

Sea World
An abundance of information about bottlenose dolphins.

Marine Mammal Vocalizations
Hear dolphins click and whistle!

Related Literature

Discovering Whales and Dolphins by Janet Craig
This quality nonfiction book is filled with information and illustrations.

Dolphin (An I Can Read Book) by Robert Ada Morris
This book follows the birth and the first months of a baby bottle-nosed dolphin.

Dolphins (Animals of the Oceans) by Judith Hodge
A good nonfiction book about dolphins.

Dolphins! by Sharon Bokoske and Margaret Davidson
This easy reader has lots of interesting information about dolphins.

Dolphins for Kids by Patricia Corrigan
This book touches on the many different kinds of dolphins.

Friendly Dolphins (Rookie Read-About Science) by Allan Fowler
This nonfiction book about dolphins also provides information on porpoises and whales.

Splash! A Book About Whales and Dolphins by Melvin and Gilda Berger
This Hello Reader book is divided into chapters, one of which is exclusively about dolphins.

Whales Can Sing and Other Amazing Facts About Sea Mammals (I Didn't Know That) by Kate Petty
Here is another nonfiction book about dolphins!

Whales and Dolphins by Peter and Connie Roop
This is an easy reader with very simple text—a good book for the children to read independently.

Whales and Dolphins by J.I. Anderson
This book covers different types of whales and dolphins, their physical characteristics, eating habits, and more.

Dolphin Theme

Dolphin Language Arts

Objective

The students will develop their own form of classroom sign language.

Materials

- information from the following Web sites: **Dolphin Language Research, Dolphin Intelligence, American Sign Language Browser,** and **Animated American Sign Language Dictionary**
- chart paper or blackboard

Procedure

1. Share information with the students from the first two Web sites listed about how dolphins have been taught a form of sign language. Lead to a discussion on American sign language and how people with hearing disabilities use sign language to communicate. View the Sign Language Web sites and teach the students a few signs.

2. Tell the students your class is going to develop their own classroom sign language. Work together to brainstorm a list of words for which it would be helpful to have a sign. For example, recess, clean-up, book, pencil, write, desk, line-up, etc. Make the list as long as appropriate for the age of the students.

3. Break the class into small groups of 3–4 students. Assign each group certain words of the brainstorm list. They should work together to create hand signs for each of the words assigned.

4. Once the groups have created their signs, they may teach them to the rest of the class.

5. Use these hand signs throughout the day (or longer) to communicate with each other. The students have created their own classroom sign language!

Extension Ideas

- Have the students write a story about an adventure swimming with a dolphin.
- Have a phonics lesson on the "ph-" sound.

©Teacher Created Materials, Inc.   #3823 Internet Activities Through the Year

Dolphin Theme

Dolphin Math

Objective

The students will measure and compare two different lengths.

Materials

- information on bottle-nosed dolphins and orcas (killer whales). Use the **Bottle-Nosed Dolphins** and **Killer Whales** sites from **Enchanted Learning.com** for background information or gather information from a book.
- 42 one-foot rulers, or 42 pieces of paper cut to one foot.
- a wide space to measure out 30 feet.
- "Dolphin Measurement" activity sheet

Procedure

1. Share the information about bottle-nose dolphins and killer whales. Point out that killer whales are a member of the dolphin family and can be 30 feet long or more. Bottle-nosed dolphins are another type of dolphin which grow to be 12 feet long at the most.

2. Pass out the rulers or pieces of paper. Have the students work together to lay the items end to end to create a 30-foot-long line and a 12-foot-long line. Have these lines begin at the same point so the students can easily compare the two lines.

3. Work as a class to answer the questions on the "Dolphin Measurement" activity sheet. For questions number 4 and 5, have some students lay down next to the lines to see about how many children it takes to equal 12 feet and how many to equal 30 feet.

Extension Ideas

- Similar to the Frog Math lesson, have the students jump along a number line (just as dolphins leap through the water) to solve math problems.
- Have the students write and solve story problems which involve numbers of dolphins in a pod. A pod is a group of dolphins.

Dolphin Theme

Name: _____

Dolphin Measurement

1. How long can a killer whale be?
   _____

2. How long can a bottle-nosed dolphin be?
   _____

3. How much longer is a killer whale than a bottle-nosed dolphin?
   _____

4. A bottle-nosed dolphin is about the same length as _____ children in my class.

5. A killer whale is about the same length as _____ children in my class.

Dolphin Theme

Dolphin Science

Objective

The students will identify and write facts about dolphins.

Materials

- pieces of paper cut in the shape of dolphins.
- books or Web sites with dolphin facts (See the Dolphin Theme Page for suggestions.)
- chart paper or chalkboard
- "Dolphin Facts" sheet (if desired)
- blue butcher paper
- tape

Procedure

1. Ask the students what they know about dolphins. Record their responses on chart paper or the chalkboard.
2. Share information with the students from books or Web sites.
3. Pass out the pieces of paper cut in the shape of dolphins. Have each student write one new fact he/she learned about dolphins on the paper. (For younger students, cut up the "Dolphin Facts" sheet into strips and have the students copy or glue the strip onto their dolphin shape. More facts may need to be added or put the students in pairs.)
4. Cut the butcher paper to look like ocean waves and mount it on the wall. Have the students take turns reading their dolphin fact and placing it on the butcher paper. The may place them so they appear to be leaping out of the water.

Extension Ideas

- As an alternative to the above lesson, compile the dolphin facts into a book and allow the students to take the book home to share with their families.
- Compare and contrast mammals and fish.
- Have the students pair up and research a specific type of dolphin.

Dolphin Facts

Dolphins are members of the whale family.

Dolphins are mammals.

Dolphins cannot breathe under water.

Dolphins breathe through a blow hole.

Dolphins use echolocation to find their way under water.

Dolphins live in the ocean.

Dolphins talk to each other by using clicks, barks, and whistles.

Dolphins have teeth.

There are more than 30 types of dolphins.

Dolphin tails are called flukes.

Dolphins move their flukes up and down to move through the water.

Most dolphins eat fish and squid.

Dolphin Theme

Dolphin Social Studies

Objective

The students will name and identify the four major oceans on a world map.

Materials

- information from the **Enchanted Learning** and **Ocean's Alive** Web sites
- a world map
- "Dolphins Live in Oceans" activity sheet

Procedure

1. Discuss with the students how dolphins live in all the major oceans of the world. (Some scientists believe there is a fifth ocean, the Southern Ocean, which is discussed at the Web sites.)

2. Share information from the aforementioned sites about the oceans and where they are located. Review the activity sheet ahead of time to be sure specific material is covered in the presentation of material.

3. Look at a world map and have the students locate the oceans as well as their home town. Which ocean do they live the closest to?

4. Pass out the activity sheet and have the students complete the sheet for reinforcement. With younger students, complete the activity sheet as a whole class.

Extension Ideas

- Using information from a book or Web site, discuss with the students how dolphins have their own way of communicating with one another through the use of clicks, barks, and whistles. Relate this to human language and how people need to communicate with one another. Would people who live in the same area be able to function if they all spoke a different language? Present the fact that people who live in the same areas speak a common language. Use a map, the "Languages Around the World" activity sheet, and the **Free Translation** Web site for a lesson on languages. Work together as a class to complete the activity sheet. The students may add other countries and languages on to the sheet as well.

- Most dolphins are social animals and help one another when hurt or in distress. Brainstorm how people who live together in the same community can help one another.

Dolphin Theme

Name:_____

Dolphins Live in Oceans

1. How many major oceans are there in the world?

   _____

2. Write down the names of the oceans.

   _____

   _____

   _____

3. Is the Earth covered with more water or more land?

   _____

4. How is ocean water different than fresh water?

   _____

   _____

5. Which ocean do you live the closest to?

   _____

©*Teacher Created Materials, Inc.* #3823 *Internet Activities Through the Year*

Dolphin Theme

Name: _____

Languages Around the World

For each country listed, write the language spoken in that country and how to say the word "dolphin."

Country	Language	How to Say Dolphin
Germany	_____	_____
Italy	_____	_____
France	_____	_____
Spain	_____	_____

Dolphin Theme

Dolphin Art

Objective

The students will create dolphin puppets.

Materials

- information from the **Dolphin Anatomy** Web site
- gray construction paper or white paper and gray paint
- craft sticks
- glue
- blue poster board
- pictures of dolphins on the Internet or in books
- cutout shapes of dolphins, if desired

Procedure

1. Share the pictures of dolphins. Talk about the different parts of a dolphin. Use the following Web site for help: **Dolphin Anatomy**.
2. Have the students create their own dolphins using the gray paper or making them on white paper and painting them gray. If the students need assistance, allow them to trace a cut-out shape of a dolphin.
3. Once the students have completed their dolphins, have them glue them onto a craft stick.
4. Working as a class, create ocean waves out of the blue poster board.
5. The students may take turns putting on puppet shows by popping their puppets out from behind the poster board. (Or the students may make their own waves by using a piece of blue construction paper.)

Extension Ideas

- As an alternative to the above lesson, have the students create rings for their dolphin puppets to jump through. The rings can be created from paper plates by cutting out the center.
- Have the students create ocean dioramas using shoe boxes, paint, construction paper and other art materials. Be sure to include dolphins in the diorama!

Dolphin Theme

Dolphin Movement

Objective
The students will act out dolphin tricks.

Materials
- information from the **Dolphin Tricks** Web site
- two or three hoola hoops
- two or three balls
- a basket or container to throw the balls into
- a wide open space allowing for movement
- a snack, such as crackers

Procedure
1. Read the information from the aforementioned Web site.
2. Set up a dolphin obstacle course in three areas and divide the class into three groups.
   - hoola hoops for the students to jump through
   - baskets/containers for the students to throw balls into
   - a wide open space for the students to imitate dolphins leaping out of the water
3. At each of the areas, offer the students a "reward" of a cracker, etc., just as dolphins are given fish.

Extension Ideas
- Play an echolocation game in which half the students are blindfolded and the other half have to call out directions to help them locate objects or make their way to a destination.

Earth Theme

Related Web Sites

The Nine Planets—Earth
This page from the Nine Planets site has a great deal of information and a number of photos of the planet Earth. Information is included on the layers of the earth, the surface of the Earth, the atmosphere, and the moon. A glossary is included to explain many of the terms used.

Earth From Space
This site consists of photographs of Earth as seen from space. Click on an area of the map to see the photographs available, then click on a thumbnail image to see the photo and read a description of the area.

Astronomy for Kids
This sit has some basic information on the planet Earth as well as the other planets. It is more kid-friendly than the previous sites. Click on a planet to go to its page and learn more about it.

Earth and Moon Viewer
This site has more good photos of Earth from space. You can view a map of the Earth showing the day and night regions at the present time, or view the earth from the sun, moon, or night side. You can also specify the latitude and longitude of a location to view it. You can also view the moon from the Earth, sun, or night side.

Helpful Hints for Planet Earth
This site presented by a first grade class has activities for taking care of Earth. Read the class' book, learn how to heal the planet, take a quiz, link to other sites for fun things to do, and more.

Children of the Earth United
This is an environmental education site where kids can learn about animals, plants, environmental issues, Native American wisdom, and much more. Games, interactive animations, and multimedia presentations are included.

DinoPal Tips to Save the Earth
The DinoPals describe simple things kids can do to help the Earth, such as plant a tree, ride a bike, save electricity, and recycle.

EEK
Environmental Education for Kids is an electronic magazine from the Wisconsin Department of Natural Resources. Learn about the Earth, plants, animals, the environment, and more. The Teacher Pages have activities and information for teachers.

Related Literature

Earth (A True Book) by Larry Dane Brimmer
This book is full of information and photographs.

The Earth and the Universe: How the Sun, Moon, and Stars Cause Changes on Earth (The Universe) by Miquel Perez
This book describes the relationship between the Earth, Sun, Moon, and Stars.

You're Aboard Spaceship Earth (Let's-Read-and-Find-Out-Science) by Patricia Lauber
This book relates being on planet Earth to being on a spaceship. Touches on the topics of available resources and their cycles.

Earth Theme

Earth Language Arts

Objective

The students will write a story which takes place in a specific environment.

Materials

- pictures of different environments (Use the "Environments" activity sheet, if needed.)
- "Story Map" activity sheet (if needed)
- paper and writing utensils
- art materials to illustrate the story, if desired

Procedure

1. Facilitate a discussion on all the different environments which make up the planet Earth. Have the students brainstorm some different environments and list them on chart paper or the blackboard. Use the "Environments" activity sheet or any pictures available to help brainstorm a list.

2. Explain to the students they may pick any environment they wish to be the setting for a story. With younger students, the class may want to decide on an environment and write a whole-class story in which each student contributes a sentence. Older students may write a story of their choice in the setting of their choice. Help the students think about what may be in the environment they have chosen before they begin writing. This may help them decide on characters and plot. A story map may be helpful in outlining the stories before they begin the writing process.

3. If time allows, have the students illustrate their stories, featuring the environment they have chosen.

Extension Ideas

- Have the students write a letter to a "Save the Earth" organization, supporting their work. Or have them write a letter to a government official urging them to work on saving the earth.
- Have the students complete the thought "The Earth is special because…"

Earth Theme

ENVIRONMENTS

Desert	Jungle
Mountain	Beach
Forest	Island

Earth Theme

Name: _____

Earth Story Map

Setting (Environment): _____

Characters: _____

_____

_____

Plot: _____

_____

_____

Event 1: _____

_____

_____

Event 2: _____

_____

_____

Event 3: _____

_____

_____

Event 4: _____

_____

_____

Earth Theme

Earth Math

Objective

The students will explore fractions.

Materials

- "Circle" activity sheet
- crayons—blue and brown
- balloons—blue and black or green—blown up so that 3/4s of them are blue and 1/4 are black or green. (Try to have about 1 balloon per student.)
- globe

Procedure

1. While holding up the globe, discuss how the Earth is covered by more water than land. In fact, almost 3/4 (71%) of the Earth's surface is covered by water.

2. Give each child one of the blown up balloons. Have them cluster the balloons together in a designated area. Discuss how the blue balloons represent the amount of water on Earth's surface and the black/green balloons represent the land. Observe how much more water than land covers the Earth. This will help create a good visual representation.

3. Pass out the "Circle" activity sheet. (For younger students, before running off this activity sheet, divide the circle into fourths to give them lines to cut on. Older students may use rulers and divide the circle into fourths on their own.)

4. Have the students color three of the fourths blue and the other fourth brown or green. Discuss how this again represents the amount of water vs. the amount of land covering Earth's surface. They should then cut out their circle into the four pieces.

5. Work as a class to explore the fractions. How many fourths make one-half? How many make a whole? The amount of depth will depend on the age of the students. Older students may be able to follow up by writing some fraction problems involving fourths. Challenge them by combining their circle parts with a partner's and writing more complex problems.

Extension Ideas

- Similar to the above lesson, work with halves by discussing the equator and how it divides the earth in half.

- Work with place value. Place value boards and manipulatives would be ideal for this lesson. All the numbers the students work with in the lesson could be numbers relating to the Earth. For example, seven (for seven continents), 365 (for how many days it takes the earth to revolve around the sun), 24 (for how many hours it takes the Earth to rotate), etc.

- Complete story problems relating to time zones. Use the **Time and Date.com** site for help.

- Have a lesson on three-dimensional shapes, including spheres, cylinders, cones, and cubes. Refer to the Bubble Math lesson for ideas.

Earth Theme

Circle

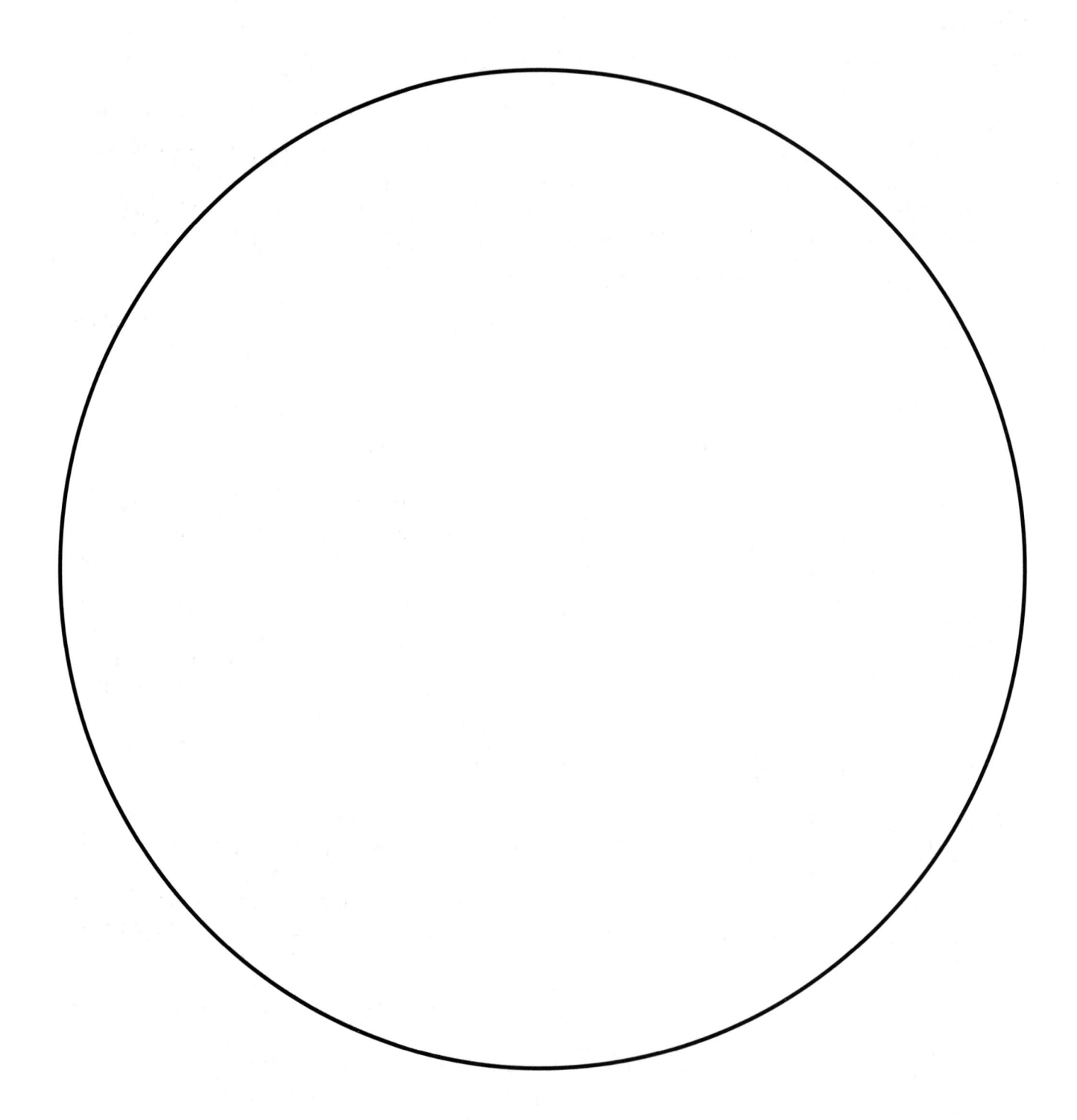

Earth Theme

Earth Science

Objective
The students will discover the different layers of the Earth.

Materials
- a book about Earth, such as *Planet Earth: Inside Out* by Gail Gibbons. Other books which may be helpful for this activity are *What's the Earth Made Of? (Starting Point Science Series)* by Susan Mayes, *Atlas of the Earth (A First Discovery Book)* by Scholastic Inc., and *Look Inside Earth (Poke and Look)* by Gina Ingoglia.
- information from the **Savage Earth Animation** Web site
- hard-boiled eggs (one per student, one per pair of students, or one for whole-class demonstration, depending on teacher's desire)
- plastic knives for the "dissection" of the egg
- "Layers of the Earth" activity sheet

Procedure
1. Read the chosen book about the Earth. Have a discussion on how the earth is made up of layers. Refer to the aforementioned link. If possible, have the students view the model on the screen and discuss again the four layers of the Earth.

2. Pass out the hard-boiled eggs. Explain they are to imagine this egg as a model of the Earth and its layers. Have the students remove the shell. Ask them what part of the Earth would the shell represent? (The crust) Next, they should remove the white of the egg, representing the mantle. Finally, view the yellow of the egg, representing the outer and inner core.

3. For reinforcement, have the students complete the activity sheet.

Extension Ideas
- Have a discussion on the three main components of Earth—land, water, and air.
- Make a human solar system, assigning students the roles of specific planets and the sun. See the movement lesson for more specifics. (This may also be laid out with balls representing specific planets.)
- Conduct some lessons on gravity. Use the following **Gravity Activity** Web site for a lesson plan.
- Conduct experiments on how day and night occur using a flashlight, a darkened room, and a globe.

Earth Theme

Name: _____

Layers of the Earth

1. List the 4 layers of the Earth.

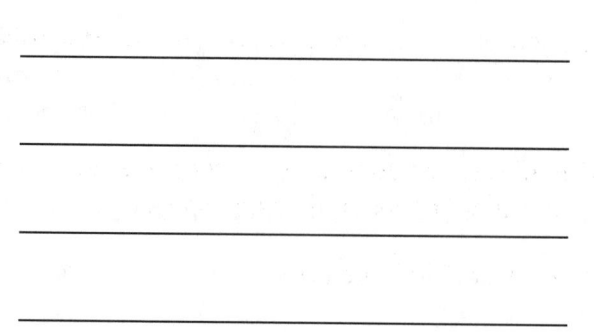

   _____

   _____

   _____

   _____

2. Draw and label the 4 layers inside this circle.

Earth Theme

Earth Social Studies

Objective

The students will utilize map skills to locate the seven continents.

Materials

- a flat world map displaying the seven continents (Use the **World Map** Web site if needed.)
- a globe
- index cards with the names of the continents on them (One card per student, with only the name of one continent on it. Three or four students may each end up with the same continent name.)
- a wide open space to make a "human map"

Procedure

1. Have a discussion on the fact that there are seven continents which make up the Earth. Define what a continent is at the level of the students. Show the students where these continents are on a globe.

2. Display the flat world map explaining how this map would be similar to peeling the map off the globe and spreading it out on a flat surface. Point to the continents on the map.

3. Have each student pick an index card with the name of a continent on it.

4. Have the students group themselves according to the card they drew.

5. Using a wide-open area, facilitate the students standing in an area to represent where the continents are placed on the flat map.

6. Discuss where the continents are in relation to one another. Review the names of the continents.

7. For reinforcement, play a "Spin the Globe Game." Have each student take a turn closing his/her eyes. Spin the globe. Have the student place his/her finger on the globe, open them and see whether they landed on a continent or on water. If on a continent, which one is it?

Extension Ideas

- Older students may play the game at the following site: **Geography Game**.
- Here's a Web site with a story to help students remember the names of the continents: **Geography/Misc**.
- Have the students pick a place on Earth where they would like to live and do some research on that place.
- Learn some ways to protect the Earth and its environment. Use one of the following Web sites for assistance: **EEK!, Simple Things You Can Do To Help, Children Of The Earth United**, or **Helpful Hints For Planet Earth**.
- Have students complete the "Tic-Tac-Earth" activity pages.

Earth Theme

Tic-Tac-Earth

Do your part! Complete any three in a row to help save our Earth. Teacher: Duplicate the card or cards that are appropriate for your class and pass them out to the students.

TIC-TAC-EARTH

Keep a tally sheet of everything you throw away over one week.	Next time you shop, bring a cloth bag with you or an old paper or plastic bag. Use this instead of getting a new one.	Write a crossword or wordsearch puzzle using ecology words you have learned. Let others try to solve it.
Make a bird feeder. Cut a grapefruit in half. Hollow it out and fill with bird seed and suet. Tie three pieces of string to the grapefruit; attach to a tree branch.	Create your own ecology project—a newsletter, fund-raising event, a play, or letter-writing campaign—to help others become ecologically aware.	Place a box at home for collecting glass; divide the different colors of glass and bring them to a recycling center when the box is full.
Clean out your closet or cupboards. Donate things you don't want any more to a needy organization.	For a week, use only cloth towels and napkins and not paper.	Turn off the lights when you are not using them.

#3823 Internet Activities Through the Year   108   ©Teacher Created Materials, Inc.

Earth Theme

Tic-Tac-Earth (cont.)

Do your part! Complete any three in a row to help save our Earth. Teacher: Duplicate the card or cards that are appropriate for your class and pass them out to the students.

TIC-TAC-EARTH

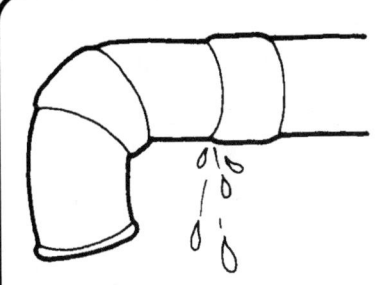

Find a water leak at home, at school, or in a local business. Report it.	Snip each section of a six pack ring before you throw it out.	Fill a 1-2 gallon plastic jug with water and some pebbles for weight. Place it in the toilet tank. This will save water every time the toilet is flushed!
Next time you find a bug in your house or classroom, help it get back outside. Don't kill it! Bugs have their place in our environment, too.	Create your own ecology project—a newsletter, fund-raising event, a play, or letter-writing campaign—to help others become ecologically aware.	Begin using a recycling box at home for paper. Place all recyclable paper there rather than throwing it out.
Construct art projects, puppets, posters, dioramas, or costumes out of recycled bags and boxes.	Turn off the water while you brush your teeth. Turn it back on for rinsing.	Share something you've learned about ecology with your parents or other adults.

©Teacher Created Materials, Inc.   #3823 Internet Activities Through the Year

Earth Theme

Earth Art

Objective

The students will create a collage of what they love about the planet Earth.

Materials

- old magazines (preferably nature magazines)
- glue
- scissors
- a large piece of butcher paper, with the outline of a circle (representing Earth)

Procedure

1. Discuss the planet Earth and all it's components—water, land, animals, people, plants, etc.
2. Discuss the term collage. Explain to the students how they will be working together to create a collage of what they love about the planet Earth.
3. Have the students cut out pictures of things they love about the Earth. (If magazines are not available, they may create their own pictures of what they love about Earth and then cut them out to be placed on the butcher paper.)
4. Create the collage by gluing the pictures inside the circle on the butcher paper. Give the collage a title and hang it in the classroom for all to view.

Extension Ideas

- Have the students make posters encouraging others to take care of the Earth. For example, "Don't Litter," "Recycle," "Don't Pollute," etc.
- Have the students make an invention out of recycled objects.

Earth Theme

Earth Movement

Objective

The students will create a representation of the solar system.

Materials

- a large open area allowing for movement.

Procedure

1. Discuss the solar system and Earth's place within it.

2. Assign students to be specific planets with the remaining students clustering together to be the sun. Have the students create a human model of the solar system. Use the following Web site reference: **Discover The Planets**.

3. Have the students rotate (spin) as well as revolve (orbit) around "the sun." Explain the difference between rotating and revolving.

4. For younger students, have them all be the Earth. Set up an object in the middle of the room to be the sun. Have all the students rotate as well as revolve around the sun.

Extension Idea

- Draw the continents (simply a sketchy rendition) in chalk on a large outside surface. Play a game where the students move from continent to continent by following teacher directions. A large class may need to be split into small groups. For example, "Group A, hop from Europe to North America!," "Group B, skip from South America to Africa," "Group C, waddle from Asia to Antarctica."

©Teacher Created Materials, Inc.

Egg Theme

Related Web Sites

The American Egg Board
This site contains nutrition information, facts, safety features, recipes, and crafts relating to eggs. Activities in the Kids and Family section give kids the chance to color eggs and take a quiz on fascinating egg facts.

Rose Acre Farms
This site also contains lots of information on eggs, including history, trivia, recipes, and crafts. It is created by an American family farm.

The Eggman
Find here some fun facts on eggs and detailed descriptions on how chickens lay eggs. Included are links to a number of sites with information about eggs.

Related Literature

Animals Born Alive and Well by Ruth Heller
This factual book is written in rhyme and covers the topic of animals born alive (not hatching from eggs). This is included on this list due to its use in the science lesson.

Chickens Aren't the Only Ones by Ruth Heller
This factual book written in rhyme covers the topic of egg-laying animals.

Egg by Robert Burton
This book is filled with wonderful photographs of 27 different animals hatching from eggs.

Eggbert: The Slightly Cracked Egg by Tom Ross
A cracked egg journeys to find the beauty of being different.

Eggs (What's For Lunch) by Claire Llewellyn
This is a nonfiction book on eggs.

Emma's Eggs by Margaret Ruurs
A hen goes to extreme lengths to try and please her owners for the types of eggs they want.

An Extraordinary Egg by Leo Lionni
Three frogs find an egg and are happy when their new "chicken" friend hatches. However, the "chicken" is actually an alligator!

From Egg to Chicken (Lifecycles) by Gerald Legg
Depicts what is happening inside an egg before it hatches.

Green Eggs and Ham and *Scrambled Eggs Super!* by Dr. Seuss
These are two great classic stories featuring eggs.

Hedgie's Surprise by Jan Brett
This Scandinavian folktale is the story of how a hen stops an egg thief with the help of a hedgehog.

One Carton of Oops! by Judy Bradbury
This story is a great math lesson on subtraction when a boy keeps breaking eggs on his way home from the store.

A Nest Full of Eggs (A Let's Read and Find Out Science Book) by Priscilla Belz Jenkins
A young boy with a Robin's nest full of eggs outside his bedroom window, watches the eggs hatch and the young birds grow.

Egg Theme

Egg Language Arts

Objective

The students will classify different pieces of literature which contain eggs as part of the subject matter.

Materials

- a poem containing an egg (such as "Humpty Dumpty")
- a folktale (such as *The Talking Eggs: A Folktale From the American South* by Robert D. San Souci or a version of "Jack and the Beanstalk" which contains a golden egg)
- a fiction book (such as *Horton Hatches an Egg* by Dr. Seuss, *Eggbert the Slightly Cracked Egg* by Tom Ross or *Rechenka's Eggs* by Patricia Polacco)
- a nonfiction book about eggs (such as *Chickens Aren't the Only Ones* by Ruth Heller or *Eggs: What's For Lunch?* by Claire Llewellyn)
- "Egg Literature" activity sheet

Procedure

1. Read each of the selections from the above list.
2. Discuss the different literary terms: poem, folktale, fiction, nonfiction.
3. Pass out the "Egg Literature" activity sheet and have the students work individually, or as a class (depending on the age), to place each piece of egg literature read in the most appropriate place. (Some of the pieces may fit into two categories, but they should work to pick the most appropriate place.)
4. Older students will be able to complete the activity sheet individually. For younger students have a whole class discussion on which was their favorite piece of egg literature and why. This could also lead into a math lesson on graphing their favorite pieces.

Extension Ideas

- Have the students write stories about lost or magical eggs on pieces of paper cut out in the shape of an egg.
- Brainstorm words that rhyme with egg.
- Have the students write stories about "mystery eggs" and what hatches out of them.
- Read *The Talking Eggs: A Folktale From the American South* by Robert D. San Souci and *Mufaro's Beautiful Daughters: An African Tale* by John Steptoe and have the students compare and contrast the two stories.

Egg Theme

Name: _____

Egg Literature

Poem _____

Folktale _____

Fiction _____

Nonfiction _____

What was your favorite piece of egg literature?
_____

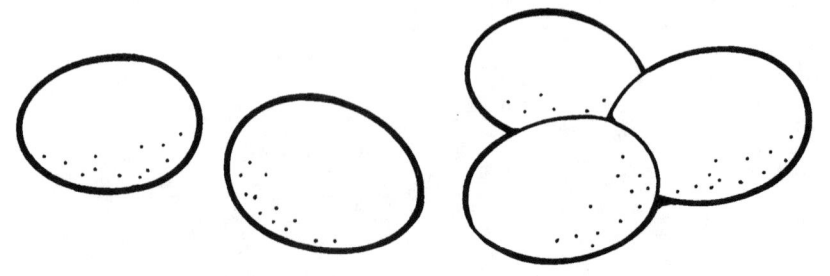

Why?
_____
_____
_____

Egg Theme

Egg Math

Objective

The students will add fractions (½ only).

Materials

- Each child or pair of children will need 10 paper eggs (or use the plastic eggs that come apart)
- "Egg Math" activity sheet

Procedure

1. Have the students cut (or pull apart if they have the plastic eggs) one of their eggs in half.
2. Have a discussion on how two halves make a whole. Have them act this out by putting their egg back together.
3. Have the students complete math problems using their manipulatives. Either call math problems out and complete them as a whole class, or have the students complete the "Egg Math" activity sheet.
4. Use some subtraction problems for older children.

Extension Ideas

- Number the inside bottom of empty egg cartons 1–12. These egg cartons can be used for a variety of math games and lessons. For example, have the students use the egg cartons similar to number lines in order to complete math equations. The students may also use the egg carton as a playing board by using dice and markers and trying to be the first to reach the number 12.
- Have a lesson on what "dozen" means.
- Older children can do multiplication or division problems to see how much an individual egg costs when a dozen costs a certain price.

Egg Theme

Name: _____

Egg Math

1. $1 + 1\frac{1}{2} =$

2. $2\frac{1}{2} + 1\frac{1}{2} =$

3. $3 + 3\frac{1}{2} =$

4. $5\frac{1}{2} + 2\frac{1}{2} =$

5. $4\frac{1}{2} + 5 =$

6. $3\frac{1}{2} + 2\frac{1}{2} =$

7. $7\frac{1}{2} + 2\frac{1}{2} =$

8. $6\frac{1}{2} + 1\frac{1}{2} =$

9. $9\frac{1}{2} + \frac{1}{2} =$

10. $8\frac{1}{2} + 1\frac{1}{2} =$

Egg Theme

Egg Science

Objective

The students will classify animals born alive versus animals which hatch from eggs.

Materials

- *Animals Born Alive and Well* and *Chickens Aren't the Only Ones* by Ruth Heller.
- "Are They Born Alive or Do They Hatch from Eggs?" activity sheet

Procedure

1. Before reading the books, brainstorm with the children all the animals they can think of that hatch from eggs and all the animals they can think of that are born alive. List these on the chalkboard or on chart paper.
2. Read the Ruth Heller books.
3. Now have the children add to the list any animals they did not think of before the reading.
4. Pass out the activity sheet and have the students complete it.

Extension Ideas

- Discuss the nutritional value of eggs.
- Learn how chickens lay eggs. Use **The Eggman** Web site for information.

Egg Theme

Name: _____

Are They Born Alive or Do They Hatch From Eggs?

Here are 5 animals that are born alive:

1. _____
2. _____
3. _____
4. _____
5. _____

Here are 5 animals that hatch from eggs:

1. _____
2. _____
3. _____
4. _____
5. _____

Egg Theme

Egg Social Studies

Objective

The students will locate countries on a world map and make (or be exposed to) an egg side dish from one of those countries.

Materials

- The following Web sites: **Recipes From Around The World (recipe from China)**, **Recipes From Around The World (recipe from Germany)**, **Recipes From Around The World (recipe from Poland)**, **Recipes From Around The World (recipe from Thailand)**

- world maps

- ingredients for one of the above recipes, or the actual food made at home ahead of time.

Procedure

1. Print out or display each of the aforementioned recipes.

2. Have the students locate the country from which the recipe comes on the maps. Look at the country in relation to where the students live. How would they get to that country? By boat, car, airplane?

3. Prepare one of the dishes and have the students critique whether they liked that food or not. (The German one is probably the easiest. It can also be made ahead at home and brought in for the students to sample).

Extension Ideas

- Have discussions on how eggs get from farms to the markets.

- Write a letter to an egg farmer and ask him/her questions about his/her job.

- Find a colonial recipe which contains eggs and discuss colonial cooking.

Egg Theme

Egg Art

Objective

The students will marble paint on egg shapes.

Materials

- shallow pans
- paint
- egg shapes cut from paper
- marbles

Procedure

1. Place the egg shape, the marbles, and some small amounts of paint in a shallow pan.
2. Have the students take turns rolling the marbles through the paint and onto their egg shape by tilting the pan. This will create designs on the egg shape.

Extension Ideas

- Decorate hard-boiled eggs by dying or painting them.
- Give each child an empty egg carton and have them create something out of it. Allow them to use their imaginations and be as creative as they can.
- Have students complete the "Eggs in a Nest" activity sheet.

Egg Theme

Eggs in a Nest

Color the picture. Cut eggs from colored paper and glue them into the nest. Cut leaves from green paper and glue them on the branches.

Birds make many kinds of nests. They lay their eggs in the nests to keep them safe.

Egg Theme

Egg Movement

Objective

The students will participate in an egg toss.

Materials

- hard-boiled eggs—one per pair of students
- outside area to conduct the game.

Procedure

1. Give each pair of students a hard-boiled egg.
2. Have the students stand close together and toss the egg back and forth. After each toss, they should take a step backwards to lengthen the distance between them. They continue tossing the egg until it is dropped and cracks.

Extension Ideas

- Have an egg rolling contest in which the students see how far they can roll hard-boiled eggs without them cracking.
- Have races in which the students balance hard-boiled eggs on spoons and try not to let them fall.
- Have an egg hunt.
- Play music and have the students mimic a bird or another animal hatching from an egg.

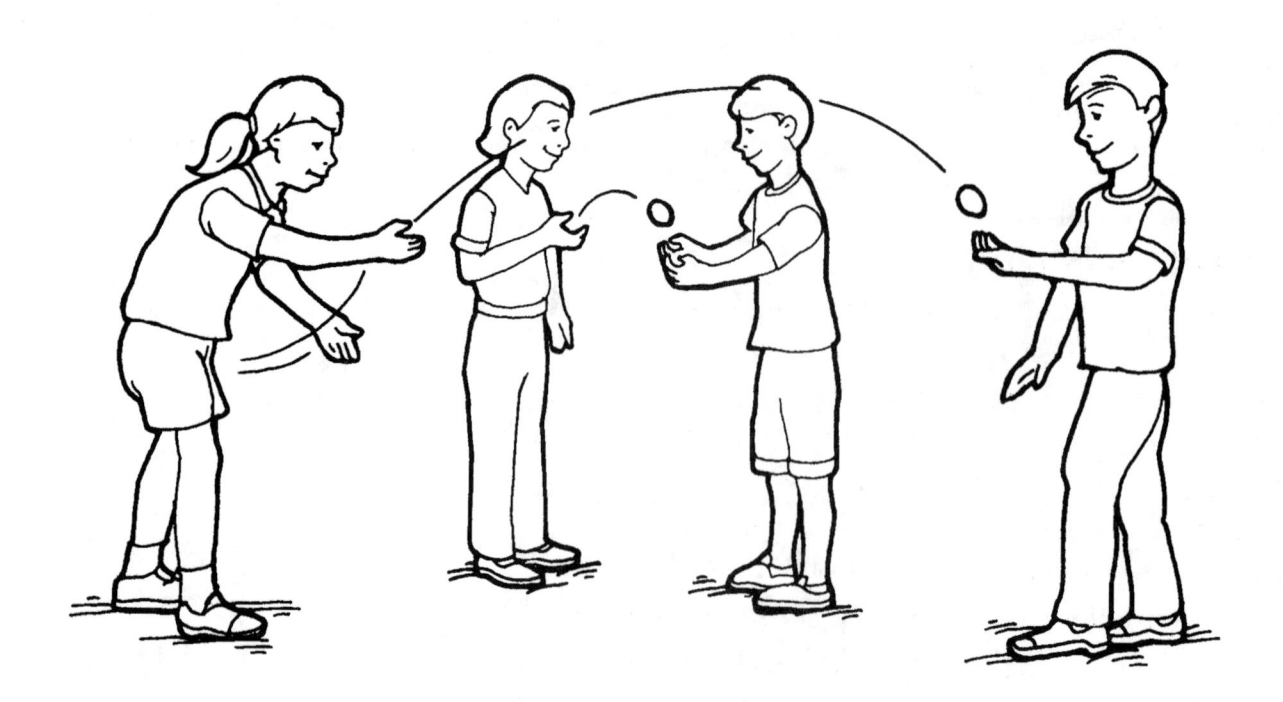

Flag Theme

Related Web Sites

Flag History
This site by PBS presents a great history of the flag, including facts, a history of the Fourth of July, and fun and games. Also found here is information such as how to fly the American Flag, how and when to salute the flag, and how to raise and lower the flag.

National Flags
This site has a nice selection of some of the national flags. The graphics are nice and large!

Flags of the World
Flags of the World claims to be the largest site on the Internet dedicated to vexillology—the study of flags—and it does have links to thousands of pages and images. The Coloring Book pages are especially nice, providing black and white outlines for the students to print and color themselves.

Flags
This site focuses on U.S. flags. There are great graphics of past U.S. flags and state flags as well, along with Federal Laws Governing the U.S. Flag, Frequently Asked Questions, and the Pledge of Allegiance.

Childfun.Com
Childfun.com's page highlights Flag Day (June 14th) activities and songs. Included are a flag to download and a large number of craft projects.

Surfnetkids
This site features a flag puzzle game. Kids have two minutes to complete a jigsaw puzzle of the American flag.

The Betsy Ross Home Page
The Betsy Ross Home Page features information on Betsy Ross and the history of the U.S. flag. Take a tour of her house, learn about her life, find out what the colors of the flag represent, and see a time line of the American flag. There are also flags available to download in PDF format.

Biography.Com—Betsy Ross
This page discusses the controversy over whether the Betsy Ross story is fact or fiction. It also tells the story of the life of Betsy Ross.

Flag Tag!
This is a game in which you are given the name of a country and two flags and asked which flag is correct. The answers are given during the game.

Related Literature

The American Flag (True book, American Symbols) by Patricia Ryon Quiri
This book provides good information on the American flag.

Did You Carry the Flag Today, Charley? by Rebecca Caudill
Will Charley ever get the privilege of carrying his classroom flag?

Eyewitness: Flag by William Crampton
Great pictures make this a good reference book.

The Flag We Love by Pam Munoz Ryan
This book is filled with nice pictures and good information.

Our Flag (I Know America) by Eleanor Ayer
Find here information on the history and the etiquette of the American Flag.

Flag Theme

Flag Language Arts

Objective

The students will write a description of a flag.

Materials

- the United States Flag or any other flag (Pictures of flags may be used as well.) Refer to the following Web sites: **Flags**, **National Flags**, or **Flags Of The World**. If the class will be doing this project individually, have enough pictures of flags so there is one per student. If you do not have a color printer, print out the coloring pages of flags at the **Coloring Book Of Flags** Web site. Show the students the color picture of their flag and have them quickly fill in the colors before writing their descriptions.

- paper

- writing utensils

- chart paper or blackboard (if done as a whole class)

Procedure

1. Decide whether the whole class will participate in writing a description, or if the students will do so individually.

2. Have the students study the flag they will be describing in their writing. This will be done by either having the entire class view the one flag they will be describing, or by handing out pictures of various flags to each individual student. What colors are in the flag? What symbols are used? Where are the colors and symbols placed in the flag? How would the students write a description of the flag for someone who cannot see it? If this project is being done as a whole class, record their descriptive sentences on chart paper.

3. If older students are doing this project individually, have them keep their flag picture a secret. Once their descriptions are written, display the flag pictures for all the students to view. Then each student may read their description while the rest of the class tries to match the description with the picture.

Extension Ideas

- As an alternative to the above, combine the Language Arts Lesson with the Art Lesson. Have the students write a description of the flag they have created during the art lesson. They may want to include a description of the process of creating their flag and what any of the symbols mean.

- Have a lesson on symbols and what they mean. Discuss the different symbols used in the American Flag. Relate this to symbols used in written language. What do the different punctuation marks mean— . , ? ! ?

- Read the Pledge of Allegiance. A great book to use for this activity is *The Pledge of Allegiance* by Francis Bellamy (Editor), Scholastic. Make a list of the unknown words and look up their definitions. If desired use "The Pledge of Allegiance" activity sheet (most appropriate for older students).

Flag Theme

Name: _____

The Pledge of Allegiance

I pledge allegiance to the flag

of the United States of America

and to the Republic for which it stands,

one nation under God, indivisible,

with liberty and justice for all.

—Frances Bellamy, 1892

Match the words with their definitions:

1. pledge
2. allegiance
3. Republic
4. indivisible
5. liberty
6. justice

_____ a country

_____ cannot be separated

_____ a promise

_____ to be fair

_____ to be loyal

_____ freedom

©Teacher Created Materials, Inc. 125 #3823 Internet Activities Through the Year

Flag Theme

Flag Math

Objective
The students will explore the number 50.

Materials
- Groups of 50 items for each pair or small group of students. (Use items such as counting bears, unifix cubes, pennies, toothpicks, beans, etc.) If working as a whole class, only one group of items will be needed.

Procedure
1. Discuss the number 50. Relate it to the U.S. flag and how there are 50 stars, one for each state.

2. Put the student in pairs or small groups. (With younger students, this lesson may want to be done as a whole class.) Give each group of students their 50 items.

3. Guide the student through a session of grouping the items in different amounts. For example, start with putting them in piles of 10s. Practice counting by 10s. Do the same for groups of 5s and 2s. Have two of the groups combine their items and count them to see what 50 + 50 =.

Extension Ideas
- Explore the number 13 (since there are 13 stripes on the flag).

- Have a lesson on symmetry. Print out pictures of symmetrical flags and ones that are not symmetrical. Use the following link for assistance in finding pictures: **National Flags**. Cut the pictures or fold them in half to demonstrate symmetry. Are both halves the same or are they different? Have the students draw one of the symmetrical flags and one of the asymmetrical flags for concept reinforcement. Using the coloring printouts at the following Web site may be helpful: **Coloring Book Of Flags**. Drawing a dotted line down the center of the flag, or folding it in half will help with concept mastery.

- Have pictures of different flags available for the students to view. Explore how patterns are used in flags.

- Have a lesson on $\frac{1}{2}$ by discussing a flag flying at half mast.

- Have the students make small flags out of straws (for the flag pole) and pieces of rectangular construction paper. Once their flags are complete, work as a whole class to create patterns in how the flags are placed. For example, a flag pointing to the left, a flag pointing to the right, etc. Or one student holding a flag over his head, another student holding a flag by his waist, etc. Therefore, the students' bodies and flags are part of the pattern.

Flag Theme

Flag Science

Objective

The students will explore the effects wind has on the environment.

Materials

- straws or craft sticks
- small pieces of fabric (in rectangles)
- masking tape
- a book about the wind, such as *Feel the Wind* by Arthur Dorros.
- "The Wind Around Us" activity sheet 1 (for older students) or "The Wind Around Us" activity Sheet 2 (for younger students)

Procedure

1. Facilitate a discussion on the wind. Have the students brainstorm different ways wind affects objects around them. List these on chart paper or on the blackboard.

2. Discuss how wind affects flags. When there is no wind a flag will hang down on its pole. However, on windy days the flag will fly out straight and may even flap in the wind.

3. Have the students make simple flags by taping pieces of fabric onto straws or craft sticks.

4. Go outside and determine whether it's a windy day or not. See if the students can make wind by blowing on their flags or waving them through the air. If it is a windy day, have the students observe other objects that are being affected by the wind. Are leaves blowing off trees? Are swings moving in the breeze? If it is not a windy day, ask the students to look around and see what objects may be affected if the wind started to blow. If needed, help lead them to the discussion on how wind affects seed travel.

5. Upon returning to the classroom, add any of the observations made outside onto the chart paper.

6. Read the book on the wind. The book may touch on some wind effects the students had not thought of earlier, which may be added to the list. Follow up with "The Wind Around Us" activity sheet 1 or "The Wind Around Us" activity sheet 2 (for younger students).

Extension Ideas

- Do more experiments with the flags they made. Which fabrics blow easier in the wind? The lighter ones or the heavier ones?

- Do a more in-depth lesson on how wind is created in different weather situations.

- Bring in a fan and experiment with the different settings (low vs. high) and how far it blows differently weighted objects. Have the students record the results.

- Do one of the wind experiments at the following link: **Wind**.

Flag Theme

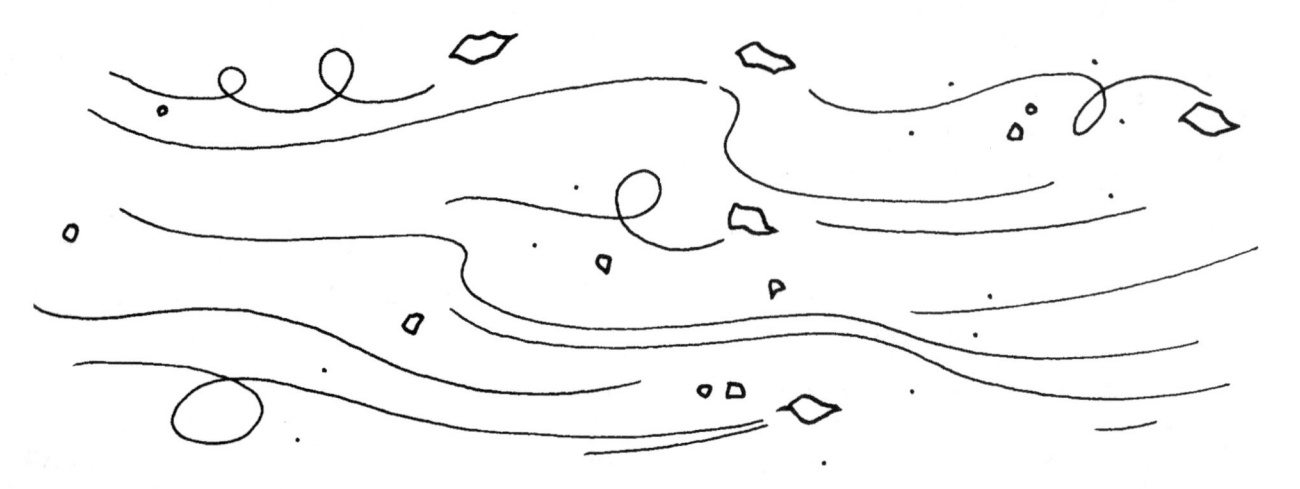

Name: _____

The Wind Around Us

List 5 ways wind moves objects in our environment.

1. _____

2. _____

3. _____

4. _____

5. _____

Flag Theme

Name: _____

The Wind Around Us

Draw 5 objects the wind moves in our environment.

©*Teacher Created Materials, Inc.* *#3823 Internet Activities Through the Year*

Flag Theme

Flag Social Studies

Objective

The students will research their state flag and locate other states on a map.

Materials

- a book with a picture of the state flag for the state your school is in, or a printout of it from the **States And Capitals** Web site. (This will give information on your state, including the flag and what its symbols mean. A color printout will work best. If this is not available to you, try and color the printout to give the students the sense of what colors are in their flag, or simply allow them to view it online.)

- a large map of the United States

- Use the **States And Capitals** Web site to get printouts of different state flags, enough so there is one per student or pair of students.) Write the name of the state somewhere on the flag, or the back of the flag. Place them in a container to be picked by the students.

Procedure

1. Brainstorm and list the different organizations and communities which have flags. For example, schools, clubs, sports teams, cities, states, countries.

2. Show the display or picture of your state's flag. Discuss what the different symbols and colors mean on the flag.

3. Have the students locate their state on a map.

4. Have each student, or pair of students, pick a flag out of the container of state flags. They may then come up to the United States map one at a time (or in their pair) and locate the state on the map. (Younger students will need more help in completing this step than older students.)

5. Attach the flag cutout to the map. If it is too big to go on the actual state, attach it off to the side and have a piece of string connecting the flag to its state.

Extension Ideas

- The above lesson can be done with the American Flag. Discuss the symbols, colors, and what they mean. (Today the flag consists of thirteen horizontal stripes, seven red and six white. The stripes stand for the original 13 colonies, the stars represent the 50 states. The colors of the flag mean the following: red symbolizes hardiness and valor, white symbolizes purity and innocence, and blue represents vigilance, perseverance, and justice.) Then the students may find different countries' flags and locate those countries on a world map.

- Have a lesson on the history of the United States Flag. The following Web site will be helpful: **Historical Flags Of The United States**.

- Have a lesson on Betsy Ross. The following Web sites will be helpful: **Betsy Ross Homepage** and **Biography.com**.

- Discuss the history of the sewing machine and how they have changed over time, increasing the ease of stitching flags. How were flags (as well as other jobs) done before machines?

- Discuss how explorers place flags when discovering or reaching new areas. For example, flags were placed on the moon, at the tops of mountains, etc.

Flag Theme

Flag Art

Objective
The students will create classroom flags.

Materials
- a variety of mediums and materials—construction paper, pieces of fabric, craft sticks, stickers, cotton balls, paint, markers, etc.
- language arts lesson plan, if desired (See Extension Ideas.)

Procedure
1. Discuss with the students how they will be creating a classroom flag. Have them think about the symbols used in the American Flag. Tell them they should incorporate symbols into their flags. (For example, gluing on 23 cotton balls for 23 students in the class.) Younger students will need more direction in this area than older students.
2. Allow them to create their flags.
3. If desired, tie this into the Language Arts Lesson. The students will then write about the flag they have created. They will include a description of the process, the flag, and what any of the symbols represent. If time allows, have the students present their flag to the rest of the class, explaining the symbols.

Extension Ideas
- Work together to create a classroom flag together. Discuss ahead of time what colors and symbols will be used. Have each student do their own section and then put them together.
- Dye fabric to create colorful flags.
- Create a 5-pointed-star in one snip. Use the following Web site: **5-Point Star In One Snip**.

Flag Theme

Flag Movement

Objective

The students will march in a parade.

Materials

- a wide, open space
- the flags made in the art lesson
- a recording of some "marching music"

Procedure

1. Discuss parades and what they entail.
2. Put on the marching music and have the students form a parade with their created classroom flags.

Extension Ideas

- Have the students imitate being a flag in different types of wind. What will they do if there is no wind, just a little wind, or big wind gusts? How will the wind affect their movement?
- Play "Capture the Flag."
- Sing "The Star Spangled Banner."
- Try any of the songs or activities at the following link: **Flag Theme Ideas**.

Frog Theme

Related Web Sites

Encarta Encyclopedia—Frog
This page from Encarta has good factual information on frogs as well as links to information about toads, salamanders, and other amphibians. Included is information on habitat, physical characteristics, behavior, life cycle, and population.

Froggy Page
The Froggy Page is all about frogs. It contains facts, songs, jokes, tales, frogs on the Internet, famous frogs, and more! You can find lots of great pictures of frogs here.

Frogland!
Frogland has information, pictures, and even a teacher's corner. You can find fun and games, and even animated GIFs on Frog TV. There are also stupid frog jokes, a froggy coloring book, and a frog of the month. Check out Pet Central for information on frogs as pets.

Minnesota Pollution Control Agency (for kids)
This site has lots of frog facts and information on how pollution is affecting frogs and their population. Find here different types of frogs and how they look and sound, coloring pages of different frogs, frog jokes, and weird stuff about frogs.

Frogs and Toads in Color and Sound
This page has great photographs as well as sounds from a wide variety of frogs! Twelve frogs are featured, including tree frogs, bullfrogs, American toads, and others. Along with each photograph is a recording of the frog's calls. Real Audio is required to hear the frog calls.

Related Literature

Tuesday by David Wiesner
This 1992 Caldecott Medal Book is an almost wordless book that depicts frogs departing on their lily pads for a magical evening journey.

An Extraordinary Egg by Leo Lionni
Three frogs find an egg and assume it has hatched into a chicken. Aren't they surprised when they find out it's not a chicken at all!

Fantastic Frogs! (Hello Reader, Level 2) by Fay Robinson
This is an informative book at just the right level for K–2.

It's a Frog's Life: My Story of Life In a Pond: Nature's Secrets Series by Steve Parker
A journal from a frog's point of view! It even includes frog's photos and journals.

The Frog Alphabet Book by Jerry Pallotta
The alphabet is used to list the different types of interesting frogs and other amphibians.

Frogs by Gail Gibbons
In classic Gail Gibbons style this book is informative and engaging for young children. It covers the frog life cycle, feeding habits, and habitats.

From Tadpole to Frog (Let's-Read-and-Find-Out-Science) by Wendy Pfeffer
This is a good introduction to the frog life cycle.

The Icky Sticky Frog by Dawn Bentley
This humorous read-aloud book includes a sticky frog tongue on the front cover!

Frog Theme

Frog Language Arts

Objective

The students will write a story about a frog.

Materials

- "The Frog Prince" by Brothers Grimm, if available.
- "Frog Story Idea Map" activity sheet
- paper, pencils, crayons, colored pencils, etc.

Procedure

1. Read "The Frog Prince" or discuss the fairy tale of a frog turning into a prince once it has been kissed.

2. Ask the students what, or who, they would want a frog to turn into if they gave it a kiss. For younger students, record their answers on chart paper. For example, "My frog would turn into _____."

3. The students will complete stories based on their maps and illustrate the stories, if time allows.

Extension Ideas

- Do a lesson on synonyms, using "hop" and "jump" as the starting point.
- Do a phonics lesson on the "fr-" sound.
- Make mini "Frog Fact" books. Tie it in with a science lesson. As an alternative, make a whole-class book in which each student records and completes one frog fact to be compiled into a book. Allow the students to check this book out of the classroom to take home and share with their families.
- Read *The Mysterious Tadpole (A Pied Piper Book)* by Steven Kellogg. In this story, a little boy waits for his pet tadpole to grow into a frog!

Frog Theme

Name: _____

Frog Story Idea Map

Plot: My frog will turn into _____
_____

Characters: _____

Setting: _____

Events: _____
_____
_____

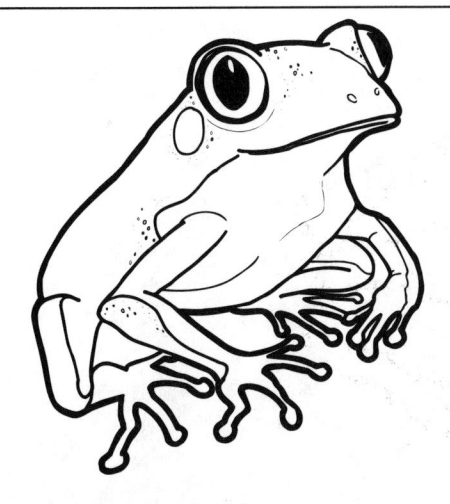

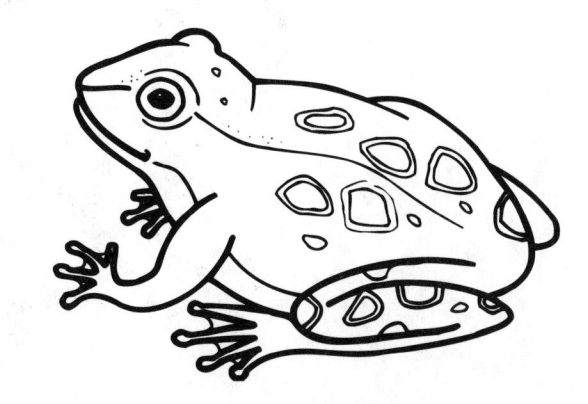

Frog Theme

Frog Math

Objective

The students will complete addition and subtraction problems using a number.

Materials

- individual number lines (1–10 or 1–20, depending on the grade level) for each student or each pair of students (There are number lines printed on the bottom of the activity sheets.) Or as an alternative, make a large number line on the classroom floor and have the students act like frogs to "hop" out the math problems.

- a "frog marker" for each student (or pair) Copy and cut out the frogs from the "Frog Marker Graphics" page.

- "Hop to the Answer! (1–10)" activity sheet or "Hop to the Answer! (11–20)" activity sheet

- If available, read the book *Ready, Set, Hop (Mathstart Series)* by Stuart J. Murphy. It's a good lesson on hopping to answer addition and subtraction problems. However, it does deal with different size hops—not equal distances for measurement.

Procedure

1. Pass out the number lines and markers.

2. Work as a class to discuss how to use a number line to figure addition and subtraction problems. Practice as a group. If you have made a number line on the floor, have the students take turns hopping out some sample problems.

3. Pass out the activity sheets and have the students complete them individually, or as a class, depending on the age level.

Extension Ideas

- For older students, have them use the number lines to complete algebra problems. For example, "If a frog is on the number 2, how many hops must he take to get to the number 5?" You may want to introduce the equation $2 + x = 5$.

- Have the students make up story problems that involve frogs.

- Have the students measure how far they can hop.

Frog Theme

Frog Marker Graphics

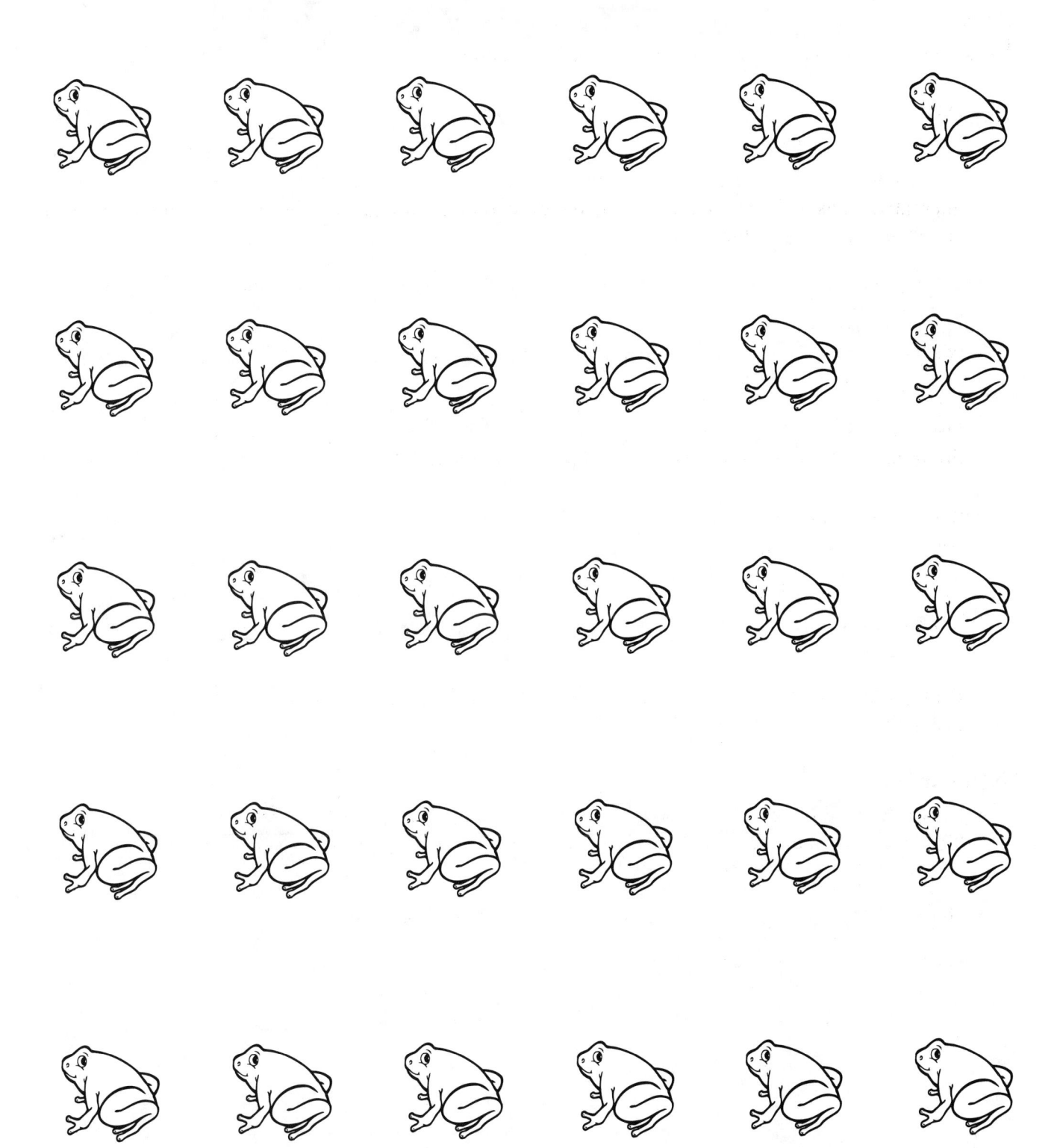

©Teacher Created Materials, Inc. 137 #3823 *Internet Activities Through the Year*

Frog Theme

Name: _____

Hop to the Answer! (1-10)

1. **2 + 1 =** _____

2. **3 + 4 =** _____

3. **1 + 6 =** _____

4. **5 + 3 =** _____

5. **7 + 2 =** _____

6. **8 + 1 =** _____

7. **3 + 7 =** _____

8. **4 + 3 =** _____

9. **7 + 0 =** _____

10. **2 + 6 =** _____

11. **9 – 2 =** _____

12. **7 – 4 =** _____

13. **8 – 4 =** _____

14. **4 – 3 =** _____

15. **5 – 2 =** _____

16. **3 – 1 =** _____

17. **10 – 5 =** _____

18. **6 – 3 =** _____

19. **5 – 4 =** _____

20. **8 – 6 =** _____

1-----2-----3-----4-----5-----6-----7-----8-----9-----10

#3823 Internet Activities Through the Year ©Teacher Created Materials, Inc.

Frog Theme

Name: _____

Hop to the Answer! (11–20)

1. **7 + 6** = _____
2. **8 + 9** = _____
3. **10 + 5** = _____
4. **5 + 9** = _____
5. **7 + 4** = _____
6. **8 + 10** = _____
7. **12 + 7** = _____
8. **11 + 9** = _____
9. **15 + 3** = _____
10. **9 + 6** = _____

11. **18 – 5** = _____
12. **15 – 7** = _____
13. **20 – 10** = _____
14. **12 – 6** = _____
15. **13 – 8** = _____
16. **17 – 5** = _____
17. **14 – 5** = _____
18. **15 – 4** = _____
19. **11 – 8** = _____
20. **17 – 7** = _____

1--2--3--4--5--6--7--8--9--10--11--12--13--14--15--16--17--18--19--20

Frog Theme

Frog Science

Objective
The students will sequence a frog changing form a tadpole into a frog.

Materials
- A book or a Web site which explains the life cycle of a frog (Good Web sites to use are **The Frog Page** and **Frogs of New England**. Good books to use are *From Tadpole to Frog (Let's-Read-and-Find-Out-Science)* by Wendy Pfeffer, or *Frogs* by Gail Gibbons.)
- glue
- scissors
- "The Frog Life Cycle" activity sheet

Procedure
1. Ask the students what they know about how frogs are born and develop. Read the chosen book or review the information given at one of the aforementioned Web sites.

2. Pass out "The Frog Life Cycle" activity sheet or plain pieces of paper. Have the students sketch or cut out the four main stages of frog development—eggs, tadpole, froglet, adult frog.

3. If the students have cut the activity sheet apart, they may glue them in the proper order on another sheet of paper. If appropriate, have the students label the stages. Older students may sketch the stages and label them on their plain pieces of paper. Older students may also want to write one fact they have learned about each of the stages on their completed paper.

Extension Ideas
- Have every student write a "frog fact" on a lily pad shape. Compile these facts into a book or display them in the classroom.

- Discuss habitats by using a book such as *The Magic School Bus Hops Home: A Book About Animal Habitats* by Patricia Relf. Classify animals by their habitats, desert, forest, ocean, pond, rainforest, etc. Make large charts to list various animals under their habitat.

- Classify animals according to the groups; amphibians, mammals, birds, reptiles, and fish. The following Web site is helpful in making definitions: **Fact Monster: Animal Groups**.

- Listen to the different frog sounds at the following site: **Frogs and Toads in Color and Sound** and have a lesson on how sound is made through vibrations and how sound travels.

Frog Theme

Name: _____

The Frog Life Cycle

Cut out the following pictures and put them in order on another piece of paper.

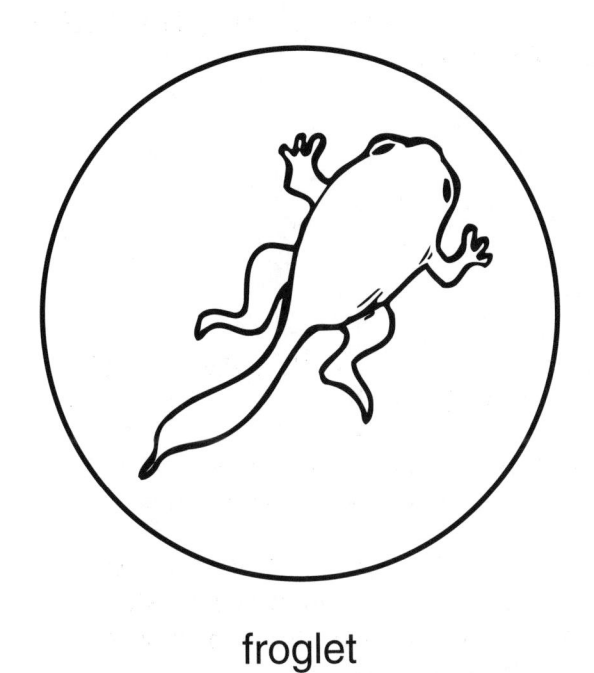

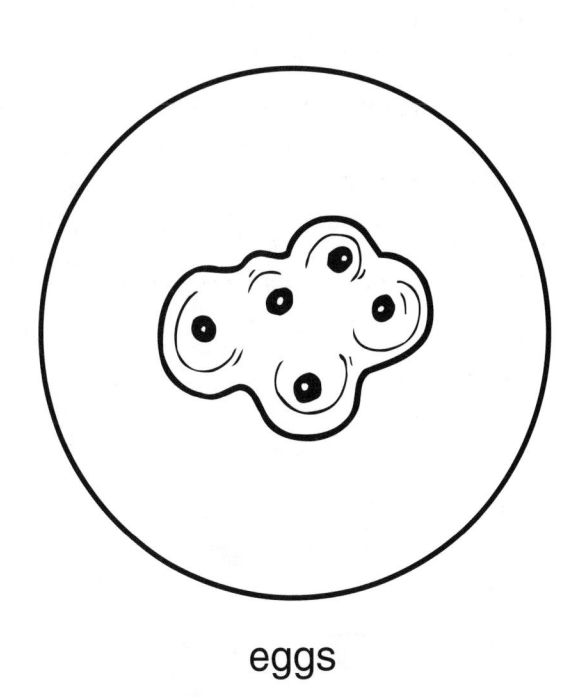

froglet

tadpole

adult frog

eggs

©Teacher Created Materials, Inc. 141 #3823 Internet Activities Through the Year

Frog Theme

Frog Social Studies

Objective
The students will classify groups according to their proximity and locate their origins on a map.

Materials
- a display or printout of one of the following sites: **The Collective Nouns** or **Collective Nouns** (for teacher reference only).
- the book *A Cache of Jewels* by Ruth Heller, if available
- large piece of chart paper, or blackboard
- "Name Those Groups!" activity sheet
- world map

Procedure
1. If available, read the book *A Cache of Jewels* to begin the lesson. Share with the students that a group of frogs living in the same area is refered to as an "army of frogs," similar to a "herd of sheep" or a "school of fish," or any of the more common phrases they may have heard. Brainstorm with the students, with the help of the above Web sites, any collective terms for animals and record them on chart paper.

2. Transition to a discussion of groups of people who live in similar communities having names as well. For example, Detroiters all live in the city of Detroit (use the name of your school's city). Expand this task onto the larger surrounding area. For example, Michiganers all live in Michigan, Americans all live in the United States of America, and earthlings all live on the planet Earth.

3. Pass out the "Name Those Groups!" activity sheets to be completed individually or as a group. Locate your city, state, and country on a map either as a whole class or individually. Older students may work this process for people who live in other cities and countries.

Extension Ideas
- Learn about pond habitats and what people need to do to protect them. The following link has helpful information: **Minnesota Pollution Control Agency (for kids)**.
- Locate on maps where certain species of frogs live.

Frog Theme

Name: _____

Name Those Groups!

1. People who live in my city are called
   _____.

2. People who live in my state are called
   _____.

3. People who live in my country are called
   _____.

4. People who live on the earth are called
   _____.

List other groups:

_____

_____

_____

Frog Theme

Frog Art

Objective

The students will create a colorful frog picture.

Materials

- "Frog Printout" or plain paper (The "Frog Printout" may be best copied on to heavier paper, such as construction paper.)
- brightly colored paints, markers, crayons, colored pencils, etc.
- information from one of the following Web sites—**Colorful Frogs** or **The Ultimate Frog Guide** (do searches on the poisonous frogs), or books with pictures of colorful frogs such as *Poison Dart Frogs* by Jennifer Owens Dewey

Procedure

1. Share pictures of the poisonous frogs from the Web sites or from books. Discuss how colorful the frogs are and the reason for their bright colors. This is how the frog warns predators that it's dangerous.

2. Pass out the "Frog Printout," or plain paper, and allow the students to create their own versions of poisonous frogs using their chosen medium.

3. Display the colorful frogs around the classroom or in the hallway. For a rainforest feel, you may want to create large trees out of butcher paper to house the frogs.

Extension Ideas

- Create a pond environment on butcher paper. Assign students different parts of the pond to create out of various art materials.
- Read the book *Tuesday* by David Wiesner and have the students create pictures of journeys they would like to take on a lily pad.

Frog Theme

Frog Printout

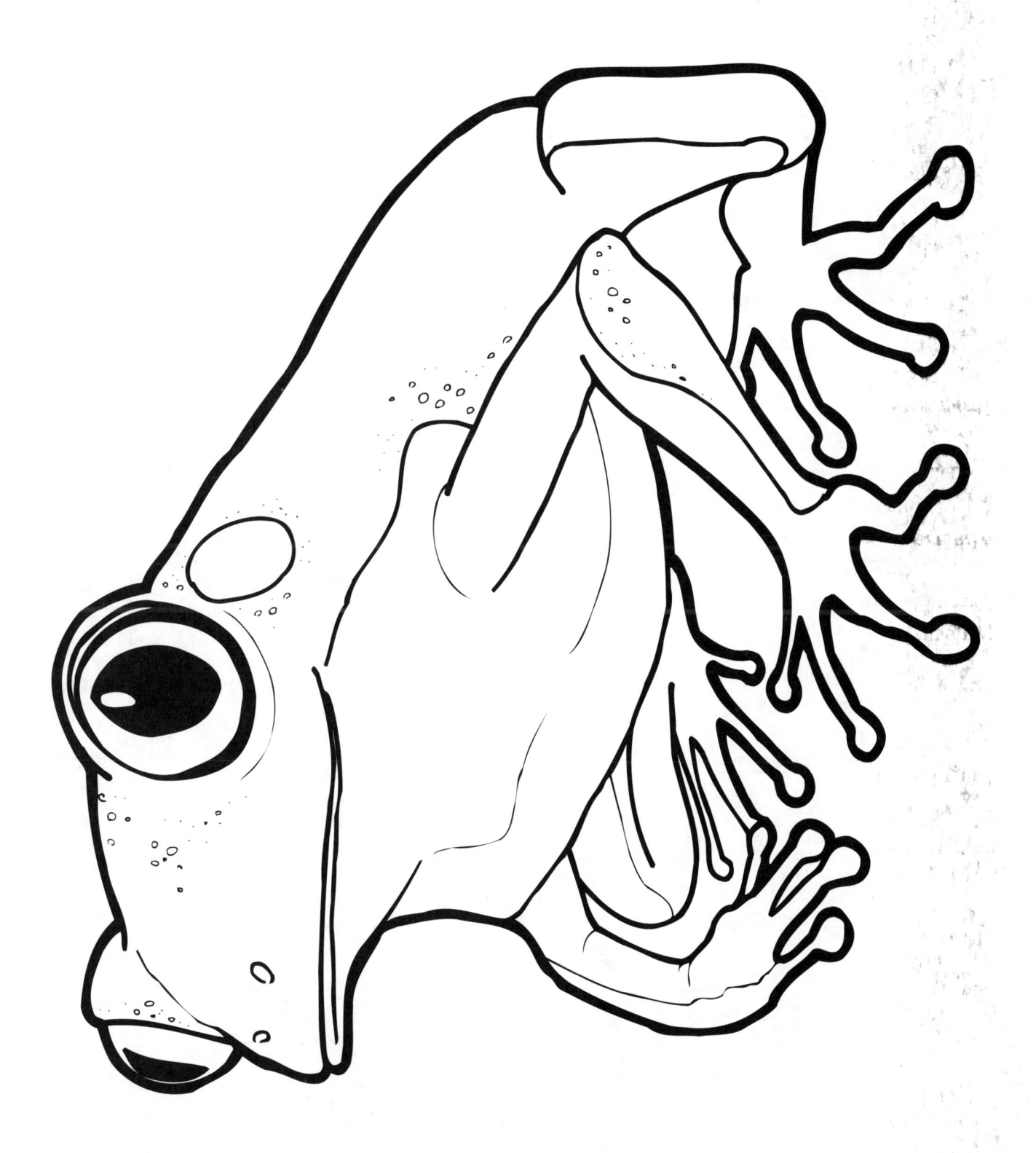

145 #3823 *Internet Activities Through the Year*

Frog Theme

Frog Movement

Objective

The students will participate in a "hopping" game.

Materials

- a large space allowing for movement
- bases, carpet squares, masking tape, or chalk to mark off "lily pads"
- a dice or spinner, if desired

Procedure

1. Set up a path of "lily pads" in a large open space. Either baseball bases, carpet squares, marking off with masking tape, or drawing them on an outside surface will work.
2. Allow the students to hop along the path.
3. If desired, turn it into a game in which the students are the moving pieces. Have the students roll a dice or spin a spinner and hop that many hops to get to the end of the path. For a larger class, it may be best to set up more than one "game board" so multiple games can be happening at once.

Extension Ideas

- Play a game of leap frog!
- Using music in the background, a selection which starts out slow and builds to a faster tempo, have the students imitate the life cycle of a frog. Curled up in a ball for the egg stage, stretching out and wiggling for the tadpole stage, small hops for the froglet, and big hops for the adult frog.
- Find the lyrics to frog songs at one of the following links: **Kermit The Frog** or **Froggy Rhymes And Songs**. Sing some frog songs!

Gingerbread Theme

Related Web Sites

All Recipes
This site includes recipes and ideas for decorating a gingerbread house. Included is a time line which guides you step by step through the planning stages. Decide what size and type of house you want to create and what sort of amenities you would like to add, then start decorating your house.

Easy Recipes for Kids
This section of "The Rainy Theme Resource Page" has a simple recipe for making gingerbread men.

Kids Domain—Miniature Gingerbread House
This site has a recipe for an easy "Miniature Gingerbread House" made from graham crackers, frosting, and small candies. Tips are included for making the gingerbread house with young children.

Awesome Clip Art
This page has a printable gingerbread man for kids to color.

Gingerbread Kids—Science Experiment Page
This page from the Kansas City Museum has a recipe for making gingerbread kids and a scientific explanation for what happens during the baking process.

Gingerbread Land's Fun for Kids Page
Gingerbread Land's Fun for Kids Page has a link to gingerbread houses to print and color, such as the Gingerbread Lady's favorite house, the grand Victorian gingerbread house, and a cut-and-paste house with all its trimmings. There is also a gingerbread song with music and lyrics. If you have Windows Media Player, you can download and listen to the song.

The White House
This link takes you directly to the White House Dining Room where you can view their own gingerbread house and read how it was made.

The Gingerbread Man
This site provides an integrated unit on the gingerbread man, with lesson plans for language arts, math, science, and more. Also included are photos of completed student work.

Related Literature

The Cajun Gingerbread Boy by Betthe Amoss
This version is set in the southwest Louisiana and has a great Cajun flare.

The Gingerbread Boy by Paul Galdone
The traditional story with great illustrations.

The Gingerbread Man by Jim Aylesworth
This version even contains a recipe.

The Gingerbread Rabbit by Randall Jarrell
This cookie is a rabbit instead of a man and ends up being alive and well.

The Gingerbread Boy by Richard Egielski
This tale is set in the city for a different twist. The pictures are wonderful!

The Gingerbread Man by Eric A. Kimmel
Another good retelling which removes some of the harshness of the traditional telling by stating "For gingerbread men return, it's said, when someone bakes some gingerbread."

Gingerbread Theme

Gingerbread Language Arts

Objective

The students will compare and contrast two different versions of the same story.

Materials

- two book versions of "The Gingerbread Boy" (Look at the literature section on the Gingerbread Theme page for suggestions.)
- "Gingerbread Stories" activity sheet.

Procedure

1. Introduce or review the terms characters, setting, and plot.

2. Read the two stories.

3. Pass out the "Gingerbread Stories" activity sheet. Depending on the level of the students either have them complete it individually or as a class. For very young students complete the activity as a whole class on the blackboard or on a piece of chart paper.

4. If the students have completed the activity sheets individually, review them as a class.

Extension Ideas

- Similar to the above lesson, use a Venn diagram to compare and contrast two versions of "The Gingerbread Boy."

- Have students make Gingerbread House Mini-books. See pages 150 through 154.

- Have the students do research in cookbooks or on the Internet to find gingerbread recipes. Make a class book of gingerbread recipes.

- Have the students write directions for creating a gingerbread house out of graham crackers. Put the students in pairs, give them the ingredients, and have them write the directions for making a house.

- Have the students write a different ending to "The Gingerbread Boy" story. Instead of getting eaten, the gingerbread boy goes on to…

- Have the students write their own version of "The Gingerbread Boy." Allow them to be as creative as they wish in picking their own setting and characters.

Gingerbread Theme

Name: _____

Gingerbread Stories

Story #1 **Story #2**

Title	Title
Characters	Characters
Setting	Setting
Plot	Plot

List the things that were the same about both stories.

_____

_____

List the things that were different about both stories.

_____

_____

©Teacher Created Materials, Inc. #3823 Internet Activities Through the Year

Gingerbread Theme

Gingerbread House Mini-book

Let's Make a Gingerbread House

Gingerbread houses were first made in a land far across the sea. You would have to ride on a boat or in a plane to get to Germany.

1

Gingerbread House Mini-book (cont.)

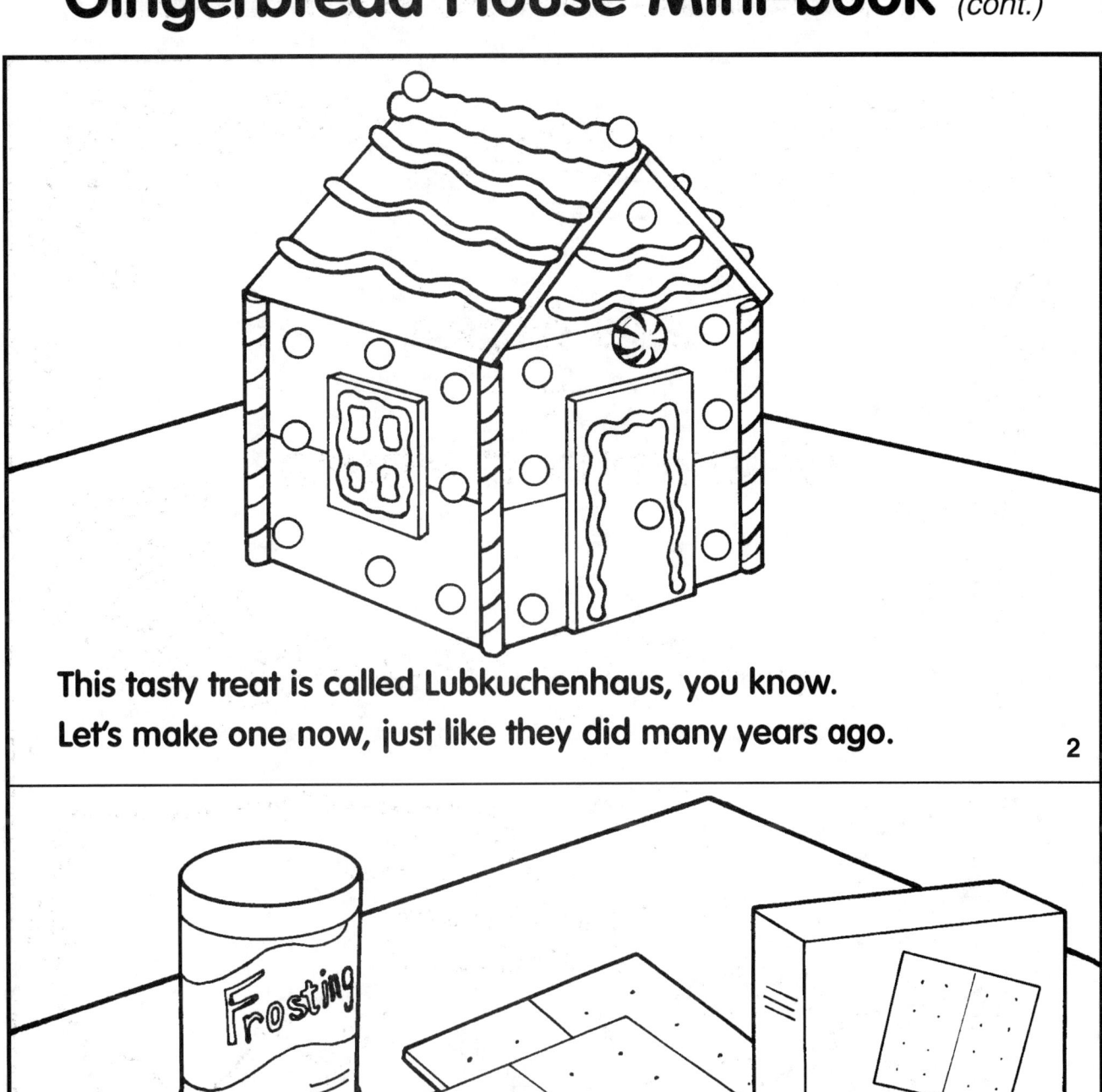

This tasty treat is called Lubkuchenhaus, you know.
Let's make one now, just like they did many years ago.

2

With frosting and crackers, we'll make this tasty treat.
Just follow these directions—be careful and be neat!

3

Gingerbread Theme

Gingerbread House Mini-book (cont.)

You need eight squares of graham crackers, and frosting from a can.
Lots of yummy candies and other sweet goodies in a pan.

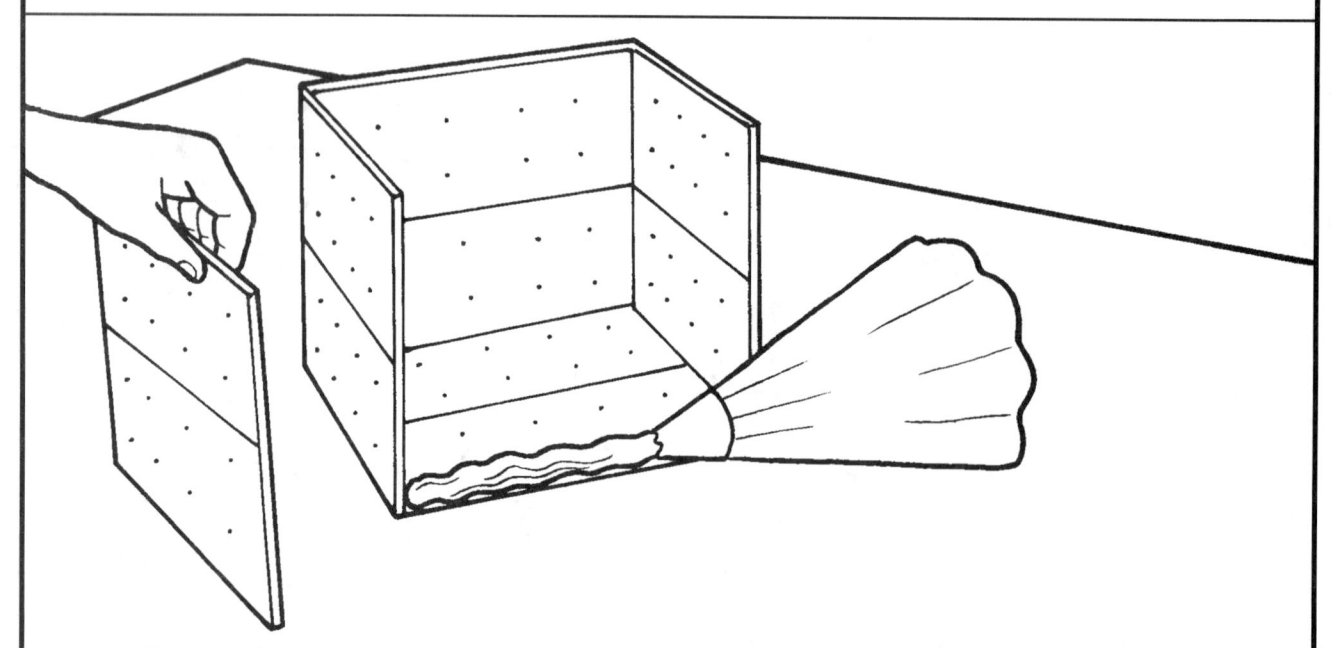

4

You'll need one cracker for the floor—place frosting around its four side edges.
Take four more crackers and stand them up for walls—now make some roof wedges.

5

Gingerbread House Mini-book (cont.)

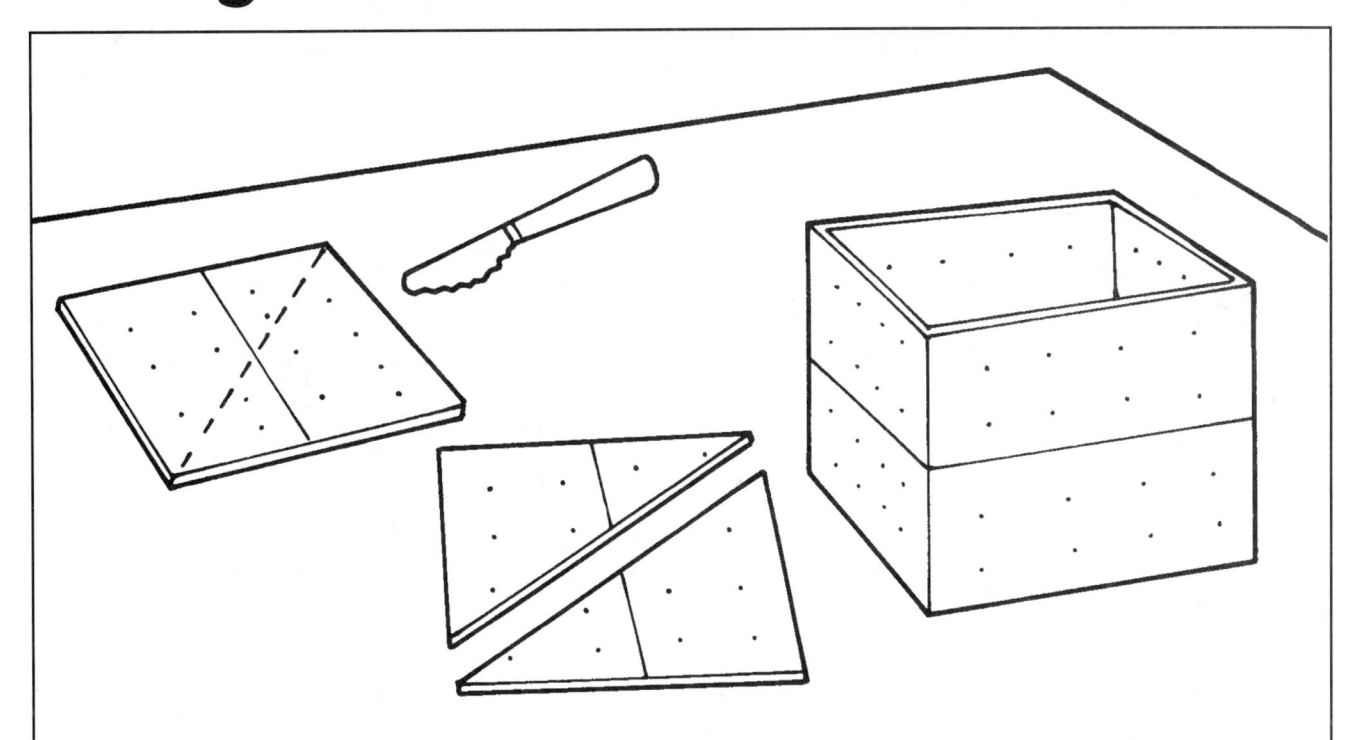

Take another square and cut it diagonally in two.
You will have two triangles, now here is what to do.

6

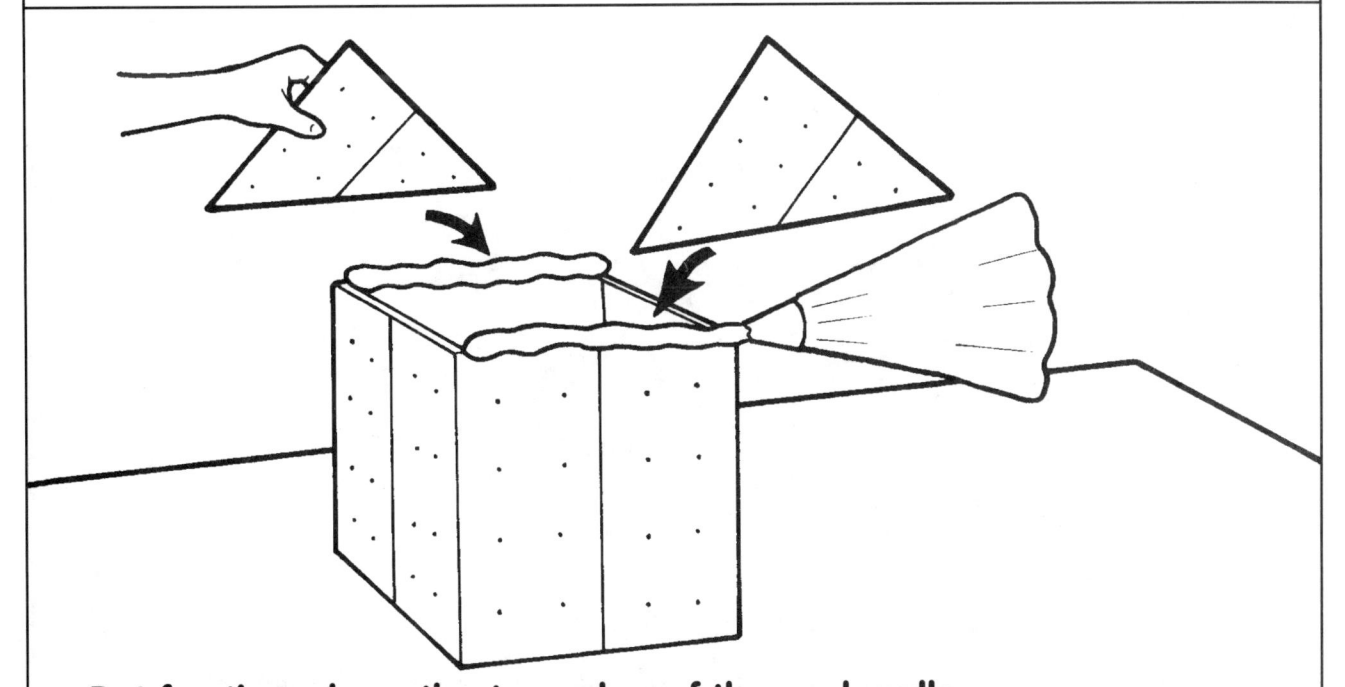

Put frosting along the top edge of the end walls.
Place the triangles on the frosting—hold in place so neither triangle falls.

7

Gingerbread Theme

Gingerbread House Mini-book (cont.)

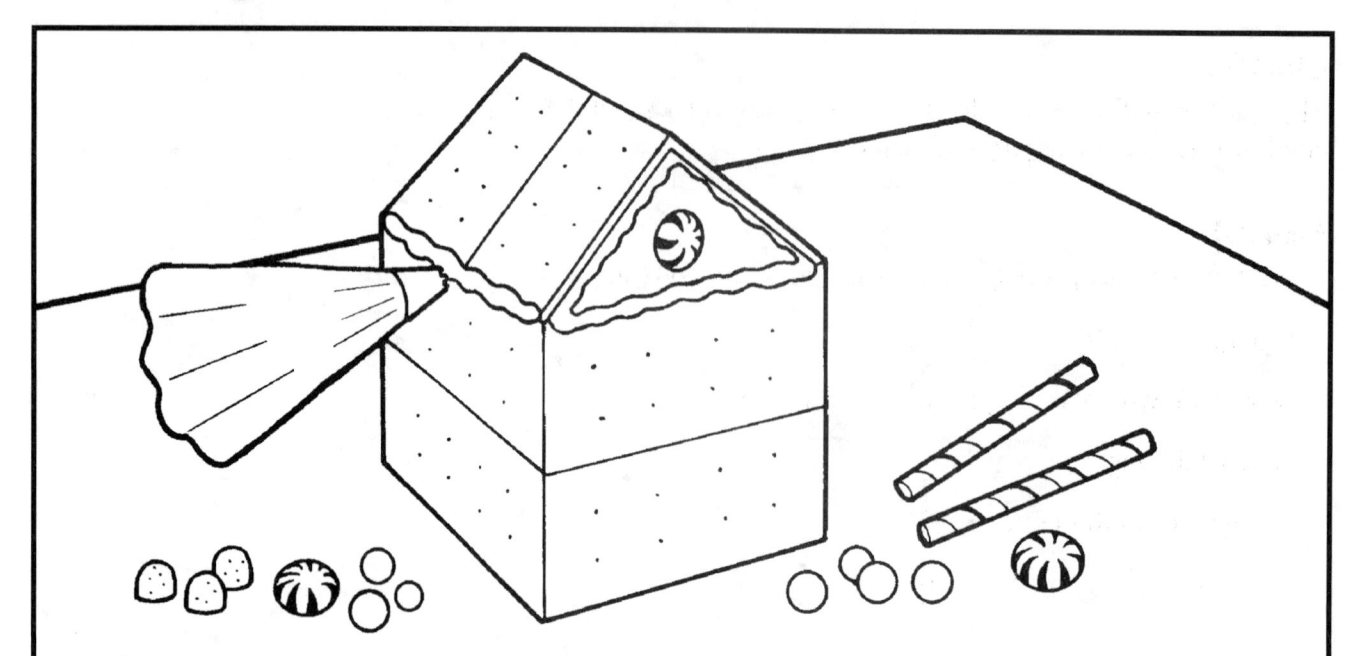

Place frosting on all the roof edges and lay down the last two squares.

Now all you need to do is decorate your house—maybe you'll make some stairs.

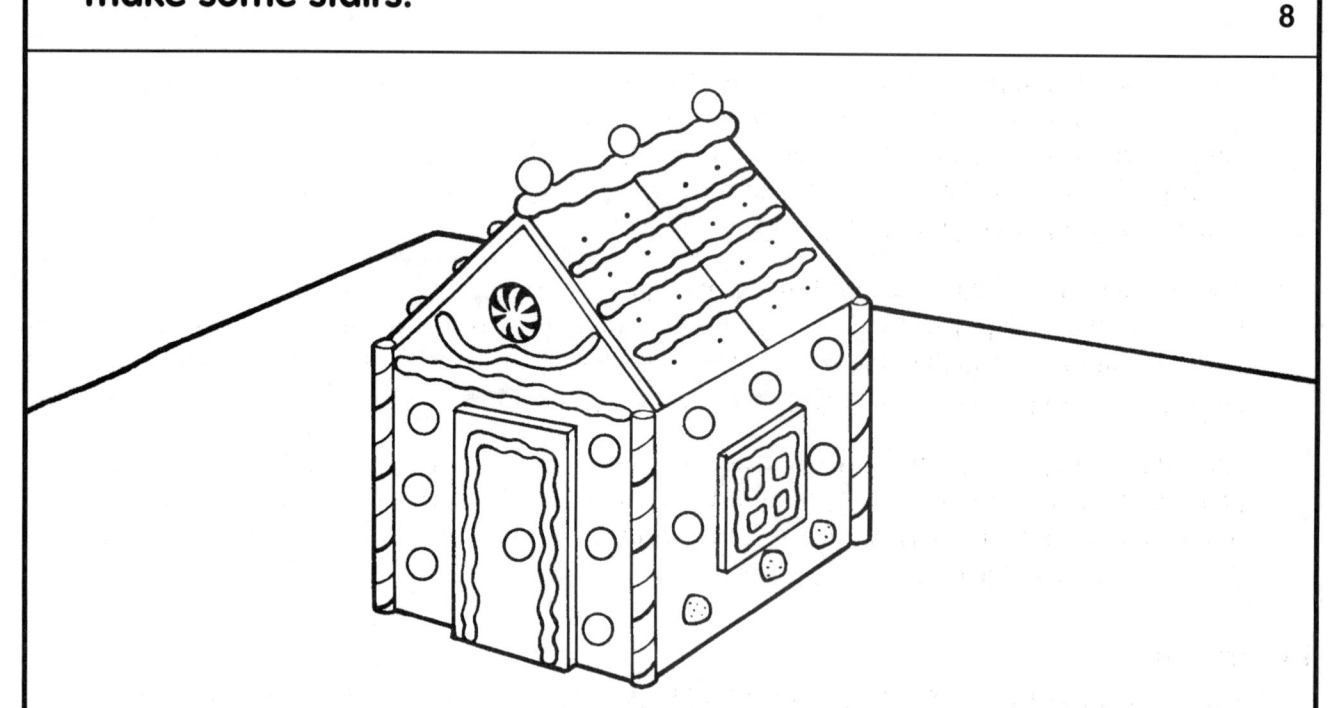

8

Dab frosting here and frosting there—add the candies that you like.

You're finished now, let's eat it up with Jimmy, Sue, and Mike!

9

Gingerbread Theme

Gingerbread Math

Objective

The students will time how long it takes an object to travel a distance. (This lesson may also be combined with the Gingerbread Science Lesson.)

Materials

- "Gingerbread Cutouts" (one gingerbread boy per student)
- straws
- a clock with a second hand or stop watch
- masking tape
- rulers or unifix cubes
- "Gingerbread Run" activity sheet

Procedure

1. Have a discussion on how to measure the length of an event using time. Starting a stop watch, looking at a clock, or counting need to be done right when an event begins. Stopping a stop watch, looking at a clock again, or stopping counting need to be done at the end of an event. Have the students think of things that can be timed, such as races, car rides, the length of a school day, etc.

2. Put the students in pairs. Pass out the gingerbread boys, the straws, the rulers or the unifix cubes, and the masking tape. Each pair of students should find a place in the classroom to set up a Gingerbread Running area. They should decide how long they want their race to be then tape a "start line" and a "finish line" on the floor by measuring it. You may want to give guidelines on how far apart the start and finish lines should be.

3. The students should then time each other blowing their gingerbread man to make him "run" from the start to the finish line. They will do this by aiming the straw at the paper gingerbread boy and blow air onto him to make him move. They may time each other by using stop watches, looking at the clock, or counting "one hippopotamus, two hippopotamus," etc.

4. Have the students record their distance and their times on the "Gingerbread Run" activity sheet. (This activity sheet has been formatted to be cut in half.) If this lesson is being combined with the science lesson, you may want to have the students complete the "Gingerbread Runs on Different Surfaces" activity sheet only.

Extension Ideas

- Graph the students' favorite way to eat gingerbread—gingerbread man cookies, gingerbread house, or gingerbread cake.

- Give every student a gingerbread man cutout. Have the class work together to calculate how many gingerbread feet, arms, buttons, etc. there are in the class. This is good practice for counting by twos.

©Teacher Created Materials, Inc.

Gingerbread Theme

Gingerbread Cutouts

Gingerbread Theme

Name: _____

Gingerbread Run

1. Our Gingerbread Run is _____ long.

2. It took my gingerbread man _____ seconds to cross the finish line.

3. It took my partner's gingerbread man _____ seconds to cross the finish line.

Name: _____

Gingerbread Run

1. Our Gingerbread Run is _____ long.

2. It took my gingerbread man _____ seconds to cross the finish line.

3. It took my partner's gingerbread man _____ seconds to cross the finish line.

©Teacher Created Materials, Inc.

Gingerbread Theme

Gingerbread Science

(This lesson is to be combined with the Gingerbread Math lesson.)

Objective

The students will experiment with friction.

Materials

- "Gingerbread Cutouts" (page 156)
- "Gingerbread Runs on Different Surfaces" activity sheet
- straws
- masking tape
- rulers or unifix cubes
- a clock with a second hand or stop watch
- different surfaces to have "Gingerbread Runs"—smooth floor, carpeted area, pavement, or grass

Procedure

1. Read the math lesson in advance.

2. The students should continue in the same manner timing their gingerbread runs. However, they should now vary the surfaces. The distance of their runs should remain the same. For example, one pair of students may time their runs on a smooth floor, on a carpeted area and then on pavement. Have the students record their times on the "Gingerbread Runs on Different Surfaces" activity sheet.

3. Incorporate a discussion on friction. Explain that friction is a force, which can help objects move more easily or with more difficulty depending on their surface. Relate your discussion to real life situations such as sliding on the ice.

Extension Ideas

- Using any of the recipe Web sites on the Gingerbread Theme page, make a gingerbread product.

Gingerbread Theme

Name: _____

Gingerbread Runs on Different Surfaces

1. Our Gingerbread Run is _____ long.

Surface	Amount of Time

2. The _____ had the greatest amount of friction.

   I know this because _____.

3. The _____ had the least amount of friction.

   I know this because _____.

4. Friction is a _____.

Gingerbread Theme

Gingerbread Social Studies

Objective

The students will make a map and give directions to help another student find a hidden object.

Materials

- "Gingerbread Cutouts" (page 156), one per student.
- "Map to the Hidden Gingerbread Boy" activity sheet

Procedure

1. Discuss how maps can help people find locations. Brainstorm times when people use maps—when traveling, when visiting a new place (such as a zoo, museum, or store map), etc.

2. Pass out the gingerbread cutouts. Put the students in pairs. Have half of each pair leave the room while remaining half hide their gingerbread men. Repeat this process with the other half of the class.

3. When all the class has returned to the room, have them draw a map of the room and write directions for where the gingerbread man is hidden. Discuss parts of maps that are appropriate for your age group. For example, including a key and using symbols for certain objects such as desks and windows. Younger students may want to draw a map and then draw a line that leads to the object. Very young students may want to eliminate the drawing and simply give verbal directions to their partner. For example, "Walk towards the front of the room. Turn towards the window. Stop by the pencil sharpener," etc. (These would also be similar directions to be written by older students, perhaps they would also use terms such as north and south or right and left.)

Extension Ideas

- Explore the history of gingerbread by using the following Web sites: **The History of Gingerbread** or **Annie's Gingerbread Page**.

- If it is close to Christmas, go to **The White House** page and view the Christmas decorations at the White House. (There is usually a gingerbread house on display.) Expand the lesson to discuss where The White House is located, who lives there, etc.

Gingerbread Theme

Name: _____

Map to the Hidden Gingerbread Boy

Here is a map of the classroom.

Here are directions to find the hidden gingerbread boy.

Gingerbread Theme

Gingerbread Art

Objective

The students will create gingerbread people.

Materials

- brown or tan construction paper
- a wide variety of art supplies such as ribbon, buttons, pieces of fabric, markers, cotton balls, yarn, etc.

Procedure

1. Pass out the art materials.
2. Allow the students to be as creative as they wish in creating a gingerbread person. For younger students, you may want to cut out gingerbread shapes in advance. Use the **Awesome Clip Art** Web site for online gingerbread art, if needed.

Extension Idea

- Make gingerbread houses using one of the Web sites on the Gingerbread Theme page.

Gingerbread Movement

Objective

The students will act out their own version of "The Gingerbread Boy." (This may also fulfill the language arts requirement.)

Materials

- At least 2 different versions of "The Gingerbread Boy." Suggestions may be found on the Gingerbread Theme page.
- A wide open space allowing for movement.

Procedure

1. Read the versions of "The Gingerbread Boy."
2. Depending on the age of the students either put them in small groups of 5–6 or work together as a whole class to act out a new version of "The Gingerbread Boy." The students will need time to plan their version, assign parts, and act it out.

Extension Idea

- Have the students play a game of tag. Certain students may be the characters trying to catch the gingerbread men and others may be the gingerbread men.

Hat Theme

Setting the Stage
Have all the students wear hats to school!

Related Web Sites

Hats in the Belfry
This is a retail site, but there are good photographs of all different types of hats that can be found here.

A Brief History of Hats
This site has basic information about hats, more for teacher review than for student reading. Also included is a glossary of hat terms.

Hat History
Find here some more basic information for teachers to share with students. The main focus of the information here is cowboy hats, and the reasons why they are worn.

The Cat's Concentration Game
This is a Cat in the Hat Computer game from the Seussville Web site. It is a very basic game in which kids can match characters from different Dr. Seuss stories. If they complete level 1, they can move on to level 2 in which they match different characters to the stories they are from.

Seussville
Here is the home page of the Cat in the Hat games and activities. The Flash 4 plug-in is required to view this site. Check out the Playground for games and storybook activities.

JanBrett.Com—The Hat Newsnotes
This section of the JanBrett.com Web site contains a letter from author Jan Brett on how her book, *The Hat*, came to be.

Colonial Kids—Clothing
This section of the Colonial Kids site has a few pictures of boys' and girls' colonial hats.

Colonial Williamsburg
This is a math lesson on making a "mob cap," which is a cap worn by girls and women in colonial times. Also included are pictures and information on why the mob cap was worn.

Related Literature

Abe Lincoln's Hat by Martha Brenner
True stories of Lincoln, set in an engaging manner. Abe Lincoln's hat is the centerpiece, yet there is good information on Abraham Lincoln, the man.

Caps for Sale by Esphyr Slobodkina
A peddler loses his hats to some irritating monkeys.

The Cat and the Bird in the Hat (Hello Reader, Level 1) by Norman Bridwell.
The story of what happens when a bird is living in a hat worn by a cat.

The Cat in the Hat by Dr. Seuss
A true classic!

The 500 Hats of Bartholomew Cubbins by Dr. Seuss
Poor Bartholomew tries to follow the king's orders and remove his hat, but there's always another underneath.

The Hat by Jan Brett
Hedgie the Hedgehog gets stuck in a wooden stocking which becomes his "hat."

Hat Theme

Hat Language Arts

Objective

The students will give and receive directions for creating a hat.

Materials

- simple outline drawing of a hat, two for each students if working in pairs, one for each student if working as a whole class with the teacher—see #4 in Procedure. (A top hat may be easiest to draw and run off on a copy machine.)
- crayons, markers, or colored pencils
- writing utensils
- paper

Procedure

1. Pass out the outline drawings of the hats. Have the students decorate one of the hats with their medium of choice, keeping their pictures to themselves, so the other students do not see them.
2. Put the students in pairs.
3. Have one student describe their hat to the other student, without revealing the picture. The other student should listen carefully and follow directions for recreating the decorations of the hat on their second outlined drawing. Once the child has finished describing the hat, he/she should reveal it to the other student to see how similar the drawings are. Then the students may switch roles for giving and following directions.
4. With younger students, the teacher may want to be the one describing a hat he/she has decorated, while all the children are listening and drawing.

Extension Ideas

- Work as a class to find items or pictures of items which rhyme with "hat" and place them in a hat.
- Work as a class to find short items and make a list inside the cutout shape of a hat.
- Read the book *Caps for Sale* and have students complete the activity on pages 166 through 167
- Read some *Cat in the Hat* books.
- Have a "Show and Tell" time for the students to talk about the hats they wore to school. As an alternative, have the students write about the hats they brought in to school. What kind of hat is it? Where did it come from? Why did they choose that particular hat?
- Read *The Hat* by Jan Brett, as well as the motivation behind her book at **All About The Hat**.
- Have the students act out *Little Red Riding Hood*.

Hat Theme

Literature Activity Cards

A. Before you read *Caps for Sale* by Esphyr Slobodkina, predict the meaning of the word *peddler*. Write your prediction on a piece of paper. Now read the story. Was your prediction correct? Look up *peddler* in the dictionary and write its meaning on the same page as your prediction.

B. Create a story web about the story. Your web should include setting, characters, problem, and solution.

Caps for Sale #1

Choose one hat from the choices provided. Imagine that this hat has been lost by its owner. You have just found it, and you must search for its owner. Write a story describing who you think the hat belongs to and how you would find that person.

Caps for Sale #2

Hat Theme

Literature Activity Cards (cont.)

In the book *Caps for Sale*, the peddler sold his caps for fifty cents each. There are many ways to combine coins to make 50 cents. Write down all of the possible combinations someone could use to buy a cap for 50 cents. Try to come up with at least eight ways to make 50 cents.

Caps for Sale #3

The peddler carried many caps on his head. He had his own checked cap, four gray caps, four brown caps, four blue caps, and four red caps. There were 17 caps in all.

Write down all of the addition sentences you can think of which equal 17.

Bonus: Make a fact family with four math sentences that include the number 17.

Caps for Sale #4

Teacher Note: A more concrete way for the students to complete activity card #3 would be to provide them with coin stamps and a stamp pad.

Hat Theme

Hat Math

Objective
The students will measure the circumference of their heads and compare the measurement to other objects in the classroom.

Materials
- cloth measuring tapes or pieces of string and straight rulers
- "My Head Measurement" activity sheet
- a variety of spherical objects placed around the room—for example, balls, pieces of fruit, a globe, etc. (Try and have some objects bigger than their heads and some objects smaller.)

Procedure
1. Ask the students how they could measure their heads to be fitted for a new hat. Have a discussion on the words circumference and spheres. Demonstrate how to measure their heads using either the cloth measuring tapes or the strings and rulers.

2. Pass out the "My Head Measurement" activity sheet and put the students in pairs. Have them help each other in measuring the circumference of their heads.

3. Once they have a measurement, or a piece of string cut to the size of their heads, have them complete the activity sheet. This will be done by having them locate the other spherical objects that have been placed around the room and measuring those objects.

4. Older students may be challenged to figure out how much bigger or smaller the objects are than their heads.

Extension Ideas
- Make a real graph for the hats brought in to school. Have the students decide which features they will use to graph the hats. For example, by color, type of hat, size of hat, etc.

- Read the book *Caps for Sale* by Esphyr Slobodkina. Have the students create their own patterns by coloring different caps. They may also make a stack of different colored caps and write math problems to accompany their stacks. For example, 3 red caps + 2 blue caps + 3 green caps = 8 caps.

Name: _____

My Head Measurement

1. The circumference of my head is _____.

Here are some objects that are bigger than my head.

Here are some objects that are smaller than my head.

_____ _____

_____ _____

_____ _____

_____ _____

_____ _____

_____ _____

Hat Theme

Hat Science

Objective

The students will discuss the reasons people wear hats and conduct an experiment on shadows.

Materials

- chart paper or a blackboard
- a strong flashlight (the bigger the better) (If the teacher is going to do a demonstration, only one flashlight is needed. If the class will break out into groups, there will need to be one flashlight per group.)
- an opaque object, such as a block or a counting bear (If possible, a small hat would be ideal to keep with the theme.) (Once again, the number of objects needed depends on whether this will be a demonstration or done in groups.)
- "Shadows" activity sheet (formatted to be cut in half)

Procedure

1. Facilitate a discussion on why people wear hats. Emphasize the following three physical reasons:
    a. protection from injury
    b. to keep warm
    c. for sun protection
2. Go into greater discussion on how the brim of a hat makes a shadow on the face, protecting it from the sun.
3. Conduct an experiment on the length of shadows in relation to a light source. For this experiment the room will need to be darkened as much as possible.
4. Have a discussion on how a shadow is made. An object must block the light source, thus creating a shadow. Relate this to the brim of a hat blocking the sun's rays from hitting one's face.
5. Gather the students around. Discuss how, due to the earth's rotation, the sun appears to move across the sky during the day. We begin with a sunrise low in the sky, at noon the sun is high over head, and then the day ends with the sun low in the sky once again.
6. While holding the chosen opaque object low and fairly close to the ground, move the flashlight in an arch shape over the object. Start out low and close to the ground, then move it up so it's directly over the object, and complete the arch down the other side.
7. Ask the students what happens to the shadow as the light source is in a different position. When is the shadow it's longest? When is it it's shortest? Relate these answers to the brim of a hat. Have a student put a brimmed hat on and move the light source over his/her head from front to back. Does the brim work when the light source is low and pointed toward the face of the student? When does the brim make the biggest shadow on the student's face?
8. Allow older students to break out into groups, with the needed materials, and experiment with the light and shadow on their own.
9. Have the students complete the short "Shadows" activity sheet as a wrap-up.

Extension Ideas

- Conduct a lesson on bicycle helmet safety. Use the **Bike Helmet.org** site for games, activities, and lesson plan ideas.
- Have a lesson on sun safety. Use one of the following sites for information: **Sun And Beach Safety Tips**, or **Sun And Safety For Kids**.

Hat Theme

Name: _____

Shadows

1. The shadow is the shortest when the light source is

   _____

2. The shadow is the longest when the light source is

   _____

Name: _____

Shadows

1. The shadow is the shortest when the light source is

   _____

2. The shadow is the longest when the light source is

   _____

©Teacher Created Materials, Inc.   #3823 Internet Activities Through the Year

Hat Theme

Hat Social Studies

Objective
The students will learn about different professions based on hats.

Materials
- "Hats and Professions" activity sheet to show pictures of different hats worn by different professions (or the actual hats themselves)
- chart paper or blackboard
- paper
- writing utensils

Procedure
1. Incite a discussion on different professions and the hats they wear. Show the pictures of hats, or actual hats, to help spark discussion.
2. Brainstorm with the class other professions and the hats they wear. Write them on the chart paper or blackboard.
3. Pass out paper and have the students write which one of the hats they would like to wear when they grow up and have as their profession. For example, "When I grow up, I want to wear a hat and be a . . . ." Younger students may draw a picture of themselves in a particular hat and write the name of the profession to the best of their ability.
4. If time allows, have the students share their papers with the rest of the class.

Extension Ideas
- Read *Abe Lincoln's Hat* by Martha Brenner. Have a lesson on Abraham Lincoln and his presidency.
- Make a time line of historical figures associated with certain hats. For example, Abraham Lincoln (stovepipe hat), George Washington (three-corner hat), Neil Armstrong (space helmet), etc.
- Brainstorm hats and the time people wear those hats to celebrate special occasions. For example, wedding veils, graduation hats, party hats, etc.
- Learn about the types of hats people wore in colonial times. Use the following site for help: **Colonial Kids**.
- Have a lesson on Mexico and do the Mexican Hat Dance. Use the following sites: **Fun Family Activities**, and **InfoPlease Atlas: Mexico**.

Hat Theme

Hats and Professions

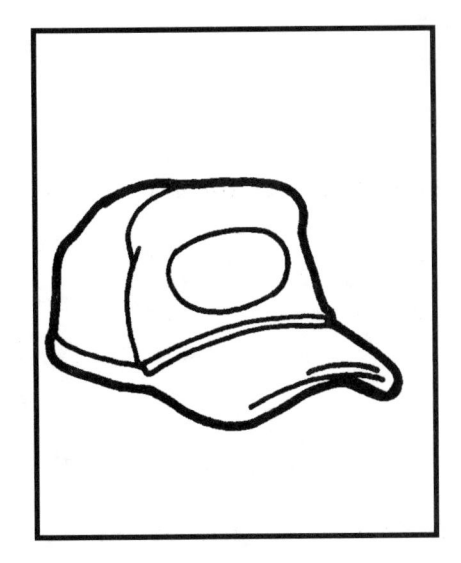

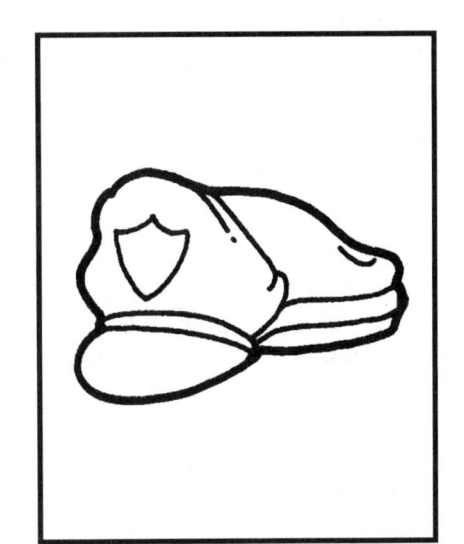

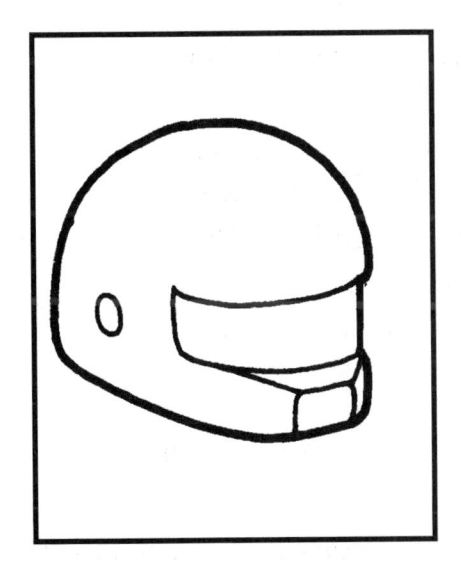

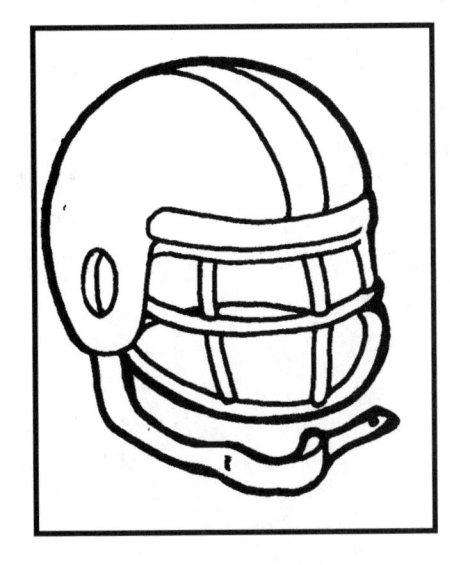

©Teacher Created Materials, Inc. 173 #3823 *Internet Activities Through the Year*

Hat Theme

Hat Art

Objective
The students will create their own hats.

Materials
- a wide variety of art supplies—construction paper, pieces of fabric, feathers, cotton balls, markers, etc.
- glue
- stapler

Procedure
1. Allow the students to be as creative as they wish to design their own special hat.
2. Assist the students, if needed, in securing a base for their hat with a stapler. Younger students may need a basic hat design already made for them, which they can decorate on their own.

Extension Ideas
- Make newspaper hats.
- Use any of the following Web sites to make one of the hat crafts: **Top Hat**, **Pilgrim Hat**, **Clown Hat**, or **Hat Crafts**.

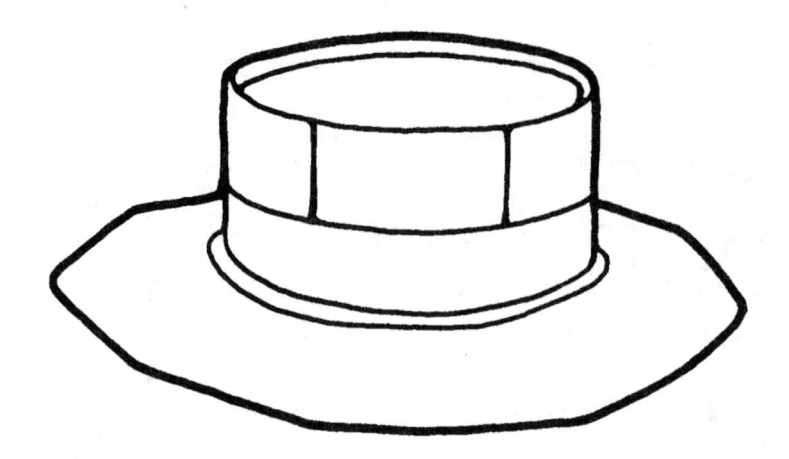

Hat Theme

Hat Movement

Objective

The students will act out different occupations.

Materials

- pictures of hats or actual hats that match various professions
- open space allowing for movement

Procedure

1. Have the students spread out in an open area.
2. Hold up individual pictures of hats, or the hats themselves.
3. Have the students act out the profession that matches the hat.

Extension Ideas

- Have the students do the Mexican Hat Dance. Use the following Web site for help: **Fun Family Activities**. This activity may also be combined with a social studies lesson.
- Have a parade wearing the hats that are made in the art lesson.

Heart Theme

Related Web Sites

Encarta Encyclopedia—Heart
This is a basic article on the heart, including the structure, function, diseases, and history.

The Heart: An Online Exploration
This site offers a wealth of information, diagrams, and actual photographs of the heart. Most of the material will need to be put in simpler terms for young children.

All About the Heart
This site is sponsored by Kidshealth.org and contains great information and diagrams geared towards kids. It is more kid-friendly than the previous sites.

Valentine Fun at Kids' Domain
This site has a wide variety of Valentine activities, including printable puzzles, online games, crafts, recipes, and more.

American Heart Association
This site from the American Heart Association contains information on the Jump Rope for Heart fundraising event. Check it out to see if you and your students might be interested in participating.

Related Literature

Many of these books deal with having a passion, a specific trait, or loving someone/something. They have been included to use for lessons suggested in the language arts area.

The Circulatory System by Helen Frost
A very simple book on the path of the blood.

Guess How Much I Love You by Sam McBratney
A father rabbit explains his love to his young rabbit.

Hear Your Heart by Paul Showers
This book is a great introduction to the heart. It includes diagrams, activities and good information.

Heart of a Tiger by Marsha Diane Arnold
A small kitten earns the name "Heart of a Tiger" by being brave.

I Like Me by Nancy Carlson
A young pig lists all the traits she likes about herself.

I Love You With All My Heart by Noris Kern
A young polar bear learns about his mother's unending love.

I'll Love You Forever by Robert Munsch
This is the story of a mother and the love for her son.

In the Heart by Ann Warren Turner
This book plays on the expression "the heart of the…" For example, "The heart of the town is my school." This would lead to an excellent lesson on brainstorming the "hearts" of different places and times.

The Jewel Heart by Barbara Helen Berger
The story of a friendship between a clown and a ballerina. The clown has a jewel for a heart which becomes lost. The ballerina then helps rejuvenate the new heart for the clown.

My Heart by Kathy Furgang
A nonfiction book about the heart.

Heart Theme

Heart Language Arts

Objective

The students will write a list of people, places, or things they like.

Materials

- pieces of paper cut out in heart shapes
- writing utensils
- a book about liking/loving someone or something (Suggestions are *I Like Me* by Nancy Carlson, *I'll Love You Forever* by Robert Munsch, or *Guess How Much I Love You* by Sam McBratney.)

Procedure

1. Read the chosen book. Have a discussion on liking/loving someone or something.

2. Have the students write about people, places, or things they love/like. The students should do their writing on the heart-shaped paper. (The writing may also be done on regular paper and then mounted onto heart-shaped paper.)

3. The writings will depend on the age level of the students. Younger students may simply draw pictures of their favorite things and, if appropriate, label their pictures. Older students may write a more detailed account about their likes.

Extension Ideas

- As a variation on the above lesson, have the students place their likes into categories of people, places, and things.

- Share books about having a passion for something, such as *True Heart* by Marisssa Moss or *The Music in Derrick's Heart* by Gwendolyn Battle-Lavert. Follow up by having the students write about a special passion or dream of their own, entitling the writing "My Heart's Desire."

- The students may write a valentine greeting to a friend or relative. Expand the lesson to include addressing envelopes.

- As a class, think of phrases that involve the word heart—"follow your heart," "change of heart," "heart of gold," etc.

©Teacher Created Materials, Inc.

Heart Theme

Heart Math

Objective

The students will add four numbers to find a sum.

Materials

- "Heart Shape" activity sheet, or a heart shape divided into four areas
- Small manipulatives, such as counting bears, beans, or candy hearts.

Procedure

1. If appropriate, review addition of two numbers.

2. Pass out the "Heart Shape" activity sheet and the manipulatives. Discuss how the heart has four chambers and that the students will be adding four numbers together to find a sum.

3. Give the students problems in which they have to add four addends to find the sum. The students will then use the manipulatives on the activity sheet to solve the problems. They will place the appropriate number of beans/counting bears/candy hearts in each chamber to find the answer.

5. Have the students create their own problems involving four addends.

6. For older students, expand this to a lesson on multiplication by fours.

Extension Ideas

- Have a lesson on symmetry. Find examples of hearts that are symmetrical as well as asymmetrical. Have the students create some of their own symmetrical and asymmetrical hearts.

- Have students practice their graphing skills with the "Mystery Picture" activity on pages 180 and 181.

- Place candy hearts in a container and have the students estimate how many hearts there are. Work together as a class to count the number and have the students figure how far off their estimates were.

#3823 Internet Activities Through the Year ©Teacher Created Materials, Inc.

Heart Theme

Name: _____

Heart Shape

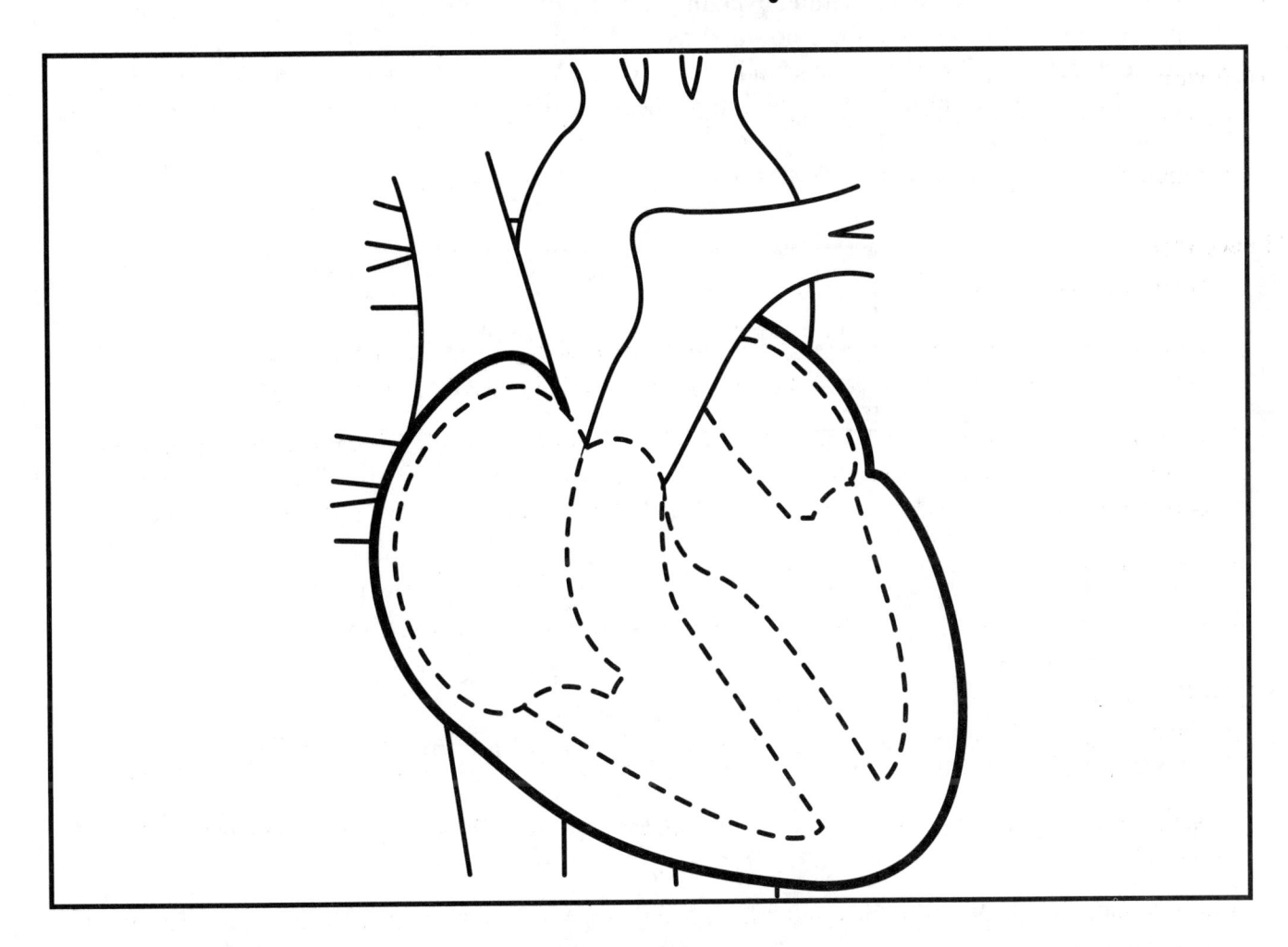

Write math equations with 4 addends below:

_____

_____

_____

_____

©Teacher Created Materials, Inc. 179 #3823 Internet Activities Through the Year

Heart Theme

Mystery Picture

Directions:

In order to complete the mystery picture, explain the directions on this page to the children, then reproduce only the color key and the coloring directions. Give each child a blank graph sheet and a copy of the directions. If the directions read: Color R/PK A6, C11, F2, the children follow up line A and across line 6 with his or her fingers until they meet on square A6. Then they color that square half and half as indicated on the color key. The children do the same to squares C11 and F2. They should cross out each letter-number as they work on it.

Color Key

LG = Light Green   PK = Pink

R = Red   PL = Purple

Color PK\LG G5 H6

Color LG G4 E6 B5 A10 D11 C7

Color PL E3 C1 A1 D1

Color R C9 E11 G10 F4

Color LG E7 D8 H10 F2 A4 A6

Color PK\R E10 F9 PL\LG H3 B8

Color PK E4 G7 LG\PK E8

Color LG D6 B11 H8 F11

Color R D9 G11 C3 E5 C10

Color LG D2 A5 B3 H9

Color LG F1 H5 A2 B6 A11 H11

Color R D3 C11 D5 C5

Color PK F8 G6 E9

Color LG F10 B9 D7 B2

Color LG\PK F7 LG\PK F6 PL\LG H2 B7

Color LG C8 G1 D10 H4 C2 A9

Color PK\LG G8 H7 LG\PL A7 A8 G2 G3

Color PL E1 E2 B1

Color LG H1 B4 C6 D4 A3 B10

Color R G9 F5 C4 F3

Heart Theme

Mystery Picture

11								
10								
9								
8								
7								
6								
5								
4								
3								
2								
1								
	A	B	C	D	E	F	G	H

©Teacher Created Materials, Inc. 181 #3823 Internet Activities Through the Year

Heart Theme

Heart Science

Objective

The student will complete fact statements about their hearts.

Materials

- non-fiction books or Web sites about the heart (See the Heart Theme page for suggestions.)
- "My Heart" activity sheet

Procedure

1. Share the books or Web sites with the students. Focus on the facts that the heart is a muscle, it pumps blood out to the body, and finding a pulse is the means to count heartbeats per minute.

2. Pass out the "My Heart" activity sheet. Depending on the age of the students, have them complete it individually or as a class. To answer the final question regarding the heart beats per minute after exercise, have the students do jumping jacks or some other physical activity for five minutes to recheck their pulse. Very young students may need adult help in finding and counting their pulse. Older students may feel their own pulse, count it for six seconds and multiply it by ten. This activity may be led by the teacher as appropriate. (This may be a good day to have a parent helper or two to help young students with the pulse part of the activity.)

Extension Ideas

- After listening to information from nonfiction books and the Internet, have the students list heart facts on heart-shaped paper.

- Have the students simulate blood circulating through the body. Set up a path in the classroom in which students pick up cards or pieces of paper with Os written on them, standing for oxygen, in the lung section of the room. They will then travel out through "the body" following artery paths, dropping off the Os and picking up CO (for Carbon Dioxide) to return to the heart following vein paths. The artery path may be marked with a red piece of yarn and the vein path with a blue piece of yarn.

- Have a cardiologist come talk to the class.

- List heart-healthy foods and activities.

- Have the students listen to each others' hearts using a stethoscope or a paper towel tube.

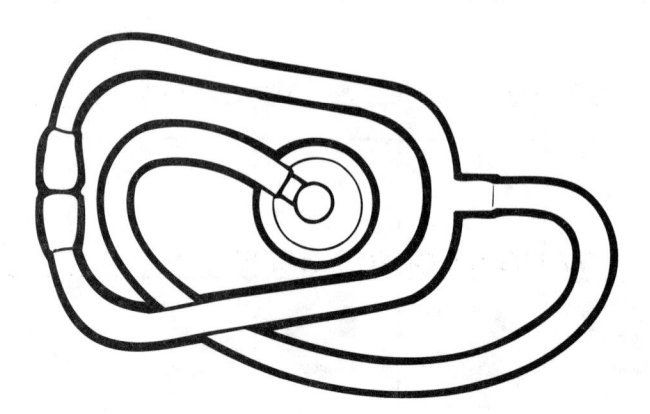

Heart Theme

Name: _____

My Heart

1. My heart is about the same size as my fist. I traced my fist below.

[blank box for tracing]

2. My heart is a _____.

3. My heart pumps _____ through my body.

4. I can feel my pulse. My heart beats about _____ times in one minute.

5. After I exercise, my heart beats about _____ times in one minute.

Heart Theme

Heart Social Studies

Objective

The students will identify destinations using cardinal directions in relationship to their home city/state.

Materials

- valentines or heart shapes with the names of states or cities written on them (One state/city per heart. Place these in a container from which the students can draw—one per student.)

- a map which includes the hometown/state of the students, as well as the other locations which have been written on the hearts (For example, if you live in the United States, you will want a map of the United States.)

Procedure

1. Have a discussion on cardinal directions. Use the map to point out the directions of North, South, East, and West.

2. Locate the home city/state of the students.

3. Have each student draw a heart shape or valentine from the container. Explain that this valentine will need to travel through the mail from its home location to the destination written on the heart.

4. Each student may then locate the state they have drawn and name it's direction in relationship to their home state. For example, if the student draws "Michigan" and he/she is from Ohio, he/she will state "Michigan is North of Ohio." Older students may use more complex directions such as Northwest, Southeast, etc.

5. Have the students write an appropriate sentence on their heart, such as "Michigan is north of Ohio," etc.

Extension Ideas

- To expand on the above lesson, have a mail carrier come in and talk about his/her job.

- Have a lesson on the history of Valentine's Day. The following Web sites may be helpful: **The History Channel** or **KidsDomain**.

- Have the student research how to say "I love you" in different languages. Use the following link for help—**WordPath**. Have the students locate countries in which people speak the different languages.

Heart Theme

Heart Art

Objective
The students will design and create a valentine.

Materials
- a variety of art materials—paper, ribbon, paint, lace, markers, etc.

Procedure
1. Have a discussion on homemade objects and how they can be very special. Direct the students to think of a special person for whom they would like to make a valentine.
2. Allow them to be as creative as they wish in designing and creating their valentine.

Extension Ideas
- Have students make valentine puzzles with the "A Puzzling Message" activity on page 186.
- Have students create "Valentine Window Houses" with the activity on page 187.
- Have the students make posters promoting heart-healthy activities.
- Have the students experiment with the colors red and white to create different shades of pink.
- Have the students draw pictures of things they like on a heart-shaped piece of paper. This could also be done in collage form by having them use magazine clippings.

©Teacher Created Materials, Inc.   #3823 Internet Activities Through the Year

Heart Theme

A Puzzling Message

Write your own Valentine message on the puzzle below. Then, cut out the pieces on the dashed lines and place them in an envelope that you have addressed to that "special person." You can write a message to your best friend, a favorite relative, or your teacher. Watch your valentine have fun putting the puzzle pieces together!

Heart Theme

Valentine Window House

Materials: pattern, scissors, pencil, crayons, glue, 9" x 11" (23 cm x 30 cm) plain white paper

Directions: Cut along the sides of the house. Cut out the windows on the dotted lines, leaving the solid line uncut so the windows and doors will open and close. This cutting can be done by pinching the paper slightly so you can make a cut with the scissors to get inside the paper and cut out the windows and doors. Glue another sheet of plain paper to the house at the edges only. Cut off the edges so that it matches the house size. On each window and the door write a word. Inside that window or door, write a word that rhymes with that word. For example, write "love" on the door and "dove" on the inside of the door. Other activities using the house include writing even numbers on the outside and odd numbers on the inside or an equation on the outside and the answer on the inside.

©Teacher Created Materials, Inc.   #3823 Internet Activities Through the Year

Heart Theme

Heart Movement

Objective
The students will engage in physical activity to increase their heart rates.

Materials
- a wide open area, allowing for movement
- jump ropes, balls, or any other equipment the students may use to get physical

Procedure
1. Have a discussion on muscles and how the heart is a muscle that is always working. It is important to exercise the heart muscle to keep it healthy and strong.
2. Have the students brainstorm healthy activities, which increase their heart rates. Explain that it is good to engage in these types of activities for 20 minutes 3 times per week.
3. Allow students 20 minutes to exercise their hearts.
4. Older students may want to take a pulse before they begin exercising and again after they exercise. (Similar to the activity in the Science Lesson.)

Extension Ideas
- Arrange a "Jump Rope for Heart" event. Details can be found at the following Web site: **American Heart Association**.
- Have a music lesson on what a beat is. Relate it to a beating heart and have the students listen to a variety of music containing different beats.

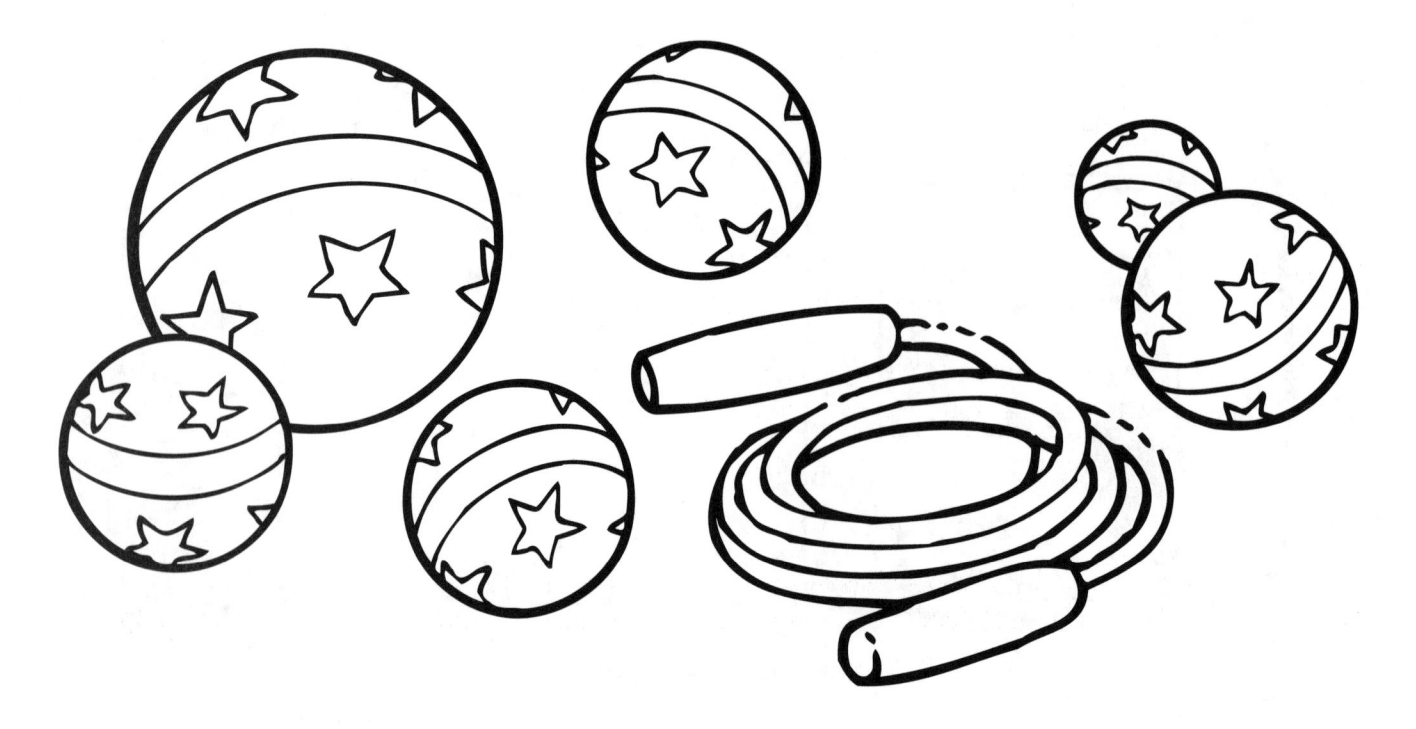

Kite Theme

Related Web Sites

Electrified Ben
This site provides information on Ben Franklin and his kite experiment.

The Electric Franklin
This is another site with Ben Franklin information.

Benjamin Franklin—Inventor
This site has information geared towards kids on Ben Franklin and his electricity experiments.

National Kite Month
This site is filled with kiting information.

The Virtual Kite Zoo
Contains terminology, construction techniques, and links to other Web sites about kites.

Learn 2 Make a Kite
Some different plans for kite making can be found at this site.

The Magic and Science of Kites
Find here history and information on what makes kites fly.

Related Literature

Curious George Flies a Kite by Margaret Rey
This familiar monkey is up to his usual antics.

The Emperor and the Kite by Jane Yolen
A young girl must save her father, the emperor, using the help of her kite.

The Great Kite Book by Norman Schmidt
A how-to book for kite-making.

Kites: Magic Wishes That Fly Up to the Sky by Demi
The story of the legend behind kite flying in China.

Kites Sail High: A Book about Verbs by Ruth Heller
A great book to use in a language arts lesson.

The Legend of the Kite: A Story of China by Chen Jiang Hong
A boy hears the legend of a kite flying festival from his grandfather.

Let's Fly a Kite—Level 2 Symmetry by Stuart J. Murphy
Great book to use in math lesson on symmetry.

Shibumi and the Kitemaker by Mercer Mayer
The daughter of an Japanese Emperor gets help from a kite-maker to build a kite big enough to help her fly.

Kite Theme

Kite Language Arts

Objective

The students will write a diamonte or cinquain poem.

Materials

- Information from the following sites: **Write Easy and Fun Poems**, **Diamonte Poems**, and **Diamonte and Cinquain Poetry**
- paper in the shape of a kite or "Kite Poetry" activity sheet.

Procedure

1. Show examples from the aforementioned Web sites. (**The Diamonte and Cinquain Poetry** site links out to lots of examples written by children.) Point out that a completed diamonte/cinquain is similar in shape to a kite. Emphasize the difference between a Diamonte and Cinquain poem. A Diamonte begins and ends with antonyms and Cinquains begin and end with synonyms.

2. Depending on the level of the students, have them write their own poems or work together as a class to compose one. Write the poems on the kite-shaped paper or on the "Kite Poetry" activity sheet.

3. For younger children, work as a class to brainstorm antonyms and synonyms. The children may then list or draw pictures of some antonyms and synonyms on their kite paper.

Extension Ideas

- Have a lesson on homonyms using tale and tail (as in a kite tail) as a starting point. The students may list the homonyms on kite-shaped paper.

- Have the students write about a place they would like to fly over as a kite. They should write the name of the place on the kite and describing words on the tail of the kite. For example, a student may write "the beach" on the kite and "sandy, wet, sunny, etc.," on the kite tail.

#3823 Internet Activities Through the Year ©Teacher Created Materials, Inc.

Kite Theme

Name: _____

Kite Poetry

My Poem

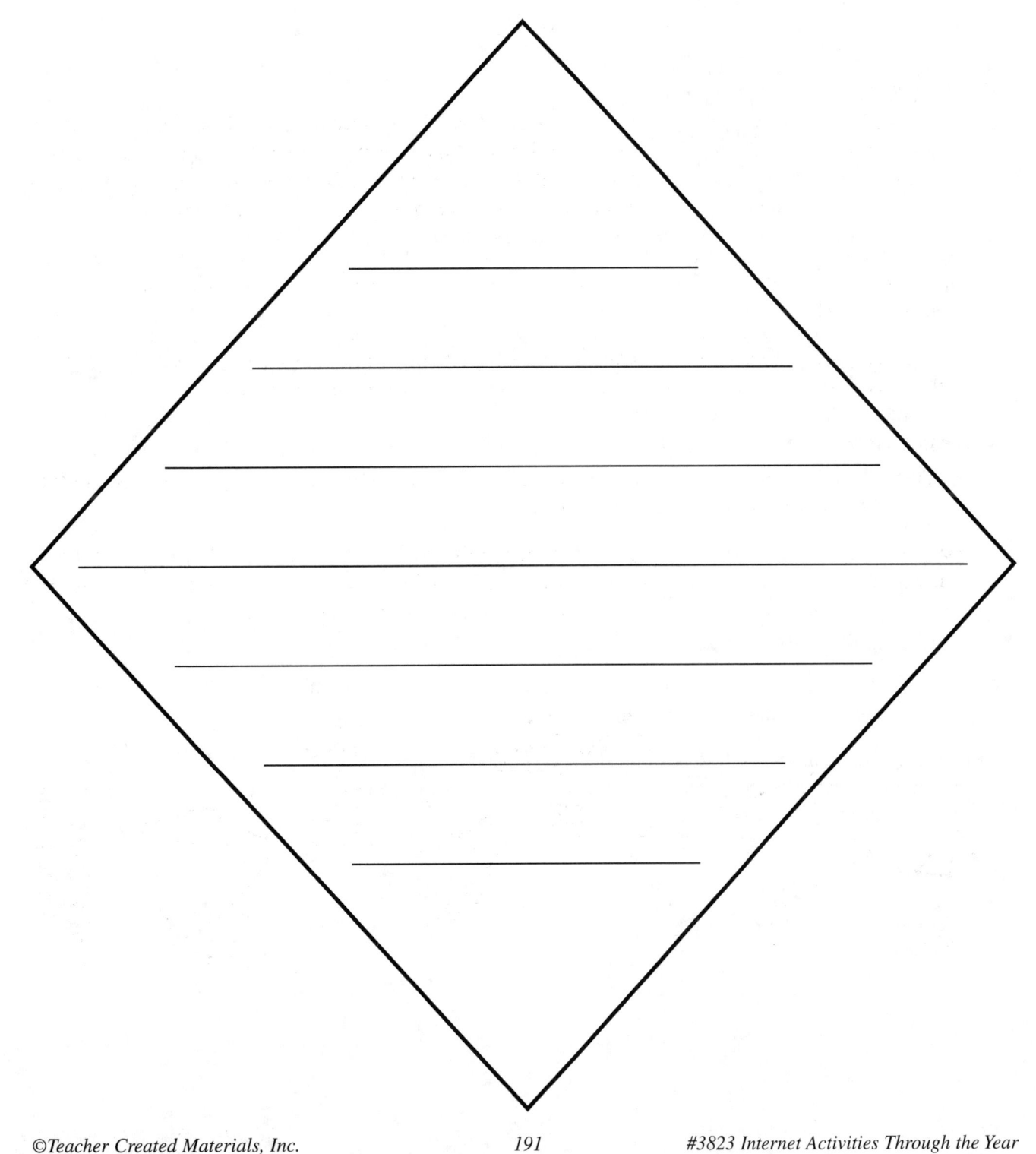

191 #3823 *Internet Activities Through the Year*

©*Teacher Created Materials, Inc.*

Kite Theme

Kite Math

Objective

The students will estimate different lengths.

Materials

- pieces of string cut to different lengths
- "How Long?" activity sheet

Procedure

1. Cut eight pieces of string ahead of time to varying lengths (label them 1–8). Some may be only a few inches long and some may be a foot or more. (The lengths will depend partly on the level of the students and their ability to measure. Younger students may work best with shorter pieces of string.)

2. Put the students in groups of three (or more or less depending on the size of the class. It will work best if there are eight groups—one per piece of string.)

3. Pass out the "How Long?" activity sheet. Hold up each piece of string and have the group decide on an estimate for the length of the string. The units used will depend on the class—inches, centimeters, or unifix cubes. The students should record their group's estimate on the worksheet.

4. Have the groups of students rotate from string to string and measure the actual length using the chosen units. They may then complete the "How Long?" activity sheet. Older students may figure the difference between their estimates and the actual lengths.

Extension Ideas

- Have students practice their counting skills and ability to follow directions with the "Counting Kites" activity on page 194.
- Have a lesson on symmetry using a symmetrical kite as an example.
- Have the students measure and create different tails for kites. They may decorate the tails with a pattern using color and/or shape in the design.
- Have the students create kites using different shapes of paper. The body of the kite may be a diamond shape and the tail made of rectangles. They may then decorate the body of the kites using a variety of shapes.

Kite Theme

How Long?

1. String #1   estimate _____

   actual _____

2. String #2   estimate _____

   actual _____

3. String #3   estimate _____

   actual _____

4. String #4   estimate _____

   actual _____

5. String #5   estimate _____

   actual _____

6. String #6   estimate _____

   actual _____

7. String #7   estimate _____

   actual _____

8. String #8   estimate _____

   actual _____

Kite Theme

Counting Kites

Read the sentence next to each row of kites, and color the kites correctly.

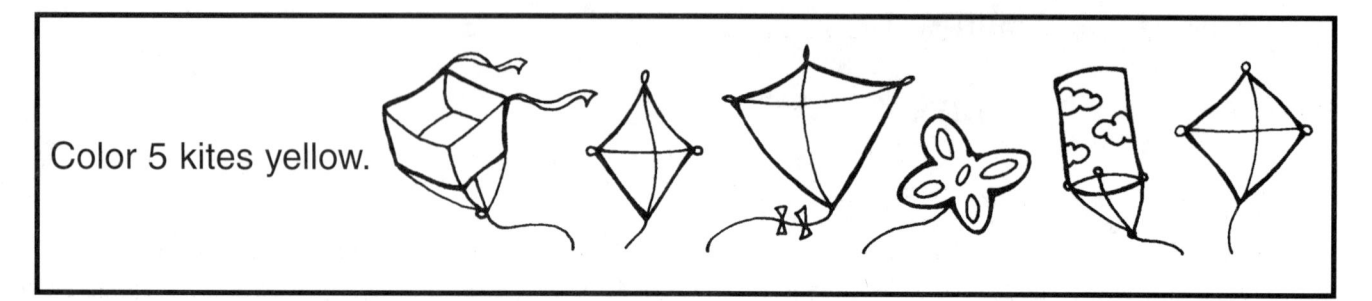

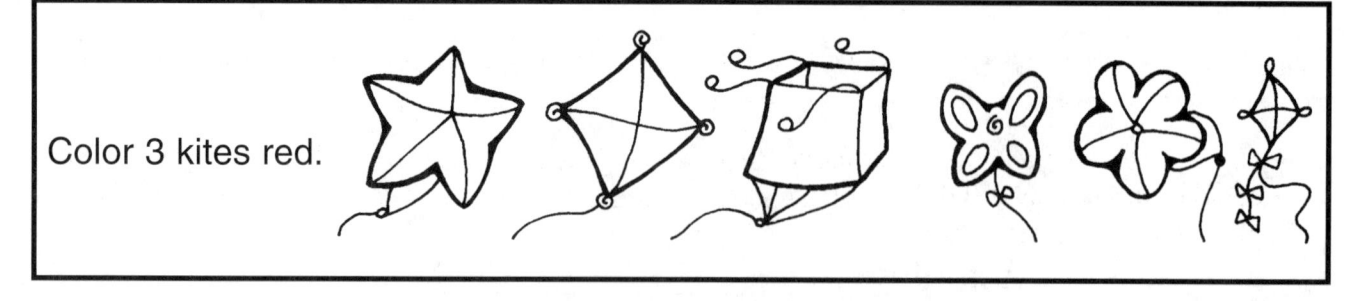

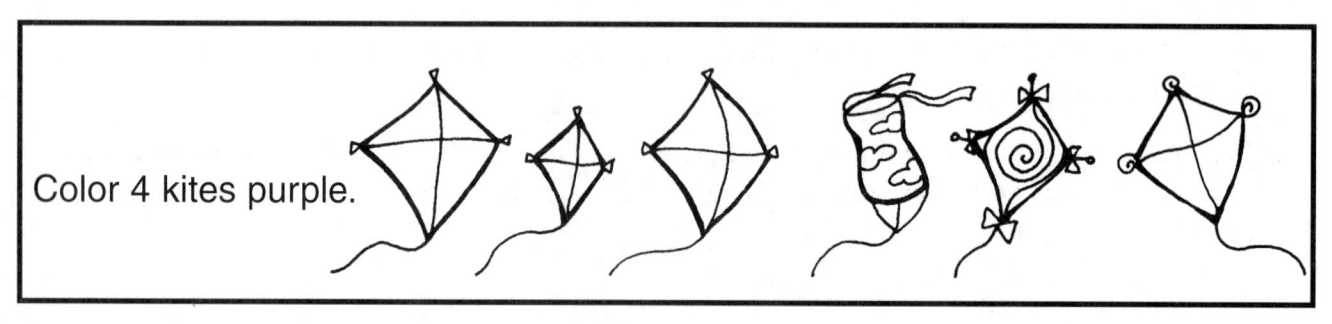

Color 2 kites blue.

Color 5 kites yellow.

Color 1 kite green.

Color 3 kites red.

Color 4 kites purple.

#3823 Internet Activities Through the Year ©Teacher Created Materials, Inc.

Kite Theme

Kite Science

Objective

The students will predict and identify which objects move the easiest in wind.

Materials

- background information on wind. The following links may be helpful: **What is Wind?**, **Kite Science** (click in "Kids" and then "Why a Kite Flies"), **Wind**.
- a fan or a hair dryer (to manufacture some wind in your classroom.)
- a variety of objects to test how far the wind can blow them. Some examples would be a tennis ball, a ping pong ball, a rock, a balled-up piece of paper, etc.
- "Wind Power" activity sheet

Procedure

1. Ask the students what they know about wind and what they would like to know. Record their responses on chart paper or the chalkboard.
2. Share the background information on what wind is and where it comes from. The amount and depth of information given will depend on the age of the students. The aforementioned Web sites will be helpful in this area.
3. Pass out the "Wind Power" activity sheet. Hold up each object which is going to be tested for the distance it can travel in the manufactured wind. Have the students record on their worksheets which object they think will travel the farthest and which will travel the shortest distance.
4. Mark off a "starting point" for the objects to be placed on and make sure the fan or blow dryer is always in the same place (for control purposes).
5. Test each object by placing them one at a time on the starting point in front of the fan or hair dryer.
6. Have the students complete the worksheet by putting the objects in order of shortest to farthest distance traveled.
7. Discuss why some objects went farther than others. Were the students' predictions correct? The depth of discussion will depend on the age level of the students. For example, friction will be discussed with older students.

Extension Ideas

- Make kites and go fly them! Many simple kite plans can be found in the links on the Kite Theme page.
- As a variation on the above lesson, have the students make small kites out of varying materials and test flying them in front of a fan. Which kites fly the best? Why?

Kite Theme

Name: _____

Wind Power

1. Which object do you predict will go the farthest distance?

   _____

2. Which object do you predict will go the shortest distance?

   _____

3. Write or draw the objects in order from the shortest to the farthest distance traveled.

Kite Theme

Kite Social Studies

Objective
The students will identify facts about Benjamin Franklin.

Materials
- information from the following Web sites: **Benjamin Franklin—Timeline**, **Electrified Ben**, **The Electric Franklin**, and **Benjamin Franklin**
- "Benjamin Franklin" activity sheet

Procedure
1. Share information from the Web sites about who Ben Franklin was. Emphasize his electricity experiment with the kite. Although there is some controversy about how accurate the legend is, it appears to be based in truth and to have occurred in June of 1752.
2. Pass out the "Benjamin Franklin" activity sheet.
3. Have the students complete the sheet and then share them with the rest of the class.

Extension Ideas
- Construct a large timeline of Benjamin Franklin's life. Use the **Benjamin Franklin—Timeline** Web site. For an extension activity have the students create a time line of their own lives.

- Have a lesson on China and the kite as a Chinese invention. Use the following web sites for assistance: **The Kite**, and **Kite History**. There are also good books on the Chinese Legends regarding kites, such as *The Legend of the Kite* by Chen Jiang Hong and *Kites: Magic Wishes that Fly Up to the Sky* by Demi. Locate China on a map.

Kite Theme

Name: _____

Benjamin Franklin

Write about or draw a picture of two of Benjamin Franklin's accomplishments.

Kite Theme

Kite Art

Objective
The students will create kites.

Materials
- information from any of the following sites for easy kite making plans/ideas: **20 Kids, 20 Kites, 20 Minutes**; **Teacher's Helper**; **Kids Kite Site**; **Basic Sled Kite**; or **Sugar Glider Kite**
- materials needed in the kite plan which you've decided upon

Procedure
1. Preview the aforementioned Web sites and decide upon the kite-making plan which best fits the students.
2. Gather the materials needed and have the students follow the directions for creating the kite.
3. If possible, go outside and fly the kites. This can be incorporated with the Movement Lesson.

Extension Ideas
- Have students find the kites in the "Hidden Pictures" activity on page 200.
- Younger students can complete the "K is for Kite" activity on page 201.
- Have the students create their own kite designs without the use of plans or directions.
- Have the students decorate kite-shaped pieces of paper to be hung from the ceiling of the classroom.

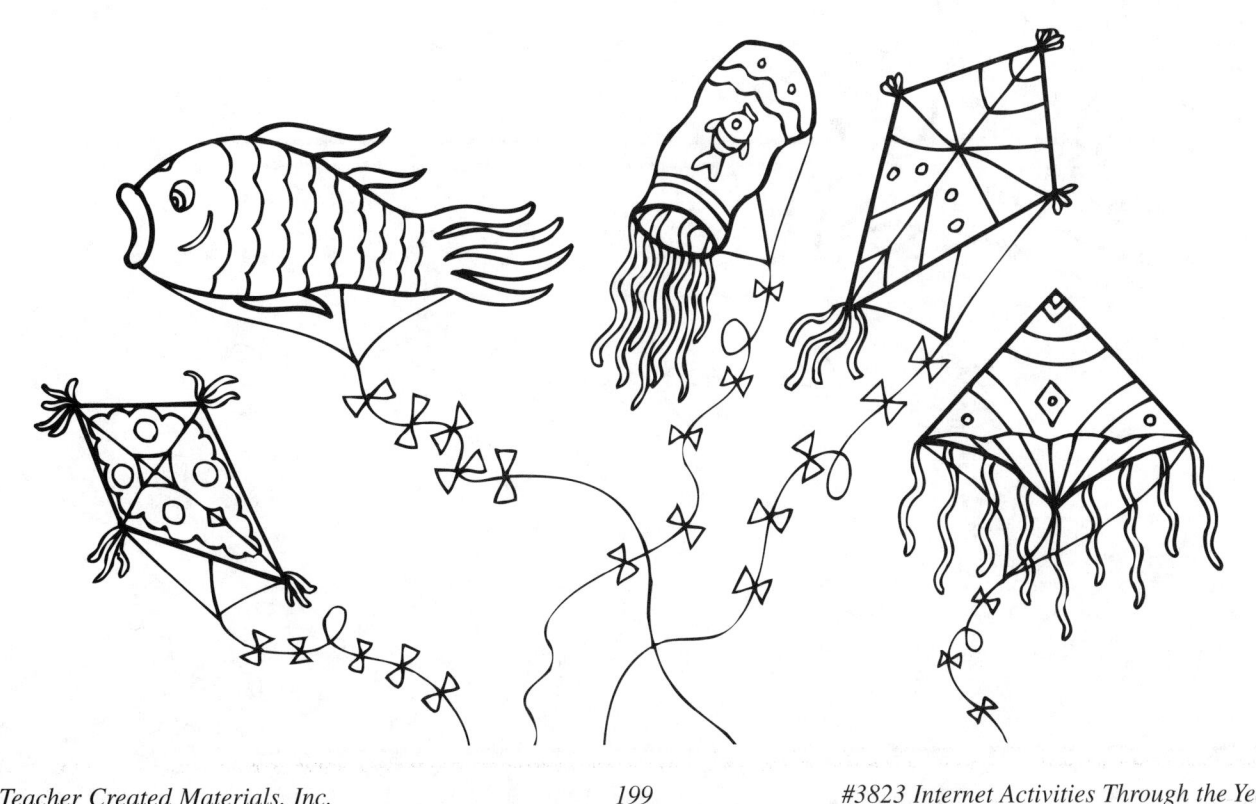

©Teacher Created Materials, Inc. #3823 Internet Activities Through the Year

Kite Theme

Hidden Pictures

Seven kites are lost in the park. Find them and color them.

#3823 Internet Activities Through the Year ©Teacher Created Materials, Inc.

Kite Theme

K is for kite

Color the kite. Glue a tail of yarn or ribbon to it.

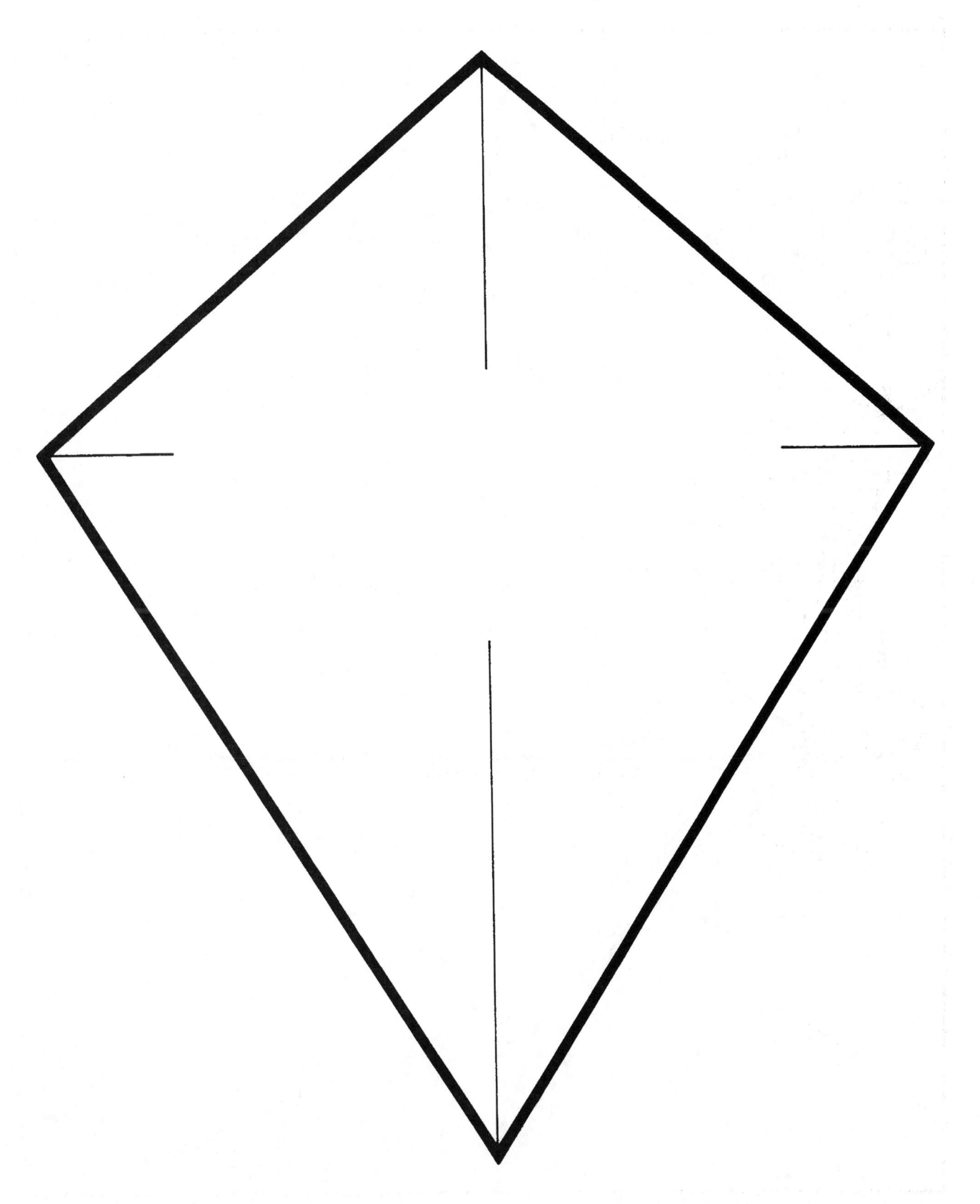

©Teacher Created Materials, Inc. #3823 Internet Activities Through the Year

Kite Theme

Kite Movement

Objective

The students will fly kites.

Materials

- kites made in the art lesson
- wde open space outside

Procedure

1. Go outside and fly the kites the students made in the art lesson.

2. If the wind is not cooperating, have the students run to make their kites fly behind them.

Extension Ideas

- Play different tempos of music and have the students pretend they are kites flying in a gentle breeze or in a heavy wind storm.

Moon Theme

Related Web Sites

The Apollo 11 Mission
This site has some basic information on the Apollo 11 mission, including the astronauts, mission objective, launch, duration, landing, and accomplishments. Recordings and pictures are included.

The History Place
This is the History Place's page on the Apollo 11 mission. More information, recordings and pictures can be found here. This page presents a time line of pictures, dates, and events. Hear the liftoff, the takeoff from the moon, Neil Armstrong's famous speech, and more.

Moon Watch
This page has great photos of the moon as well as news, trivia, facts, and frequently asked questions. It also shows the current phase of the moon, updated every four hours.

The Apollo Program—Apollo 11
This site has more good information and pictures about the Apollo 11 mission, including the mission summary, facts, crew, spacecraft, landing sites, images, and audio/video. Links to other Apollo missions can be found here.

Kid's Astronomy
This site has great information and pictures of the moon. The text is more kid friendly than the previous sites listed. Lots of other solar system information can be found here!

Related Literature

Airmail to the Moon by Tom Birdseye
When the tooth that she was saving for the tooth fairy disappears, Ora Mae sets out to find the thief and send him "airmail to the moon."

Berenstain Bears on the Moon by Jan and Stan Berenstain
Brother and Sister Bear travel to the moon in this rhyming story.

The Best Book of the Moon by Ian Graham
This book is filled with facts and folklore about the moon. It would be excellent for introductory research.

The Boy Who Ate the Moon by Franklyn M. Branley
After eating the moon, a boy takes a strange journey.

The Church Mice and the Moon by Graham Oakly
Two church mice are kidnapped to be trained as astronauts and sent to the moon.

Flower, Moon, Snow by Kazue Mizumura
This book of Haiku includes several poems about the moon.

Half a Moon and One Whole Star by Crescent Dragonwagon
The summer night is full of wonderful sounds and sights as Susan falls asleep.

Maggie's Moon by Martha G. Alexander
A little girl and her dog set out to capture the moon and bring it home with them.

Me and My Place in Space by Joan Sweeny
This book explains to children what they see in the sky, including the moon and planets.

The Moon by Isaac Asimov
Included is a good glossary and index as well as pictures describing the phases of the moon.

Moon Theme (cont.)

Related Literature (cont.)

The Moon by N.S. Barret
Photos and text describe the moon's physical characteristics based on information obtained from the Apollo lunar missions.

The Moon by Paulette Bourgeois
Including a glossary and index, as well as facts, experiments, stories and legends, this would be a good book to use to enrich a social studies lesson. It introduces the beliefs different cultures have held about the moon.

The Moon by Carmen Breedson
This is a history of human beliefs about the moon over time, including current scientific knowledge and information on the Apollo space program

The Moon Book by Gail Gibbons
This book is filled with good information about the moon

The Moon Seems to Change by Franklyn Masfield Branley
Learn about the changes that happen to the moon's appearance as it travels around the earth.

Moon Landing: The Race for the Moon by Carole Stoll
This book details Apollo moon missions, including a good index and fact glossary.

Moonwalk: The First Trip to the Moon by Judy Donnelly
This book provides a detailed description of the Apollo 11 mission to the moon.

My Place in Space by Robin and Sally Hirst
A brother and sister give their address to the bus driver and then learn their place in the universe.

Neil Armstrong: Young Flyer by Montrew Duham
This is a good biography of Neil Armstrong.

Papa, Please Get the Moon for Me by Eric Carle
This is the story of a father and daughter and the changing size and shape of the moon.

Space Busters: The Race to the Moon by Phillip Wilkinson
Good information can be found here about the Apollo missions to the moon (includes a glossary).

Sun, Moon, and Planets by Lynn Myring and Sheila Snowden
Includes facts about the moon and moon missions.

Touch the Moon by Marion Dane Bauer
This is a fantasy story about the moon.

The Truth About the Moon by Clayton Bess
An African boy is told several tales about the moon, but he still feels he has not learned the truth.

What's Out There: A Book About Space by Lynn Wilson
Included is information about the phases and orbit of the moon, the planets, and Apollo 13.

Moon Theme

Moon Language Arts

Objective

The students will explore the tall tale genre. They will be introduced to the idea of man explaining observed natural phenomena through the use of story telling.

Materials

- *The Truth About the Moon* by Clayton Bess
- "Story Puppet" activity sheet or moon, sun, river, and star shapes cut out for each child
- tape/glue
- popsicle sticks
- crayons, colored pencils, or markers

Procedure

1. Pass out the cutout shapes of the "Story Puppet" activity sheet.
2. Have the students color and label the shapes.
3. The students should then create puppets by gluing or taping the shapes onto the popsicle sticks.
4. Read the book *The Truth About the Moon* by Clayton Bess. (Summary: An African child is told several stories about the moon, and at the end he still feels he has not learned the truth.)
5. While reading the story, have the students use the appropriate puppets to act out the three tall tale stories. Teacher direction will be needed to guide the students through this activity.
6. As an alternative, have the class break into three groups after reading the story. Then let each group make their own props and act out the tall tale they have been assigned or have chosen themselves.

Extension Ideas

- Read an alternate story from the related literature list and have the students brainstorm and write a list of moon vocabulary.
- Give the story starter "If the moon were made of _____ I would…"
- Have the students write a letter to an astronaut.
- Do a phonics lesson on the "oo" sound.
- Write moon poems on cutout moon shapes.

Moon Theme

Story Puppets

Moon	Star
River	Sun

#3823 Internet Activities Through the Year ©Teacher Created Materials, Inc.

Moon Theme

Moon Math

Objective

The students will discover that fractions make up part of a whole.

Materials

- The lesson may be prepped with one of the following books (if desired): *The Moon Seems to Change* by Franklyn M. Branley, *The Best Book of the Moon* by Ian Graham, *What the Moon is Like* by Franklyn M. Branley.

- For each pair of students, have one whole moon cut out of blue paper, one yellow moon cut in half, one green moon cut in fourths. The halves and fourths should equal the whole.

Procedure

1. Give each pair of students their moon shapes. Discuss the terms whole, half, and one-fourth.

2. Have the students place the half shapes on top of the whole shape. Ask questions such as "How are the two halves and the whole the same?" and "How are they different?"

3. Then have them place the fourths over the yellow (whole) piece and ask similar questions.

4. Then they should place the fourths over the half shapes. Ask questions again.

5. Finally, allow the students to continue exploring the materials and brainstorm other fractions ($2/4 = 1/2$, $4/4 = 1$ whole, etc.)

6. The pieces may be stapled together and labeled to form a small flap book.

Extension Ideas

- Practice counting by odds and evens, or fives and tens, by using half and whole moons on a number line.

- Use actual moon pies as a snack and break them into fractions before eating them.

- Using the rhyme "Hey Diddle Diddle," measure how far each child can jump. This can be used as a combination math and movement activity. Use 6-inch diameter paper moons to measure the distance jumped.

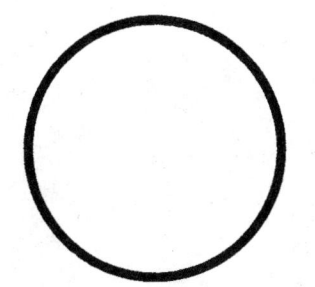

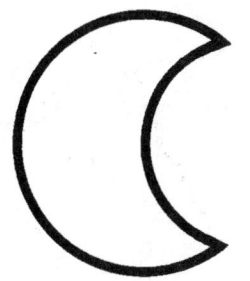

Moon Theme

Moon Science

Objective

The students will act out the orbit of the moon and Earth in relation to the sun.

Materials

- (based on a class of 20) one white balloon, five blue balloons, 15 yellow balloons
- a large area allowing for movement

Procedure

1. Choose students to hold the balloons.
2. Cluster them together in groups to form the moon, Earth, and sun. Discuss with the students the fact that the Earth and the sun are larger than the moon (this is represented with the number of balloons used.)
3. Have the student with the white balloon (the moon) orbit around the Earth balloons (blue).
4. At the same time have the Earth (blue balloons) orbit around the sun (yellow balloons).

Extension Ideas

- Using a mirror and flashlight, explore the reflective light qualities of the moon.
- Find out how many moons other planets have.
- Do a lesson on what an eclipse of the moon entails. Use the **What Causes an Eclipse** Web site for information.

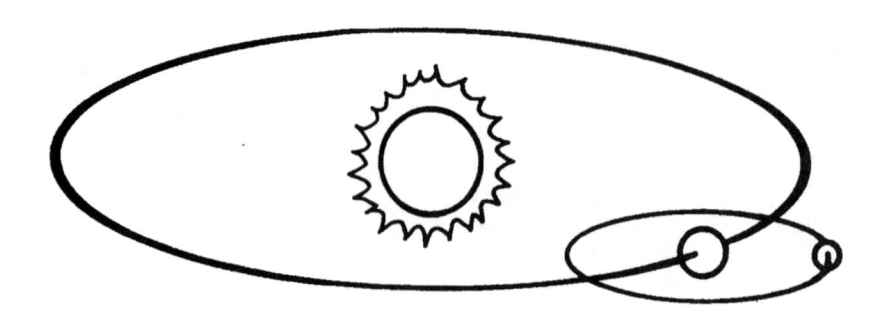

Moon Theme

Moon Social Studies

Objective

The students will discover the history of the first manned mission to the moon. They will gain experience with the use of a time line to study an event in history in relationship to the present day and themselves.

Materials

- A book about the first landing on the moon (*Moonwalk* by Judy Donnelly would be a possible choice).

- The Web site **The Apollo 11 Mission** to be displayed for the students.

- A printout of a picture of Apollo 11 or the astronauts who were on that mission.

- A baby picture of the teacher and each of the students (these can be actual photos or drawings).

- A photo or drawing of each student on their first day of kindergarten, first grade, second grade, etc. (go as high as to the current grade they are now in.)

- A long piece of butcher paper to be labeled with dates and photos/drawings for the time line.

Procedure

1. Read the story about the first landing on the moon.

2. Display the link mentioned in the materials list above. This will give an actual sound recording of Neil Armstrong's first step onto the lunar surface.

3. Discussion will follow the story and Web site visit. Be sure to talk about the impact that this landing had on the country and the world. Compare it to other events in the world today: the Olympics, an election, etc.

4. Now help the class construct a time line on the butcher paper that begins with an event before the moon landing. It could be the teacher's birthday, the Principal's birthday, or a U.S. President's birthday (attach a photo/drawing of this person on the correct date). The next event will be the lunar landing date (attach the printout of Apollo 11), then the students' birthdays, followed by the date of the first day of K, 1st, or 2nd grade and today's date. Choose any other dates that are significant to the students. The students will attach their photos/drawings on the appropriate place on the time line.

5. Ask questions about the completed time line. The complexity of the questions will depend on the age of the students. For example, "Were you born before or after Apollo 11's mission?," "How old was the principal/teacher/president when Apollo 11 landed on the moon?," etc.

Extension Idea

- Read the book *The Moon* by Carmen Bredeson, which gives the history of human beliefs about the moon over time and includes current scientific knowledge.

Moon Theme

Moon Art

Objective

The students will explore the use of color and color mixing. They will also make an emotional and visual connection between color, poetic rhythm, and musical harmony.

Materials

- Enya CD or other new age instrumental music
- water color paint
- white painting paper
- paint brushes
- the book *Half a Moon and One Whole Star* by Crescent Dragonwagon (or some other poems about the moon)

Procedure

1. While reading the book or similar poetry, play the music in the background.
2. Instruct the students to listen to the reading.
3. Have the students then use the painting materials to create pictures inspired by the reading/music. Direct the students to mix the colors to create new colors and scenes that remind them of the reading/music.

Extension Ideas

- Allow the children to use alternative materials, such as cotton, yarn, pasta shells, beans, etc., to complete the phrase "If the moon were made of . . . (material of their choice)."
- Make paper maché moons and hang them from the ceiling.
- Give the students black construction paper and have them create a night sky using white chalk or white tempera paint.

Moon Theme

Moon Movement

Objective

The students will practice jumping.

Materials

- a 6-inch paper circle that represents a moon
- an open space

Procedure

1. Recite the rhyme "Hey Diddle, Diddle."
2. Have the students jump from a starting line.
3. Measure how far the jump in distance is using the paper moon.

Extension Ideas

- Play New Age or outer space sounding music and have the students imitate a moonwalk with a feeling of weightlessness.
- Assign students to be particular planets and have them act out the rotation of the planets (similar to the science lesson).
- Have the students practice counting backwards from 10–1 and have them pretend they are rockets blasting off to the moon.
- Play Spud using the word "moon" instead of "spud."

Pancake Theme

Related Web Sites

Pancake Kids
This site is sponsored by the International House of Pancakes. There are a few games to play, such as a pancake puzzle, and coloring pages to print.

Dole 5 A Day
Click on Kid's Cookbook when you get to this site sponsored by Dole to find a recipe for Banana Raisin Pancakes.

International Pancake Theme
This site has information on a race between Liberal, Kansas and Olney, England in which women run with pancakes in a skillet. Read the history of this race, see pictures of past races, and read their official pancake recipe, which will serve about a thousand people!

Pancake Recipes
Here is a collection of all types of pancake recipes, including a recipe for creamed corn pancakes.

Related Literature

Curious George Makes Pancakes by Margaret Rey
Curious George gets involved in making pancakes at a fundraiser for the Children's Hospital.

If You Give a Pig a Pancake by Laura Joffe Numeroff
A great story involving cause and effect by the same author of *If You Give a Mouse a Cookie* and *If You Give a Moose a Muffin*.

Mr. Wolf's Pancakes by Jan Fearnley
Mr. Wolf attempts to get help from his nursery rhyme friends to make some pancakes. When they end up being rude to him, yet still demand some of the pancakes, he teaches them a lesson! Caution: the ending has the wolf gobbling up the other characters. However, it is done in a lighthearted way.

Pancakes for Breakfast by Tomie dePaola
This is a wordless picture book in which a little woman must go through lots of trouble to get her morning pancakes.

The Pancake Theme (Get Ready, Get Set, Read!) by Kelli C. Foster
This phonics book reviews the long vowel sounds.

Pancakes, Pancakes! by Eric Carle
A young boy has lots of work to do in order to help his mother make some pancakes!

Penelope Penguin's Pancake Party by Debbie Pollard
The first day of Kindergarten needs to start out with a breakfast of pancakes. But what happens if you forget to eat your pancakes?

Sugaring by Jessie Haas
This book follows the process of making maple syrup with a little girl and her grandpa.

Pancake Theme

Pancake Language Arts

Objective
The students will write recipes for pancakes and place the recipes in alphabetical order.

Materials
- "Pancake Recipe" activity sheet, chalkboard and chalk, or chart paper
- A sample pancake recipe:
    - 1 ½ cups flour
    - 1 teaspoon salt
    - 3 tablespoons sugar
    - 1 teaspoon baking powder
    - 2 eggs
    - 3 tablespoons melted butter
    - 1 cup milk

Directions
1. Combine the flour, salt, sugar, and baking powder in a bowl.
2. Add the eggs, butter, and milk.
3. Mix the ingredients.
4. Cook the pancakes in a hot pan.

Procedure
1. Share the pancake recipe with the class by writing it on the chalkboard or chart paper. For younger students, you may want to write the sample recipe on the recipe activity sheet before copying it. Therefore, the students will only have to write the name of their recipe and the added ingredient.
2. Have a discussion on the components of a recipe—ingredients, steps to follow, etc.
3. Have the students copy the basic recipe onto their recipe activity sheets and add in any special ingredients they would like in their pancakes. Allow them to be as creative as they would like to be. An important step will be to give a name to their pancake recipe. For example, "Chocolate Chip Pancakes," "Bubble Gum Pancakes," "Peanut Butter Pancakes," etc.
4. Once the recipes are complete, list the titles of the recipes on chart paper or the chalkboard. Depending on the level of the students, either work together as a class or individually to put the recipe names in alphabetical order.
5. If desired, compile the recipes with a table of contents into a class Pancake Recipe Book.

Extension Ideas
- Read and compare the two books *Pancakes, Pancakes!* by Eric Carle and *Pancakes for Breakfast* by Tomie dePaola.
- Have the students write words to accompany the book *Pancakes for Breakfast* by Tomie dePaola.
- Have a lesson on adding –ing to short vowel words. Use flip—flipping as a starting point.
- Have a compound word lesson, using pancake as an example.
- Explore collective nouns for groups of food. For example, stack of pancakes, batch of cookies, bushel of apples, etc. Incorporate Ruth Heller's book *A Cache of Jewels*.
- Read *If You Give a Pig a Pancake* by Laura Joffe Numeroff. Discuss cause and effect. The students may make their own stories following the theme "If You Give a _____ a _____."

Pancake Theme

Name: _____

Pancake Recipe

Title:

_____

Ingredients:

_____   _____

_____   _____

_____   _____

_____   _____

Steps:

1. _____

2. _____

3. _____

4. _____

5. _____

6. _____

Pancake Theme

Pancake Math

Objective

The students will compile sets of numbers and count them to figure answers to addition problems.

Materials

- "Pancakes" activity sheet or five paper circles per student or pair of students.
- containers of small manipulatives, such as beans, to pose as blueberries, chocolate chips, etc. (These will be placed on the "pancakes.")
- "Adding with Pancakes" activity sheet (most appropriate for older students)

Procedure

1. Give each student, or pair of students, their five "pancakes" and a container of manipulatives. They may cut their pancakes out or leave them intact on the activity sheet.

2. Work as a class to solve problems such as "I have three pancakes and they each have two blueberries on them. How many blueberries are there altogether?" The difficulty of the problems will depend on the age of the students.

3. Allow time for older students to create their own problems on the "Adding with Pancakes" activity sheet.

Extension Ideas

- Conduct a lesson in diameter by having students measure different size pancakes.
- Measure distances by having students see how far they can flip a pancake. Cut the "pancakes" from heavy cardboard or craft foam. Have the students flip the pancakes across an open area in the classroom or outside. Use a spatula or have them flip it directly from a pan.
- Do any type of addition in which stacks of pancakes are involved. A stack of three pancakes plus a stack of two pancakes, equals how many pancakes altogether? Or figure out how many pancakes would be needed for everyone in the class to have two, three, or more.

Pancake Theme

Pancakes

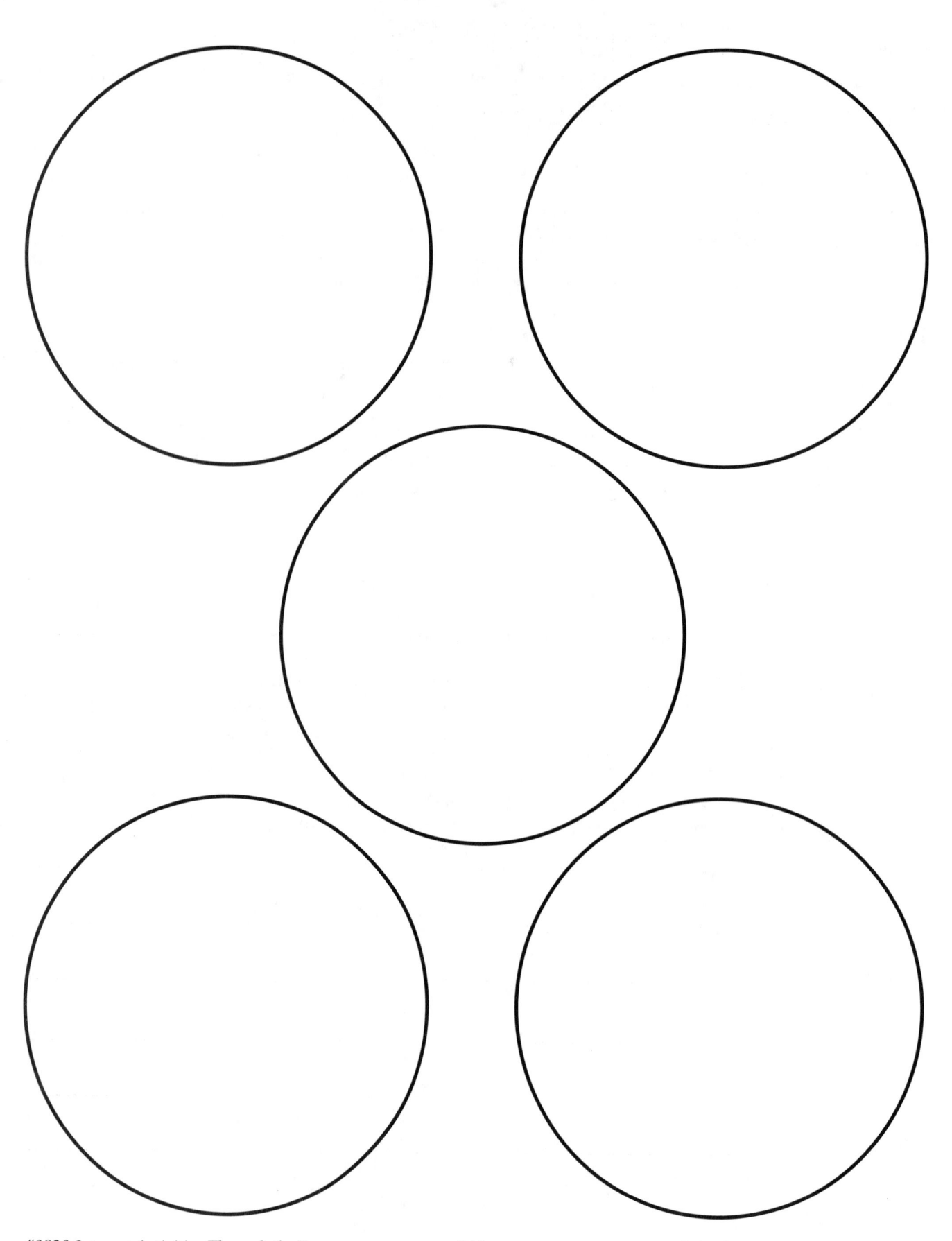

#3823 Internet Activities Through the Year 216 ©Teacher Created Materials, Inc.

Pancake Theme

Name: _____

Adding With Pancakes

Write some pancake story problems.

1. _____
   _____
   _____

2. _____
   _____
   _____

3. _____
   _____
   _____

4. _____
   _____
   _____

5. _____
   _____
   _____

6. _____
   _____
   _____

Pancake Theme

Pancake Science

Objective
The students will identify different foods that come from trees, emphasizing maple syrup.

Materials
- a book or a Web site on maple syrup (One of the following sites may be helpful: **Making Maple Syrup in Indiana**, **Michigan Maple Syrup**, and **Massachusetts Maple Producers**.)
- chart paper or blackboard
- "Foods We Get from Trees" activity sheet

Procedure
1. Ask the students to brainstorm different foods that come from trees. Record their responses on the chart paper or blackboard.
2. If maple syrup is not one of the given responses, lead to a discussion on maple syrup.
3. Present the information on how maple syrup is produced with the help of one of the above Web sites or a book. Include information of tree sap and the different parts of a tree. Use the following Web site for background help on tree sap: **Discovery School—Sap** (most appropriate for teacher preparation).
4. Pass out the "Foods We Get from Trees" activity sheet for reinforcement. Younger students may draw pictures of foods that come from trees.

Extension Ideas
- Make pancakes in the classroom! Focus on following a recipe and measuring the amounts correctly.
- Have a lesson on solids, liquids, and gases. Relate different aspects of pancakes to these states of matter. For example, milk (an ingredient of pancakes) is a liquid, pancakes are solids, and the process of making maple syrup involves the boiling off of water (example of gas).

Pancake Theme

Name: _____

Foods We Get From Trees

List some foods which come from trees:

_____

_____

_____

_____

_____

_____

_____

_____

_____

_____

Pancake Theme

Pancake Social Studies

Objective
The students will explore how making butter has changed over time.

Materials
- information from the **Making Butter** Web site
- baby food jars (one per student or pair of students)
- cream (enough to place 1 tablespoon in each jar)
- *Pancakes for Breakfast* by Tomie dePaola or *Pancakes, Pancakes!* by Eric Carle.

Procedure
1. Share information with the students from the above Web site on the process of butter making. If desired, also share the sections of *Pancakes for Breakfast* and/or *Pancakes, Pancakes!* which show the butter being churned. Lead to a discussion on how before machines were invented, people had to churn butter by hand.

2. Pass out the baby food jars with the cream inside of them. Have the students shake the jars until they have formed a small amount of butter.

3. When they have completed "churning their butter," have a discussion on how much easier machines have made our lives. Brainstorm machines which have made our daily lives easier.

Extension Ideas
- Make a pancake recipe, which originates from a different part of the world. For example, make German Potato Pancakes or thin French Crepes. Locate the country on a map and share some information about its culture.

- Locate on maps the states which produce maple syrup.

- Share the Native American Legend of how Maple Syrup was discovered. Use one of the following links: **Maple History** or **Native Americans and Maple Syrup**.

Pancake Theme

Pancake Art

Objective

The students will create a stack of pancakes using various art supplies.

Materials

- paper plates
- tan construction paper
- glue
- brown paint
- small paper cups or containers—one per student or pair of students (The glue and brown paint will be mixed in the containers to create "syrup.")

Procedure

1. Have the students cut circles out of the tan construction paper to serve as "pancakes" and glue them onto their paper plates.
2. Depending on the age of the students, they may mix their own brown paint and glue in a small container or have this done ahead of time.
3. The students should pour the glue and paint mixture over their "pancakes" to create "syrup."

Extension Ideas

- Design spatulas to be used for flipping pancakes. Offer a wide variety of materials, so the student may be as creative as possible.
- Have the students create pictures of pancakes to accompany the language arts lesson.

Pancake Theme

Pancake Movement

Objective

The students will participate in a pancake flipping game.

Materials

- "pancakes" made from thick cardboard or craft foam, about 4" in diameter (one per five students)
- spatulas (one per five students)
- a wide open space allowing for a relay race

Procedure

1. Divide the class into teams of five students. Set them up in a relay race format, using markers (such as cones or chairs) at the opposite end of the space for them to round before coming back to the starting place.

2. The first person in each team should be given a spatula and a pancake. They should begin by flipping the pancake out in front of them as far as they can. They then run up to the pancake, place it back on the spatula and continue flipping and chasing it around the marker and back to the next person. This game may be set up as a competition or not, depending on teacher preference.

Extension Idea

- As a variation on the above game, have students take turns trying to flip imitation pancakes into a frying pan. They may begin by standing right in front of the frying pan (to be placed on the floor or a low table). With each successful land in the frying pan, the students may take a step back to get farther and farther away from the pan.

Penguin Theme

Related Web Sites

Virtual Antarctica Science: Penguins
Good background information for teachers on penguins can be found here. Included is information on different species of penguins, such as the Emperor Penguin and Crested Penguin, along with behavior, breeding, locomotion, and colonies.

Penguins Around the World
This site is filled with information on all different types of penguins. Kids can view a slide show, learn about penguin habitats, learn fun facts, and take a quiz. It even has a section for teachers with lesson plans and collaborative ideas.

Pete and Barb's Penguins Pages
Lots of information on penguins can be found here. There are over a hundred pages, along with photographs and maps. Included are book suggestions, ideas for teachers, and fun pages. The authors of this site are true penguin enthusiasts and provide a diary of one of their trips to Antarctica.

Penguins
This site sponsored by Sea World provides some basic information about penguins.

Monterey Bay Aquarium: Focus on Penguins
This page from the Monterey Bay Aquarium focuses on penguins. Included is information about the aquarium's penguins, care and feeding, and the behavior of penguins in captivity and in the wild. Learn why the "tuxedo" that the penguins wear helps them avoid predators, how they keep warm in the cold climates they live in, and why they are in danger. Be sure to check out the live Penguin Cam and the video of penguins swimming!

Penguin Planet
Features photographs and excerpts from a book by a wildlife photographer. Included is a Kids' Corner with printables, links, and a video of penguins in action!

Related Literature

Antarctic Antics: A Book of Penguin Poems by Judy Sierra
A collection of penguin poems!

Cuddly Dudley by Jez Alborough
This lovable penguin tries to find some peace and quiet.

Mr. Popper's Penguins by Richard Atwater
This classic chapter book could be read over a long unit on penguins.

The Penguin (Animal Close-Ups) by Beatrice Fontanel
Good information.

A Penguin Pup for Pinkerton by Steven Kellogg
This popular great dane attempts to incubate a football in his paws, after hearing how Penguins do the same with their eggs.

Whiteblack the Penguin Sees the World by Margaret Rey
This book is brought to you by the much loved "Curious George" team. It was not discovered until after the death of Margaret Rey, although it was written in 1937. It is the story of a penguin who set off to see the world in order to have stories to tell.

Tacky Books (Series) by Helen Lester
This series of books revolves around a penguin named Tacky.

Penguin Theme

Penguin Language Arts

Objective

The students will write an invitation.

Materials

- colored paper, construction paper, and card stock (The "Penguin Party" activity sheet and "Penguin Stationery" on pages 225 and 226 can also be used for this activity.)
- envelopes
- writing utensils
- examples of invitations (if available)

Procedure

1. Facilitate a discussion on penguins and their coloring. Discuss how penguins appear to be wearing tuxedos. Ask the students at what times people wear tuxedos and get dressed up in their best clothes. One of the answers may be when going to a party.

2. How do people know they are invited to a party? By receiving an invitation. Explain to the students they will be having a "Penguin Party" at the end of their school day (or whenever is appropriate). Therefore, they need to write invitations to the event.

3. Discuss the elements that are important to include on an invitation: Time, Date, Place, etc. Discuss the specifics of your "Penguin Party."

4. Pass out the chosen paper and envelopes. Expand the lesson to include addressing envelopes with the return address, etc. Pair the students up so they may address their envelopes to a fellow classmate.

5. Allow the students time to complete their invitations and envelopes. This lesson may also be combined with an Art Lesson to have the students fully decorate their invitations.

Extension Ideas

- Use the "Black and White" Day activity on pages 227 and 228 to make invitations for a Black and White day in the classroom.

- Have a lesson on alliteration and have the students complete sentences such as "Penguins pack _____ in their parcels," or "Penguins pick _____ to give as presents."

- The students may listen to nonfiction books and information from web sites listed on the Penguin Theme Page. Have them write penguin facts on egg-shaped pieces of paper to serve as "penguin eggs." Make a class book.

Penguin Theme

You are invited to a Penguin Party!

Penguin Theme

Penguin Stationery

Penguin Theme

Black and White Day

Have a Black and White Day in your classroom. Wear black and white clothing. Invite parents or another classroom to join you for part of the day for a Penguin Performance. Give a Readers' Theater, read original stories and poems, sing some penguin songs, and share projects completed during the unit. Send out invitations. Ask parents to send black and white snacks—black jelly beans, black licorice, black olives, white marshmallows, chocolate sandwich cookies, vanilla or chocolate chip ice cream, cauliflower, white milk—to serve for refreshments.

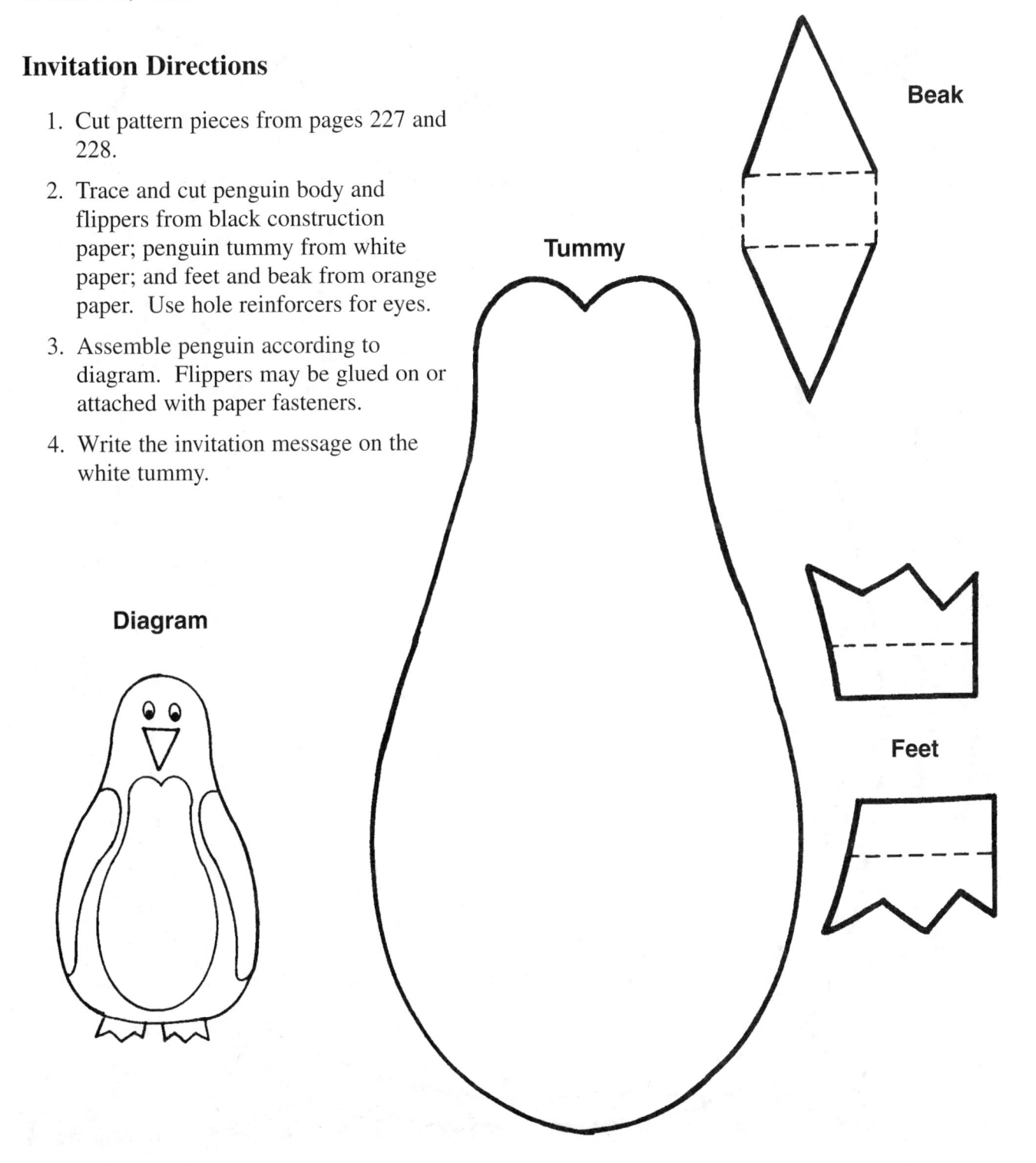

Invitation Directions

1. Cut pattern pieces from pages 227 and 228.

2. Trace and cut penguin body and flippers from black construction paper; penguin tummy from white paper; and feet and beak from orange paper. Use hole reinforcers for eyes.

3. Assemble penguin according to diagram. Flippers may be glued on or attached with paper fasteners.

4. Write the invitation message on the white tummy.

Diagram

Tummy

Beak

Feet

©Teacher Created Materials, Inc.   227   #3823 Internet Activities Through the Year

Penguin Theme

Black and White Day *(cont.)*

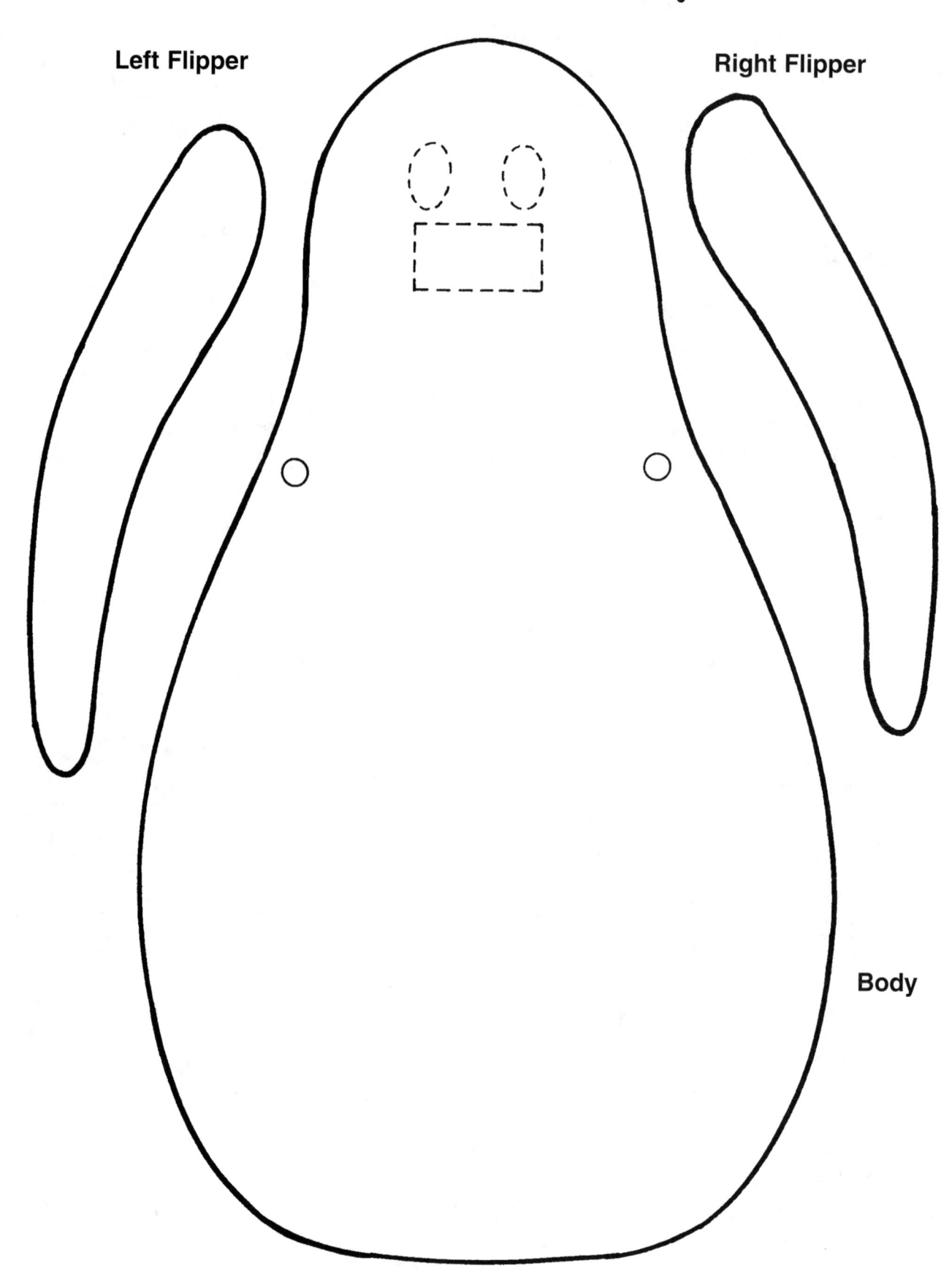

Left Flipper

Right Flipper

Body

#3823 Internet Activities Through the Year 228 ©Teacher Created Materials, Inc.

Penguin Theme

Penguin Math

Objective

The students will measure heights and arrange them from shortest to tallest.

Materials

- measuring tapes or rulers
- "Average Penguin Heights" activity sheet
- string or yarn

Procedure

1. Divide the class into pairs or groups of three.
2. Discuss how there are many different species/types of penguins. Liken this to different types of dogs. Each species has its own characteristics including height. Some species are taller/shorter than others.
3. Give each pair of students a slip of paper with the type of penguin and its height. The slips of paper may be cut from the "Average Penguin Heights" activity sheet. Decide ahead of time whether you will be using centimeters or inches.
4. Have the students measure a piece of string to that height and cut it off.
5. Reconvene as a class and have the students arrange their strings in order from shortest to tallest. Tape the string on the wall in the classroom or hallway and mark the name of the species and its height above each string.

Extension Ideas

- Continue to plan your "Penguin Party" from the language arts lesson. Have the students determine how many items will be needed for the party. For example, if everyone has one cup of juice, how many cups are needed? Or if every guest has two cookies, how many cookies will be needed?, etc.
- Make story problems using penguins, and/or penguin eggs as the main factor. For example, if five penguins are on the ice and two jump off to swim, how many are left?

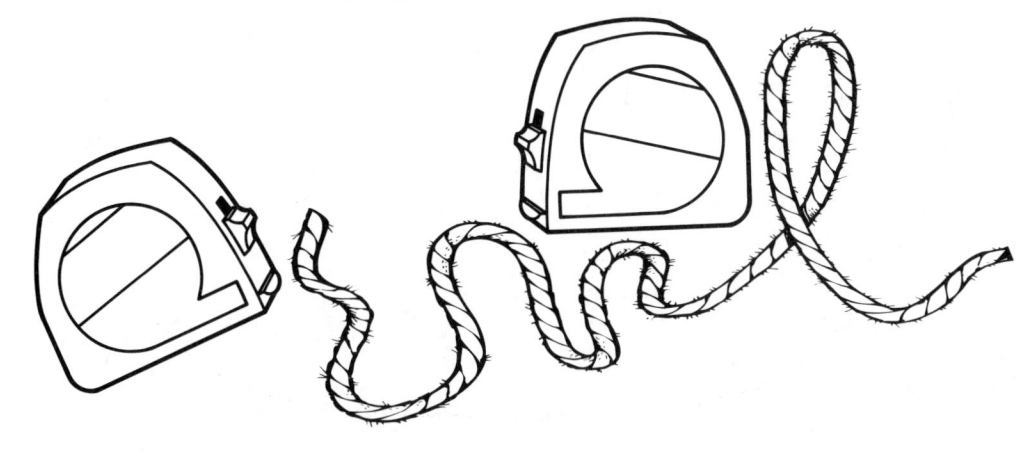

Penguin Theme

Average Penguin Heights

Emperor Penguin 120 cm.

King Penguin 90 cm.

Gentoo Penguin 80 cm.

Chinstrap Penguin 70 cm.

Adelie Penguin 70 cm.

Yellow-Eyed Penguin 70 cm.

Macaroni Penguin 70 cm.

Royal Penguin 70 cm.

Erect Crested Penguin 65 cm.

Blackfoot Penguin 60 cm.

Rockhopper Penguin 50 cm.

Snares Crested Penguin 50 cm.

Galapogos Penguin 45 cm.

Fairy Penguin 40 cm.

Emperor Penguin 47 inches

King Penguin 35 inches

Gentoo Penguin 31 inches

Chinstrap Penguin 28 inches

Adelie Penguin 28 inches

Yellow-Eyed Penguin 28 inches

Macaroni Penguin 28 inches

Royal Penguin 28 inches

Erect Crested Penguin 26 inches

Blackfoot Penguin 24 inches

Rockhopper Penguin 20 inches

Snares Crested Penguin 20 inches

Galapogos Penguin 18 inches

Fairy Penguin 16 inches

Penguin Theme

Penguin Science

Objective

The students will list facts about penguins.

Materials

- nonfiction books and Web sites about penguins (See the Penguin Theme page for Web sites.) Suggested literature titles include *Penguins (Animals of the Ocean)* by Judith Hodge, *Penguins* by Lunn M. Stone, *Seven Weeks on an Iceberg* by Keith R. Potter, *These Birds Can't Fly (Rookie Read-About Science)* by Allan Flower, *The Emperor's Egg* by Martin Jenkins, *Looking at Penguins* by Dorothy Hinshaw Patent, *Penguins!* by Gail Gibbons, and *Penguin (See How They Grow Series)* by Mary Ling.
- "Penguin Facts" activity sheet
- chart paper or chalkboard

Procedure

1. Ask the students what they know about penguins. List these facts on chart paper or the chalkboard. If desired, ask the students what they would like to learn about penguins and record these questions.

2. Share some of the nonfiction books or Web sites about penguins. There are many fascinating facts about penguins, including the reasons for their coloring, their nesting habits, and the way they socialize.

3. After exploring the information with the students, allow them to complete the "Penguin Facts" activity sheet by listing four new facts they have learned about penguins. Older students may be able to do the investigating of materials on their own. Younger children may need to copy four facts from the chart paper or draw pictures of what they learned.

4. As an alternative, have the students record their facts onto pieces of paper cut out in the shape of penguins. Display these facts on a wall called "Our Colony of Penguin Facts." (Groups of penguins are called "colonies.")

Extension Ideas

- Make lists of penguin vocabulary. Have the students find definitions of words such as "rookery," "molting," and "creche."
- Conduct an experiment with heat absorption and reflection in relationship to color. This relates to the coloring of penguins. Black absorbs heat, while white reflects it.
- Have a lesson on friction. Penguins "toboggan" down icy slopes. Would they reach similar speeds if the slope were covered with grass?
- Compare penguins to other birds.
- Investigate the Antarctic habitat through books and Web sites. *Antarctica (Sunburst Book)* by Helen Cowcher is a good book to start with.

Penguin Theme

Name: _____

Penguin Facts

List 4 facts about penguins.

1. _____

2. _____

3. _____

4. _____

Penguin Theme

Penguin Social Studies

Objective

The students will identify the Northern and Southern Hemispheres, as well as the equator.

Materials

- world maps or globes
- "Dividing the Earth" activity sheet
- information from the **Penguins Around the World** Web site.

Procedure

1. Have a discussion about where penguins live on the Earth. Share the aforementioned Web site. Included is a map, which gives information on penguin species and on which continents they live.

2. Discuss with the students how penguins only live in the Southern Hemisphere. Continue with the discussion by defining the equator, the Northern Hemisphere, and the Southern Hemisphere. Use the maps and/or glove as a visual aid.

3. Pass out the "Dividing the Earth" activity sheet and have the students follow the directions.

Extension Idea

- Have a lesson on Antarctica. Utilize the following Web sites for information and photographs: **Zoom School** or **Live From Antarctica 2**.

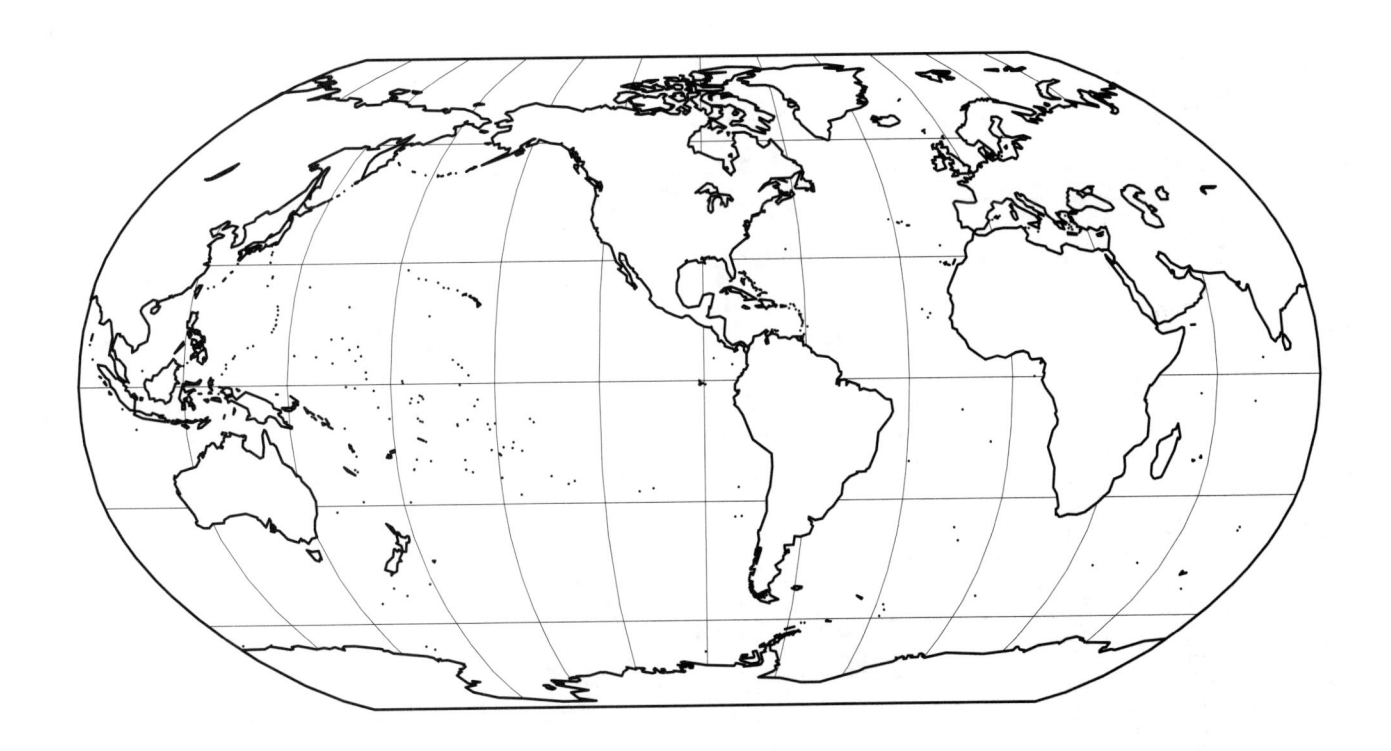

Penguin Theme

Name: _____

Dividing the Earth

Follow the directions for dividing the Earth.

1. Draw a line across the middle of the Earth.

2. Color the Northern Hemisphere blue.

3. Color the Southern Hemisphere green.

4. Draw a penguin in the Southern Hemisphere.

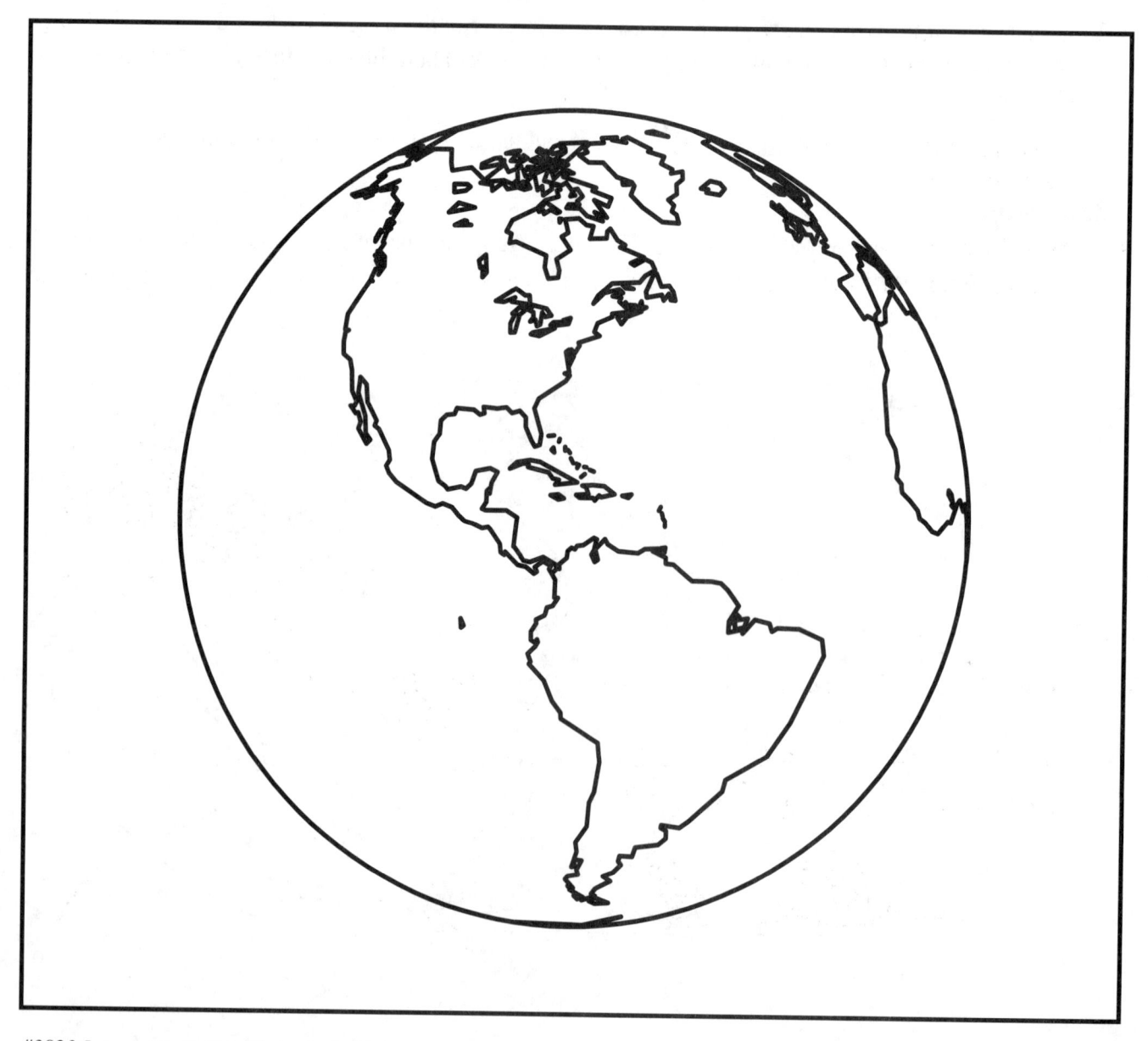

Penguin Theme

Penguin Art

Objective

The students will experiment with creating shades of gray.

Materials

- black and white paint
- paper and paintbrushes
- pictures or photographs of penguins

Procedure

1. While showing the pictures or photographs, discuss the coloring of penguins and how they all are primarily black and white.

2. Give each student some black paint and some white paint. Have them experiment mixing black and white to create various shades of gray. Ask questions about making the shades lighter and darker.

3. Have the students paint a scene which includes a black and white penguin and the various shades they have created.

Extension Idea

- In conjunction with the language arts lesson, have the students decorate the invitations they wrote.

Penguin Theme

Penguin Movement

Objective

The students will participate in a variety of penguin games.

Materials

- tennis balls (or some other balls of similar size)
- bean bags or stuffed animals (to represent penguins)
- a large open area allowing for movement

Procedure

1. Follow through on the invitations which were written in the language arts lesson and have a "Penguin Party."

2. The party may consist of the following three games (or more to be created by the students):

    a. Egg Carry—Have the students try to walk (or shuffle from one point to another balancing a tennis ball on the tops of their shoes. The tennis ball represents a penguin egg being incubated by its father.

    b. Penguin Slide—Using the stuffed animals or bean bags, have the students try to slide the item as far across the floor as possible. This will work best on a smooth floor for the least amount of friction. The sliding objects are similar to penguins sliding across the ice/snow.

    c. Waddle Walk—Have the students waddle from one point to another, similar to the walk of a penguin.

Extension Idea

- Expanding on the lesson above, have the students create their own "Penguin Party Games."

Pig Theme

Related Web Sites

Pork4Kids
A great site with information, games, and activities for kids, teachers, and parents! Kids can play the food pyramid game, take a farm tour, meet a farm kid, make their own chef's hats, and build cyber-sandwiches. There is a lot of information about farms and farm life to be found here.

MathStories.Com
This page has a work sheet of math problems pertaining to the story of "The Three Little Pigs."

The World Swine Web
This "Pigs in Print" page contains a nice book list of fiction and nonfiction books about pigs.

Pig-Mania: A Pig Theme Unit
This site provides information and links to other pig sites with factual information, fun and games, teacher pages, and lesson plans and activities.

Related Literature

The 3 Little Pigs by Marie-Louise Gay
This is a traditional telling of the classic story.

Alaska's Three Pigs by Arlene Laverde
This retelling of the classic story is Alaskan style!

Albert & Lila by Rafik Schami
A pig and an old hen are the focus of this story of friendship.

All Pigs Are Beautiful (Read and Wonder) by Dick King-Smith
Contains facts about pigs and compares pigs to people!

Oliver and Amanda or any of the Amanda/Oliver Pig Books by Jean Van Leeuwen
This is a series of books about a family of pigs.

Chester, the Worldly Pig by Bill Peet
Chester is a pig who wants to be more than a meal.

City Pig by Karn Wallace
A city pig finds true happiness (and it's not in the city)!

Pigs by Gail Gibbons
This is a simple nonfiction book with lots of good information about pigs.

The Three Little Javelinas by Susan Lowell
This is a southwestern-style version of the classic story.

Three Little Hawaiian Pigs and the Magic Shark by Donavee Laird
This version has a Hawaiian twist.

The Three Little Cajun Pigs by Berthe Amoss
Louisiana is the setting of this version of the story.

Charlotte's Web by E.B. White
This is the classic novel about a pig named Wilbur and a spider named Charlotte.

Pig Theme

Pig Language Arts

Objective

The students will complete story maps and compose their own fictional stories about pigs.

Materials

- any version of "The Three Little Pigs"
- "Story Map for 'The Three Little Pigs'" activity sheet
- blank "Story Map" activity sheet
- paper
- "idea box" (explained below in step #5)

Procedure

1. Read or retell the "The Three Little Pigs."
2. Discuss the terms *characters*, *setting*, *plot*. Plot may be broken down into Events 1, 2, 3, etc.
3. Have the students complete a story map for the "Three Little Pigs." This could be done as a whole class, in pairs, or individually, depending on the grade level.
4. Give each student a story map to create their own stories. (The kindergarten level may want to do this as a whole-class activity.) Tell them one of the characters needs to be a pig, but they may choose their other characters, the setting, and the plot.
5. As an alternative for younger children, or those who need help thinking of ideas, have "idea boxes" created ahead of time. There will be a "Character Idea Box," a "Setting Idea Box," and a "Plot Idea Box." Have slips of paper in each box with appropriate suggestions written on them. Here are some examples:
    - Character Ideas—A dog, an alien, a whale, a child, a bear, a cow…
    - Setting Ideas—Are meeting each other for the first time, are fighting over a toy, are looking for something to eat, are inventing a special machine… Allow the students to pick an idea out of the boxes.
6. Once the story map is complete, the students will write their stories using the map as a guide.

Extension Ideas

- Have a lesson on adjectives, listing words used to describe pigs.
- Have the students write a sequel to "The Three Little Pigs."
- Have a phonics lesson on the letter "P," or on "ig" family words.
- Write some "Pig Poetry."

Pig Theme

Name: _____

Story Map for "The Three Little Pigs"

Characters: _____

_____

_____

Setting: _____

_____

_____

Plot

Event 1:_____

_____

Event 2:_____

_____

Event 3:_____

_____

Event 4:_____

_____

Pig Theme

Name: _____

Story Map

Characters: _____

_____

_____

Setting: _____

_____

_____

Plot

Event 1: _____

_____

Event 2: _____

_____

Event 3: _____

_____

Event 4: _____

_____

Pig Theme

Pig Theme

Pig Math

Objective
The students will count money.

Materials
- "Piggy Bank" activity sheet
- "Piggy Bank Story Problems" activity sheet
- money or manipulatives used to represent money
  (The number and types of coins will depend on how much the students have worked with money so far. For example, kindergarten students may only each need ten pennies to manipulate. Second grade students may need a wider variety of quarters, dimes, nickels, and pennies. If it is not possible to supply students with money or representations of money, draw a "piggy bank" on the chalkboard. Then as the story problems are read to the students, draw the "money" in the piggy bank for the students to look at and use for a visual.)
- a list of money story problems appropriate for the class, prepared by the teacher (These problems will be read to the students.)

Procedure
1. Give each student a "Piggy Bank" activity sheet to use as their "piggy bank" and money or money manipulatives. (Or draw the piggy bank on the chalkboard.)
2. Read story problems for the students to complete using their money. Some examples for younger students may be: "You have three pennies in your piggy bank, you add three more. Now how many pennies do you have?" Some examples for older students would be: "You have two dimes in your piggy bank, you add a nickel. How much money do you have now?"
3. Give each student a "Piggy Bank Story Problems" activity sheet and have them work in pairs and record some of their own money math problems and answers.
4. Allow the pairs to share one of their problems with the rest of the class. The complexity of these problems will depend on the age of the students.

Extension Ideas
- Similar to above, have the students practice counting by ones, fives, and tens using pennies, nickels, and dimes. How many of each does it take to reach $1.00?
- Find a see-through container to label your "piggy bank." Fill it with pennies and have the students estimate how many pennies are in it. Work as a class to determine how many there actually are.
- Play a "Piggy Bank Game." Have the students play in pairs. Each student is given 1 die and a "Piggy Bank." They take turns rolling their dice. For each roll, they may place that number of pennies in their "bank" (use the "Piggy Bank" activity sheet). Whoever has the most pennies at the end of the game is the winner.

©Teacher Created Materials, Inc.

Pig Theme

Piggy Bank

Name: _____

Piggy Bank Story Problems

Write some money story problems.

1. _____
_____
_____
_____
_____

2. _____
_____
_____
_____
_____

3. _____
_____
_____
_____
_____

Pig Theme

Pig Science

Objective

The students will identify different animal tracks.

Materials

- the **Animal Tracks Den** Web site or a book about animal tracks, such as *Big Tracks, Little Tracks: Following Animal Prints (Let's-Read-And-Find-Out Science. Stage 1)* by Millicent Selsams
- "Pig Tracks" activity sheet
- "Animal Tracks" activity sheet (answers are below)

Procedure

1. View the above link with the students or read the book to them.
2. Discuss different animal feet—claws, webs, hooves, etc.
3. Show the page of pigs' tracks.
4. Hand out the "Animal Tracks" activity sheet.
5. Have the students predict which animal left each track. After the students have had time to make their predictions, give them the answers. The answers are as follows (from left to right): dog, duck, elephant, raccoon, fox, mountain lion, zebra, turkey, pig.

Extension Ideas

- Do a lesson on the sense of smell. Pigs have a tremendous sense of smell. Put some different scents in small paper cups. Cover them with a mesh material the students cannot see through and have them guess the smell.
- Have the students make fact books about pigs. Read nonfiction books about pigs and create books about their characteristics.
- Research some of the different types of pigs.
- Have the students match animals with animal babies. For example, pig—piglet, goat—kid, cow—calf, etc.
- Have the students spend time at the **Pork4Kids** Web site which provides information on pigs and pigs farms.

Pig Theme

Pig Tracks

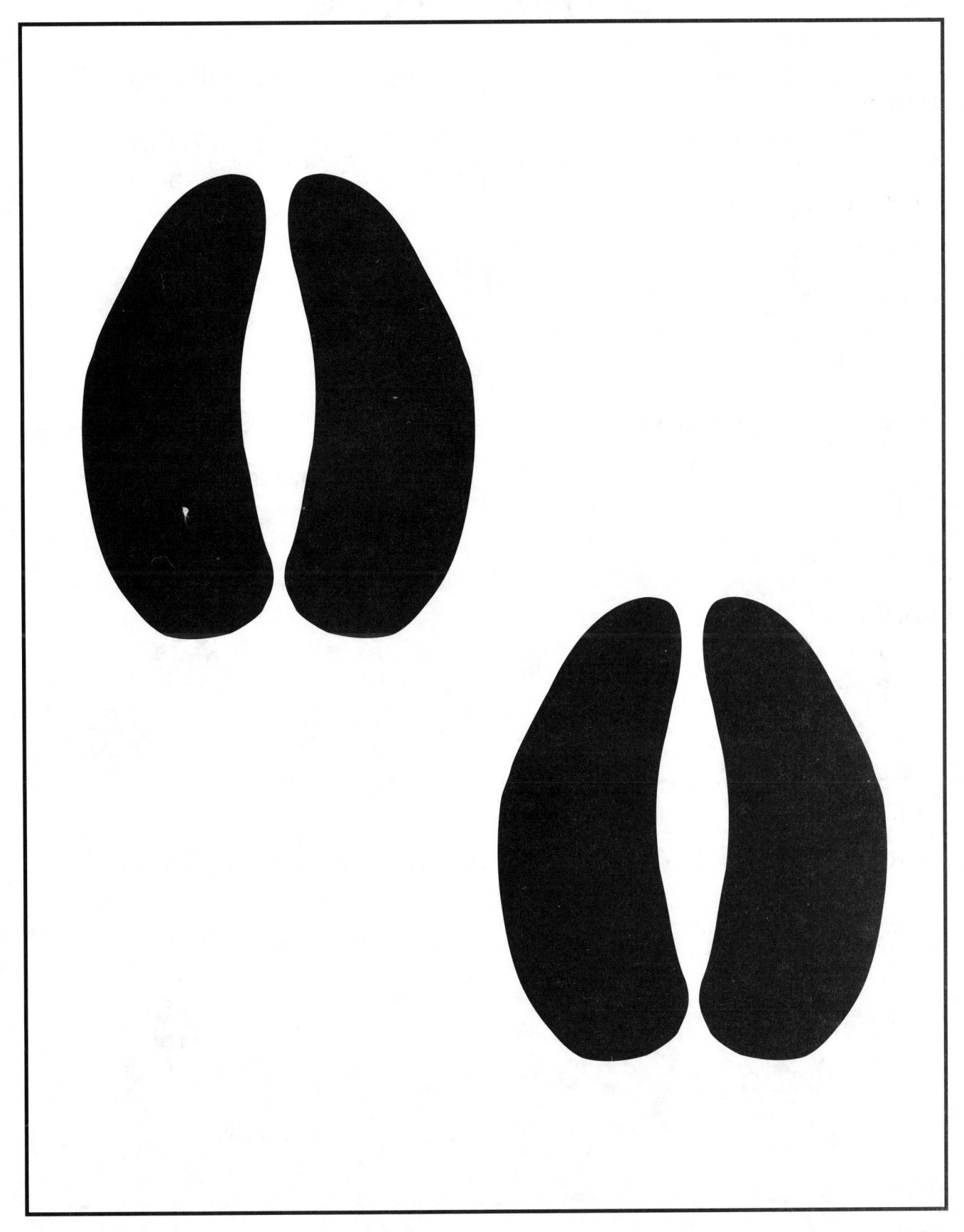

©Teacher Created Materials, Inc. #3823 *Internet Activities Through the Year*

Pig Theme

Name: _____

Animal Tracks

Predict which animal left each track. Choose from the following animals:

Mountain Lion	Raccoon	Zebra
Duck	Turkey	Elephant
Dog	Fox	Pig

Prediction: _____ Prediction: _____ Prediction: _____

Actual: _____ Actual: _____ Actual: _____

Prediction: _____ Prediction: _____ Prediction: _____

Actual: _____ Actual: _____ Actual: _____

Prediction: _____ Prediction: _____ Prediction: _____

Actual: _____ Actual: _____ Actual: _____

Pig Theme

Pig Social Studies

Objective

The students will locate areas on a map from which different versions of "The Three Little Pigs" originated. The students will also compare different cultural versions of "The Three Little Pigs."

Materials

- *The Three Little Javelinas* by Susan Lowell
- *The Three Little Cajun Pigs* by Berthe Amoss
- *Three Little Hawaiian Pigs and the Magic Shark* by Donavee Laird
- maps
- "The Three Little Pigs Around the Country" activity sheet

Procedure

1. Introduce and read each of the three versions of "The Three Little Pigs."
2. Discuss the three areas in the United States from which these versions originated: Arizona, Louisiana, and Hawaii.
3. Have the students locate these three areas on a map of the United States.
4. Discuss how the versions were alike and how they were different.
5. Have the students complete the "The Three Little Pigs Around the Country" activity sheet.

Extension Ideas

- Discuss the fact that many pigs live on farms. Compare and contrast living on a farm to living in the city. Use the **Pork4Kids** Web site, which provides a cyber tour of a pig farm. Some comparisons to consider would be: transportation, the number of people, the number of buildings, types of housing, types of animals, distance to schools and stores, noise level, etc. Make a chart of these differences.

- Have a lesson on Christopher Columbus and his 2nd voyage to the New World in 1493. It is believed he brought pigs on this trip and introduced them to the New World. Later, pigs were imported from England.

Pig Theme

Name:_____

The Three Little Pigs Around the Country

Write the name of the state from which each story originated.

Choose from the following states:

| Hawaii | Arizona | Louisiana |

1. "The Three Little Javelinas" by Susan Lowell _____

2. "The Three Little Cajun Pigs" by Berthe Amoss _____

3. "Three Little Hawaiian Pigs and the Magic Shark" by Donavee Laird _____

4. List 3 similarities in the stories:

   _____

   _____

5. List 3 differences in the stories:

   _____

   _____

6. Which story was your favorite?

   _____

7. Why?

   _____

   _____

Pig Art

Objective
The students will mix paint to create different shades of pink.

Materials
- red and white paint
- white construction paper
- paint brushes
- "Pig Pattern," if desired

Procedure
1. Give each student a piece of paper to cut out a pig. If desired, copy the "Pig Pattern" from page 250 onto white construction paper and have the students cut out that pig.
2. Give each student some red and white paint and a paintbrush.
3. Allow the students to mix the paint to achieve the shade of pink they would like their pig to be. Discuss with the students what made the shade lighter or darker.
4. Once the pigs are complete, look at all the different shades, which have been created. The students may want to sequence them from lightest to darkest.
5. Display the pigs in a pig pen in the hallway or somewhere in the classroom. The pig pen may be a fence cut out from brown butcher paper.

Extension Idea
- Have the students create piggy banks. They could be made from paper mache, shoe boxes, or plastic bottles covered with torn tissue paper and adhered with a mixture of glue and water painted on the top.

Pig Theme

Pig Pattern

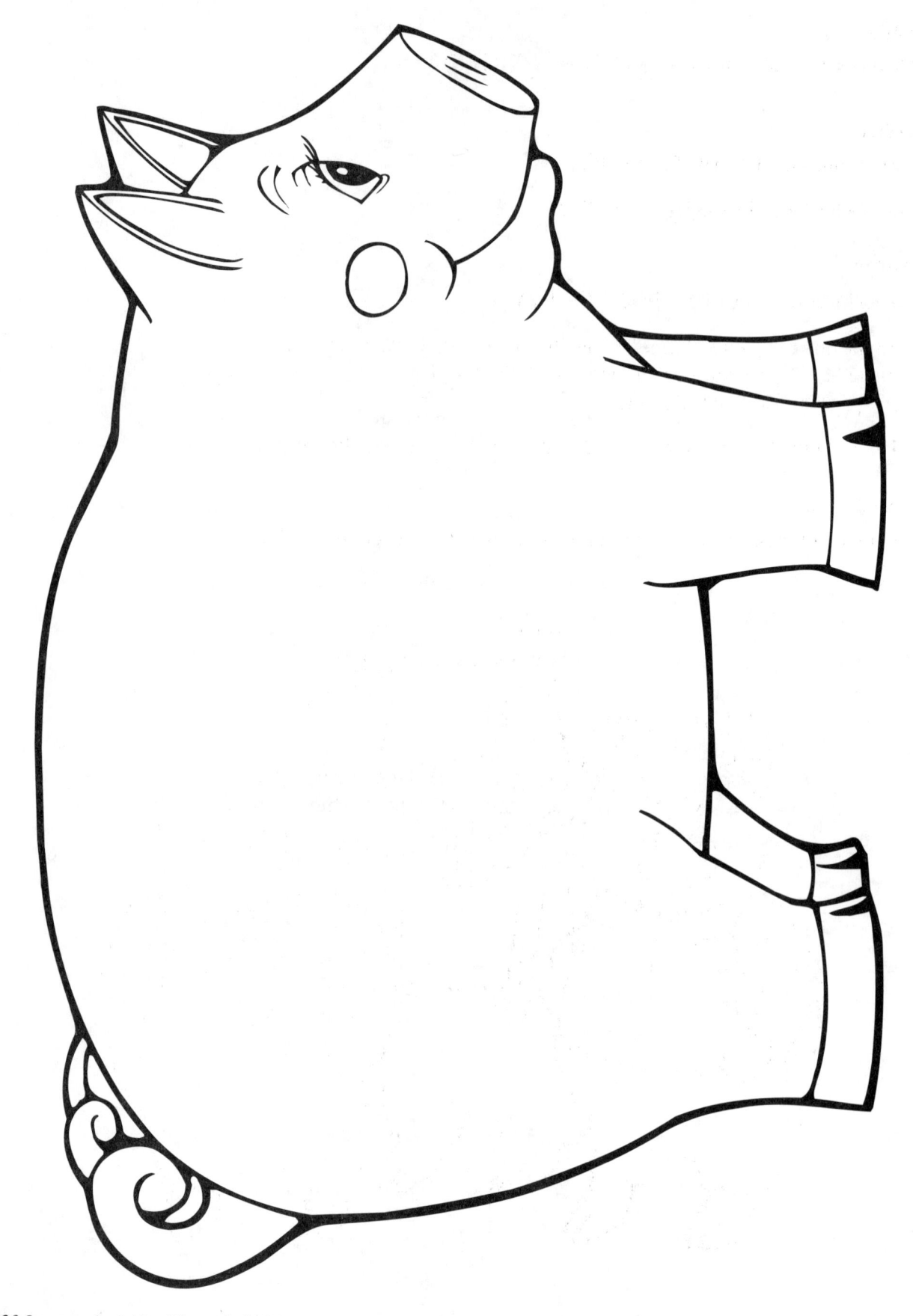

Pig Movement

Objective

The students will act out the story of "The Three Little Pigs."

Materials

- a retelling of "The Three Little Pigs"
- an open space allowing for movement

Procedure

1. Retell the story of "The Three Little Pigs."
2. As the story is retold, have the students act out motions to accompany the story. For example, the students can pretend they are building houses, trying to blow the houses down, and running from one pig's house to another, etc.
3. The students may each act this out individually, or have parts assigned to them for the acting.

Extension Idea

- Find a soft area for rolling and pretending the students are pigs rolling in mud.

Pizza Theme

Setting the Stage
If possible, plan a pizza party to finish off this fun day. The pizza may either be made by the class, or ordered from a local restaurant.

Related Web Sites

Pizza Farm
The pizza farm is a "living demonstration" which teaches kids about agriculture. Included is an online tour.

Nuttin' But Kids
This site contains links to some pizza songs.

Time for Kids
Find here an article on the most popular pizza toppings.

Garden Gate
This site has directions for planting a "pizza wheel" garden.

Meals.Com
Here is a history of pizza.

The History of Pizza
Find out about the roots of pizza.

About Pizza
Included are recipes, history, and links about pizza.

Related Literature

Curious George and the Pizza by Margaret Rey
Curious George gets in trouble when he tries making a pizza.

Extra Cheese, Please!: Mozzarella's Journey from Cow to Pizza by Cris Peterson
This book introduces the students to cheese making. Follows the process from the dairy farm to the top of a pizza.

Hi, Pizza Man! by Virginia Walter
A little girl and her mother imagine what type of delivery person/animal is going to show up at their door.

The King of Pizza : A Magical Story About the World's Favorite Food by Sylvester Sanzari
This king goes on an adventure to discover pizza.

Little Niño's Pizzeria by Karen Barbour
A father learns a lesson about spending time with his family when he closes down his small pizzeria to open a fancy restaurant.

The Little Red Hen (Makes a Pizza) by Philemon Sturges
This is an updated version of the original Little Red Hen fable.

Pizza Party (Hello, Reader, Level 1, Preschool-Grade 1) by Grace MacCarone
This early reader is about a pizza party.

Pizza Pat by Will Terry
This cumulative story is similar to "The House that Jack Built."

Pizza Theme

Pizza Language Arts

Objective

The students will write sentences to answer a series of questions.

Materials

- "May I Take Your Order?" activity sheet
- paper
- writing utensils
- a fictional book about pizza, such as *Sam's Pizza: Your Pizza to Go* by David Pelham

Procedure

1. Read the story to spark the students' interest in pizza and pizza toppings.
2. Pass out the "May I Take Your Order?" activity sheet.
3. Put the students in pairs and have them ask one another the questions. They should record their partner's answers. Allow the students to be as creative and silly as they wish.
4. If appropriate, have the students use the activity sheets to write complete sentences describing the type of pizza their partner has ordered. They should write these sentences on a separate sheet of paper, concentrating on starting each sentence with a capital letter, finishing with a period, etc.
5. Younger students may need to be guided more through the worksheet and be allowed to draw pictures and attempt to label them with words.

Extension Ideas

- Ask the students to respond to the following statements: "Write a color word that starts with the letter 'P'." "Write an animal that starts with the letter 'P'." "Write a food that starts with the letter 'P'." Then have the students fill their responses in to the following sentence: The _____(color) _____(animal) likes _____(food). An example of a completed sentence might be "The pink panda likes peanut pizza." Have the students illustrate their sentences.
- Write pizza recipes.
- Write the steps for dialing the phone and ordering a pizza.
- Put the students in groups and have them write commercials or ads for pizza. They may think up a name and a slogan for their pizza. Combine it with the art lesson and have the groups decorate a large piece of cardboard to be their pizza box top.
- Read some pizza books and have the students vote on their favorite one. Remember to have them give reasons for why a certain book was their favorite.
- Read *Pete's a Pizza* by William Steig. Have the students make up a similar story using their own names. For example, Sam's a sandwich, Mary's a muffin, etc.

©Teacher Created Materials, Inc.   #3823 Internet Activities Through the Year

Pizza Theme

Name:_____

May I Take Your Order?

1. What size pizza would you like? _____
   _____
   _____

2. What toppings would you like on your pizza? _____
   _____
   _____

3. What would you like to drink?_____
   _____
   _____

4. What would you like for dessert? _____
   _____
   _____

Pizza Theme

Pizza Math

Objective
The students will combine fractions to make a whole.

Materials

- five large circles (about 12" in diameter) These will be "pizzas." Cut the circles into the following fractions (which will pose as "slices" of pizza):
    - Circle #1—cut in half
    - Circle #2—cut in thirds
    - Circle #3—cut in fourths
    - Circle #4—cut in sixths
    - Circle #5—cut in eighths

    Make sure the "slices" of each circle are even. This will make 23 "slices" of pizza. If there are more than 23 students in the class, adjust the fractions so each student will have one slice of pizza. For example, do two or more circles cut in half.

- "Pizza Math" activity sheet

Procedure

1. Mix up all the "slices" of pizza which have been cut out ahead of time. Pass out the slices so that each student has at least one slice of pizza.

2. Direct the students to move about the room and find other students with the exact same size slice of pizza as theirs. They should then all gather together with their similar size slices to put together and make a whole "pizza."

3. Allow the students time to find the other students in their group.

4. Once these groups have gathered together, pose a series of questions. For example, "How many people are in your group to make up a whole pizza?" "Which group has the biggest pieces of pizza?" "Which group has the smallest pieces?" The students may complete the "Pizza Math" activity sheet at the same time.

5. Introduce and/or review the terms one-half, one-third, one-fourth, etc. If appropriate, illustrate writing fractions.

6. As an extension, have older students combine groups together and lay their slices on top of each other. They may then discover relationships between fractions, such as $1/4 + 1/4 = 1/2$.

Extension Ideas

- Have the students practice more math skills with the "More or Less" activity sheet on page 257.

- Give each student a circle piece of paper and manipulatives to pose as pizza toppings. For example, unifix cubes for green pepper, beans for mushrooms, pennies for pepperoni, etc. The students may then write math equations to coincide with the pizzas they create.

- Graph the students' favorite toppings.

- Assign slices of pizza a price and have the students complete money equations.

©Teacher Created Materials, Inc.   255   #3823 Internet Activities Through the Year

Pizza Theme

Name:_____

Pizza Math

1. How many people are in your group? _____

2. How many people are in the group with the biggest slices of pizza? _____

3. How many people are in the group with the smallest slices of pizza? _____

Name:_____

Pizza Math

1. How many people are in your group? _____

2. How many people are in the group with the biggest slices of pizza? _____

3. How many people are in the group with the smallest slices of pizza? _____

Pizza Theme

More or Less

Color, cut out, and paste the pictures from the bottom of the page in the correct boxes. Answer the question below each box.

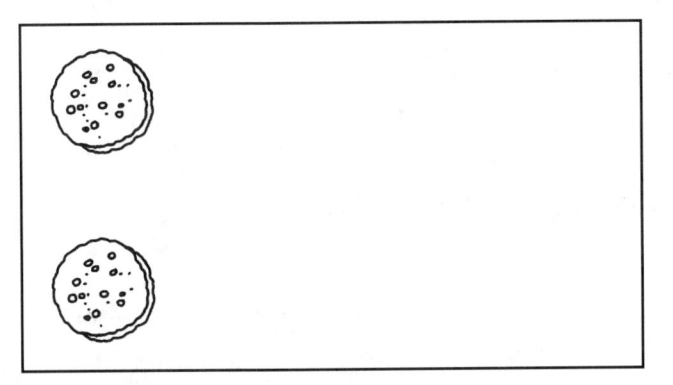

Are there *more* or *less* than 10 pepperoni?_____

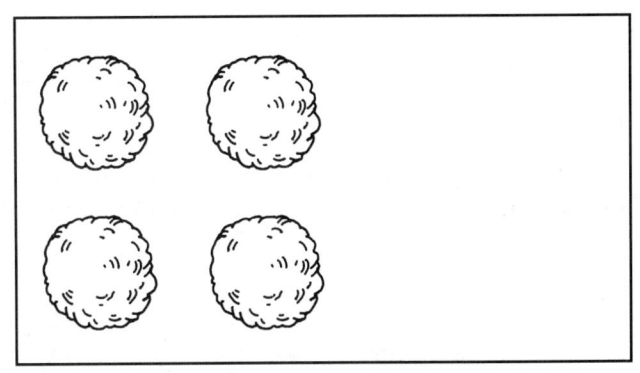

Are there *more* or *less* than 10 meatballs?_____

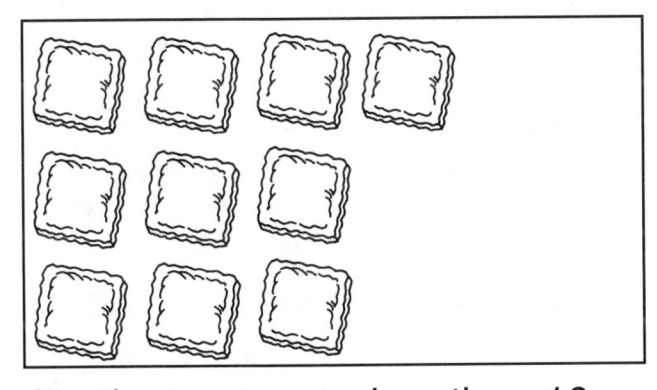

Are there *more* or *less* than 10 ravioli?_____

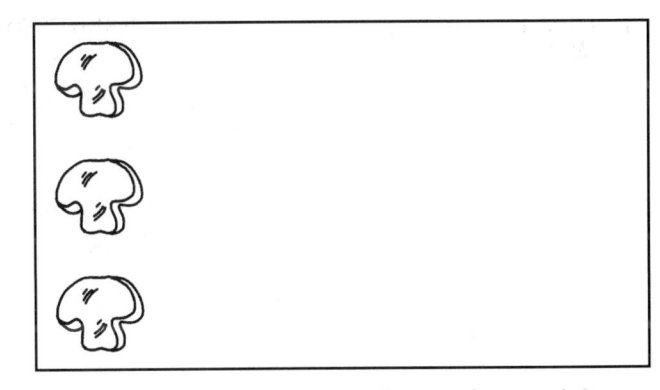

Are there *more* or *less* than 10 mushrooms?_____

©Teacher Created Materials, Inc.   257   #3823 Internet Activities Through the Year

Pizza Theme

Pizza Science

Objective
The students will classify foods into their proper group.

Materials
- information from one of the following sites: **KidsHealth** or **USDA** (They both have good information on the Food Pyramid for kids.) Another good resource is the book *Hold the Anchovies: A Book About Pizza!* by Shelley Rotner, which has real photographs of food.
- a large piece of butcher paper outlined with the food pyramid
- the "Foods for the Food Pyramid" activity sheet cut up into small slips of paper, with one food on each sheet of paper, and one slip per student (Some extra foods may need to be added depending on the size of the class.)

Procedure
1. Using information presented at the aforementioned Web sites, discuss the Food Pyramid with the students. Go over the different sections and the amounts that are recommended for each group.
2. Pass out the slips of paper so each student has one slip.
3. Have each student read their food items. (Some are real pizza toppings and some are silly pizza toppings.) The student should then place his/her slip in the proper area of the butcher paper food pyramid. Discuss how many of the food groups can be contained in one single pizza.
4. As an extension, have the students draw a picture or list their favorite toppings for pizza. They may then write the food group each topping falls into.

Extension Ideas
- Make pizza. Simple pizzas are easy to make using English Muffins. Try the recipe at the **English Muffin Pizzas** Web page. Have the students follow the recipe and watch how the ingredients change once they are baked (i.e., cheese melting.) If possible, make the dough from scratch and have a lesson on the properties of yeast. A good book to use for this activity is *The Pizza that We Made* by Joan Halub, which includes a recipe.
- Have a lesson on how the different toppings get to a pizza. For example, vegetables are grown, meat comes from animals, cheese comes from the milk of an animal, etc.

Pizza Theme

Foods for the Food Pyramid

	tomato		cheese
	pepperoni		ham
	sausage		mushroom
	pizza crust		green pepper
	onion		pineapple
	broccoli		cauliflower
	chicken		banana
	bacon		yogurt
	crackers		fish

Pizza Theme

Pizza Social Studies

Objective
The students will identify Italy as one of the origins of pizza.

Materials
- a world map or globe
- a link to one of the following Web sites: **Very Best Baking**, **The History of Pizza**, or **The History and Origins of Pizza** or book which contains the history of pizza, such as *Pizza!* by Teresa Martino.

Procedure
1. Share the information of the history of pizza from one of the Web sites or from the book. Discuss the country of Italy and locate it on the map or globe. The level of the discussion will depend on the age of the students.

2. Extend the lesson to a discussion on different countries and their foods. Use the **Recipes from Around the World** Web site for different examples of recipes from other countries.

3. Brainstorm as a class some other favorite foods which have a heritage with certain countries. Some examples would be tacos from Mexico and egg rolls from China.

4. Locate these countries on the map or globe.

Extension Ideas
- Many pizza toppings are grown on farms. Have a lesson on agriculture. Use the **4-H Virtual Farm** site for assistance.
- Have the students deliver pretend pizzas to different parts of the school. They will need to follow a map or write directions for going to places such as the principal's office, the library, etc.

#3823 Internet Activities Through the Year   260   ©Teacher Created Materials, Inc.

Pizza Art

Objective

The students will create a pizza utilizing a variety of art materials.

Materials

- paper plates or round pieces of poster board
- red paint
- a variety of materials to serve as "the toppings" (For example, shredded paper or yarn for cheese, buttons or round paper for pepperoni, brown tissue paper for mushrooms, etc.)

Procedure

1. Pass out the paper plates or poster board "the crust."
2. Have the students put the red paint on for the sauce.
3. They may then add their desired "toppings" to create their pizza.

Extension Idea

- Have the students design and create a pizza box top on a large piece of cardboard. This lesson may be combined with the language arts lesson for creating their own pizza shop names and slogan.

Pizza Theme

Pizza Movement

Objective

The students will imitate kneading and tossing pizza dough.

Materials

- play dough—either store bought or homemade, enough so each student receives a good size piece (The **Kids Homemade Play Dough** site contains a recipe for homemade play dough.)

Procedure

1. Discuss what it means to knead dough. Demonstrate for the students kneading and tossing the dough.

2. Pass out the play dough and allow the students time to knead and toss their own dough.

Extension Ideas

- Extend the above lesson by having the students get into pairs and toss their pizza dough back and forth between one another. Similar to a balloon toss, have the students stand close together and slowly back apart from one another to see how far they can go before dropping the dough.

- Have the students have a pizza delivery relay race. The teams will have to carry a cardboard box and hand it off to one another in order to complete the race.

- Read *Pete's a Pizza* by William Steig. Pair the students up and have them make each other into a pizza, similar to the book.

Polar Bear Theme

Related Web Sites

Polar Bears International
This is a nonprofit organization dedicated to the protection of polar bears. The site contains lots of good information and photographs of polar bears.

The Bear Den
This link will take you directly to a fact sheet on polar bears. This site is sponsored by the American Zoo and Aquarium.

Sea World Education Department—Polar Bears
This site provides you with a wealth of information on the polar bear! Contents include Scientific Classification, Habitat and Distribution, Physical Characteristics, Senses, Adaptations for an Aquatic Environment, Behavior, Diet and Eating Habits, Reproduction, Birth and Care of Young, Communication, Longevity and Causes of Death, Conservation, References and Bibliography, Books for Young Readers, Specific Index, and Wild Arctic Activities.

Encarta Encyclopedia—Polar Bear
This is an article with concise, factual information on the polar bear.

Nature—Great White Bear
Information presented by PBS's Nature Program entitled "Great White Bear." Included is information on the habitat of the polar bear, how scientists track polar bears, life in the arctic, and online and print resources.

GeoZoo—Polar Bears
This site is geared toward children making the definitions and explanations easy to understand. Contents include Polar Bears in Action, Home/Habitat, Diet, Family Life, Polar Bears & People, a GeoQuiz about Polar Bears, Books, and Links to other bear sites.

Arctic Animals
This site contains information on polar bears and other types of arctic animals. Included are facts, stories, activities, and links to other resources.

Polar Bears
This site has lots of good lesson plan ideas on polar bears. There are also many individual activities for students to try.

Related Literature

The Bear by Raymond Briggs
In this book, a little girl has an interesting house guest!

A Boy and a Bear: The Children's Relaxation Book by Lori Lite
You may wish to use this book at the end of the Movement Lesson in order to relax your students. It is a very calming book.

Great Crystal Bear by Carolyn Lesser
Most appropriate for older children, this book is poetic as well as informational about a year in the life of a Polar Bear.

Klondike & Snow: The Denver Zoo's Remarkable Story of Raising Two Polar Bear Cubs by David Kenney, et. al.
This is an interesting and educational story for older children.

Polar Bear Theme (cont.)

Related Literature (cont.)

Little Polar Bear, Take Me Home! by Hans De Beer
This is one in a series of well loved books.

Little Polar Bear Finds a Friend by Hans De Beer
Little Polar Bear finds a friend in another well-loved series book.

Polar Bear: Growing Up in the Icy North (Reader's Digest All-Star Readers Level 3) by Sarah Jane Brian
This book follows two bear cubs growing up.

A Polar Bear Journey by Debbie S. Miller
Follow a mother and two polar bear cubs through a year in their life together.

Polar Bear, Polar Bear, What Do You Hear? by Eric Carle
Most appropriate for younger children, this is a classic book on animal sounds.

Polar Bears (A New True Book) by Emilie U. Lepthien
This book is filled with facts about polar bears!

Polar Bear: Habitats, Life Cycles, Food Chains, Threats by Malcolm Penny
Good information and photographs can be found in this book on polar bears.

Polar Bears Past Bedtime (Magic Tree House 12, paper) by Mary Pope Osborne
The main characters in this book get transported to the Arctic and have to solve a riddle.

Snow Bear by Jean Craighead George
An Arctic adventure begins for an Eskimo child and a polar bear.

Polar Bear Theme

Polar Bear Language Arts

Objective

The students will write a collaborative story about an adventure with a polar bear.

Materials

- *The Bear* by Raymond Briggs, if available
- paper and pencils or chart paper

Procedure

1. Read the book *The Bear* by Raymond Briggs. If the book is not available, have a short brainstorming session on different fantasy adventures one could have with a polar bear.
2. Have the entire class sit in a circle (older students may be divided into groups of 4–5).
3. Have each student contribute a sentence or two about an adventure with a polar bear.
4. Record the story on chart paper as the students dictate their sentences. Older students may select a "secretary" from their group to record the sentences. These smaller groups may also contribute more than a sentence or two.
5. Proceed with the process of editing and publishing this class (or small group) book. The students may illustrate the pages they authored.

Extension Ideas

- Have the students write factual reports on polar bears.
- Have a lesson on the letter "P."
- Complete a Venn Diagram comparing a polar bear to another kind of bear.

Polar Bear Theme

Polar Bear Math

Objective

The students will measure distances using 12" units.

Materials

- "Polar Bear Track" activity sheet
- "How Many Polar Bear Tracks?" activity sheets
- rulers

Procedure

1. Enlarge the "Polar Bear Track" activity sheet on a copy machine so it measures 12". It would be best to use the track on the left side of the paper for enlargement. Make enough copies so each pair of students may have a track.

2. Pass out the "Polar Bear Track" activity sheet, rulers, and the "How Many Polar Bear Tracks?" activity sheet to each pair of students.

3. Explain that the average adult polar bear track can be this size. Have the students measure the track to see how long it is.

4. Using the tracks, have the students work in pairs to complete the activity sheet. (Younger students may need to work as a whole class, with the teacher as the lead, to complete measurements of some classroom items.) Be sure to discuss measurement words such as length, width, height, etc.

Extension Idea

- Do a lesson on weight. Find out how much an average adult polar bear weighs and see how many average students would equal that weight.

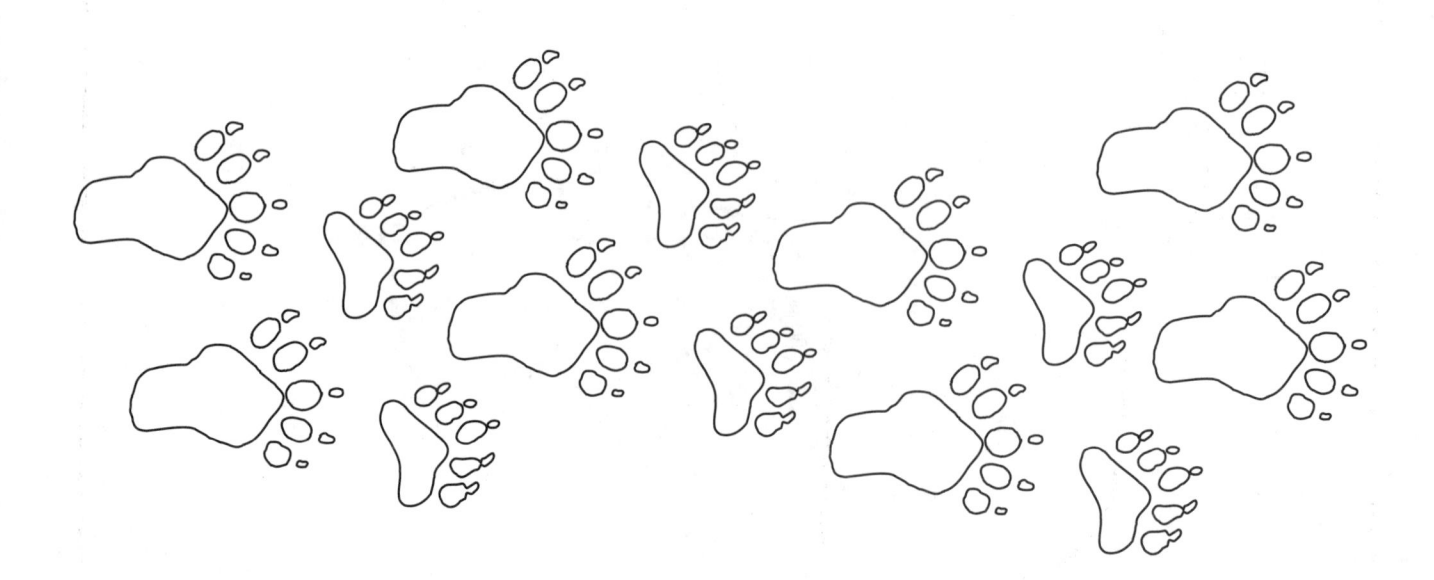

Polar Bear Theme

Polar Bear Track

©Teacher Created Materials, Inc. 267 #3823 Internet Activities Through the Year

Polar Bear Theme

Name:_____

How Many Polar Bear Tracks?

A Polar Bear track is _____ inches long.

1. I am _____ Polar Bear Tracks tall.

2. My arm is _____ Polar Bear Tracks long.

3. My leg is _____ Polar Bear Tracks long.

Here are some other items in the classroom with their Polar Bear Track measurements. (Some ideas are a desktop, the height of a desk, the width of the door, the distance from your seat to the teacher's desk, etc.)

Item	**# of Polar Bear Tracks**
_____	_____
_____	_____
_____	_____
_____	_____

Polar Bear Theme

Polar Bear Science

Objective

The students will conduct an experiment to determine how blubber helps keep polar bears warm.

Materials

- Vaseline™ or shortening
- about 12 ice cubes (one per each pair of students)
- paper towels or tissues (to clean up Vaseline™).
- "How Do Polar Bears Keep Warm?" activity sheet

Procedure

1. Ask the students how they think polar bears keep warm in the Arctic climate. You may want to share information from the **Polar Bears Alive** Web site or read a book on how polar bears keep warm. Lead the students to a discussion on blubber.

2. Put the students in pairs and pass out an ice cube, the activity sheet, and a spoonful of Vaseline™ or shortening. Have one student cover one of the index finger fingertips of their partner with a thick layer of the Vaseline™ or shortening. That student will then place both index fingertips against the ice cube. Which fingertip gets colder faster? The one with or without the covering? The students will then switch roles for the other student to try the experiment.

3. Have the students complete the activity sheet.

4. As an option to the above experiment, a more in-depth blubber experiment can be found at the **Blubber Glove** Web site.

Extension Ideas

- Do a lesson on camouflage. Discuss with students how polar bears blend in with their environment.

- Make polar bear fact books (can be tied in with a language arts lesson). Have the students write their facts on cutouts of the polar bear tracks. They may each make their own books, or work to create a class book.

- Do a lesson on the Arctic habitat. The following Web sites may be helpful: **Arctic Circle**, **Animals Of The Arctic**, and **Arctic National Wildlife Reserve**.

Polar Bear Theme

Name:_____

How Do Polar Bears Keep Warm?

1. Have your partner place the Vaseline™ or shortening on one of your index fingers.

2. Place both index fingers on the ice cube.

3. Answer the following questions:

    - What is the Vaseline™ or shortening similar to on a Polar Bear?

        _____
        _____
        _____

    - Which finger felt cold the fastest?

        _____
        _____
        _____

    - What are some other ways Polar Bears keep warm?

        _____
        _____
        _____
        _____

Polar Bear Theme

Polar Bear Social Studies

Objective
The students will explore maps and gloves to determine where polar bears live.

Materials
- information from the **Polar Bears** Web site (click on "Habitat and Destinations"), or a book which has a map of Polar Bear habitats.
- world maps or globes

Procedure
1. Read the book or the information from the Web site giving information on where polar bears live.
2. If there are enough maps/globes, pass out and work as a class to find the areas where polar bears live. Have the students locate their hometown and where it is in relation to arctic regions.
3. For younger children, simply discussing how the Arctic is at the top of the earth and the Antarctic is at the bottom of the earth is sufficient. Point out that polar bears live in arctic regions.

Extension Idea
- Using Styrofoam balls as the "earth," have each student label the Arctic area and the Antarctic area.

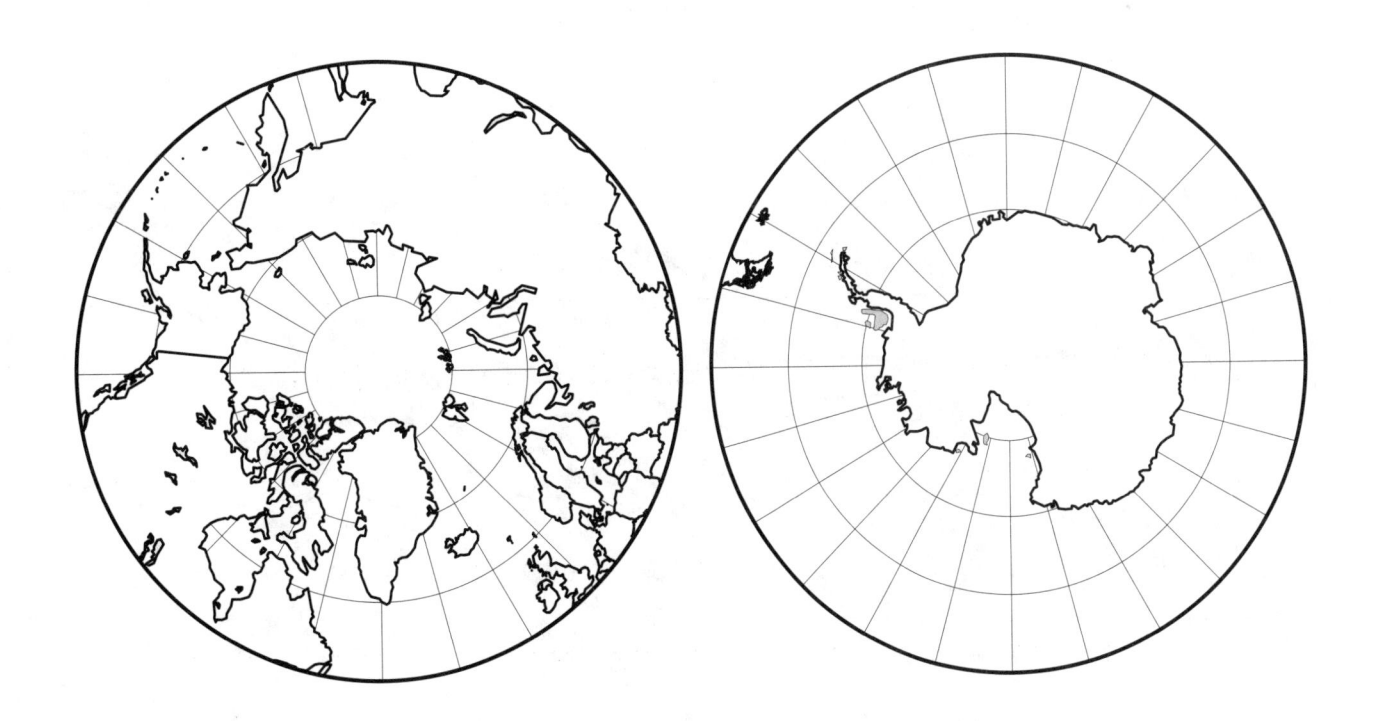

Polar Bear Theme

Polar Bear Art

Objective

The students will create a polar bear using their choice of medium.

Materials

- dark colored construction paper for the background
- white paint, sponges, chalk, cotton balls, white construction paper, white felt, etc.

Procedure

1. Allow the students to choose from what type of medium they would like to create their polar bear. Some examples would be, sponge painting with white paint, gluing cotton balls to create a polar bear, tearing white construction paper (for a torn paper look), cutting out felt.

2. Once the creations are complete, discuss how different mediums created different looks. Display the work in your "Polar Bear Museum."

Extension Ideas

- Make a whole-class mural of an Arctic habitat, including snow, ice floes, tundra, different Arctic animals, etc.
- Have the students create "bear dens" out of shoeboxes. Create a polar bear mom and cubs to inhabit the den.

Polar Bear Movement

Objective
The students will imitate bear movement.

Materials
- a large open area allowing for movement
- Designate some of the area as ocean water and other areas as ice floes. If possible, use chalk or tape to mark off the floes.

Procedure
1. Have the students imitate bear movement. Discuss what it means to "lumber around." They can move like bears and "jump" from ice floe to ice floe without "falling in the water."

Extension Idea
- Play a game of tag in which ice floes are "safe zones."

Popcorn Theme

Related Web Sites

The Popcorn Board

This site has lots of information on the history and growth of popcorn. The Kids page has coloring sheets and work sheets for students to complete. Also included are teacher pages, nutrition information, and recipes. The "Encyclopedia Popcornica" has trivia, historical information, and an FAQ.

Popcorn Snack Recipes

Find here a group of popcorn recipes that would be easy to make in the classroom! There are caramel corn, chocolate popcorn, kettle corn, and popcorn ball recipes, among others.

Related Literature

The Huckabuck Family and How They Raised Popcorn in Nebraska and Quit and Came Back by Carl Sandburg

This book follows the Huckabuck family through the ups and downs of trying to raise popcorn.

Popcorn by Alex Moran

This is an easy-reader, rhyming book.

The Popcorn Book by Tomie dePaola

Ttrue facts on popcorn and its history can be found in this fun book.

The Popcorn Dragon by Jane Thayer

This is the story of how a dragon makes some friends by popping corn with his fire breathing mouth.

Popcorn at the Palace by Emily Arnold McCully

Blending fact and fiction, this is the story of a young girl and her father who travel to London to try and interest the English in popcorn.

Popcorn Plants by Kathleen V. Kudinski

This is a nonfiction book with an abundance of information and real photographs of popcorn plants.

Science Fun With Peanuts and Popcorn by Rose Wyler

This book is filled with fun experiments, recipes, and activities to be done with popcorn and/or peanuts.

Why Does Popcorn Pop?: And Other Kitchen Questions by Catherine Ripley

A collection of questions and answers to some commonly asked "kitchen questions" make up this nonfiction book.

Popcorn Theme

Popcorn Language Arts

Objective
The students will list words which imitate sounds (onomatopoeia).

Materials
- an excerpt from a book or poem which gives an example of onomatopoeia
- "Sound Words" activity sheet

Procedure
1. Discuss with the students how certain words imitate sounds. For example, "pop" for the sound of popping corn, "hiss" for the sound of steam or what a snake says, "hum" for the sound of a fan, "snip" for the sound of scissors. . . . If the children are old enough, introduce the word *onomatopoeia*. It may be helpful to have an excerpt from a book or a poem which is a good example of onomatopoeia.
2. Working as a class, in pairs, or individually, have the students complete the "Sound Words" activity sheet by listing items and their matching "sound words."

Extension Ideas
- Have students practice more language arts skills with the "Popcorn Poetry" and "Popcorn Story Starters" activity pages on pages 277 and 278.
- As a variation on the above plan, pass out cards with pictures of different items or animals and the students could take turns giving the word for the sound the item or animal makes. On a piece of butcher paper or on the chalkboard list these "sound words." This would be better suited for younger children.
- Do a lesson on compound words, using "popcorn" as an example.

Popcorn Theme

Name:_____

Sound Words

Item   **The Sound it Makes**

_____   _____

_____   _____

_____   _____

_____   _____

_____   _____

_____   _____

_____   _____

_____   _____

#3823 Internet Activities Through the Year   ©*Teacher Created Materials, Inc.*

Popcorn Theme

Popcorn Poetry

Pop, Pop, Pop!

Little _____ Popcorn,
       (Child's Name)
Sitting in a pot.
Moving and a Jumping,
Pop, _____ Pop!
    (Child's Name)

Popcorn

Popcorn
White, Fluffy
Heating, Jumping, Popping
Buttered, Salted
Tasty!

Popcorn Flakes

I saw popcorn flakes
Sitting in a bowl.
"Munch-Munch" went my mouth,
until I was full!

Popcorn Rain

Popcorn raining all around,
Hitting the treetops, hitting the ground.
Hitting my umbrella here,
Hitting my umbrella there.
What happens when it finally stops?
It starts raining lollipops!

Popcorn Surprise

On top of my popcorn, all fluffy and white,
I poured on the butter, and started to munch.

When all of a sudden, and to my surprise,
As I started eating, I heard a loud crunch.

So I checked my loose tooth, and guess what I found,
Not only was it missing, it must have gone straight down!

*Teacher Note: Students can create their own poetry for the Popcorn Pillowcase Poems.

Popcorn Theme

Popcorn Story Starters

Reproduce as many starters as needed. Cut out and place starters in a popcorn sack or cup. Let each student draw a starter and begin to write!

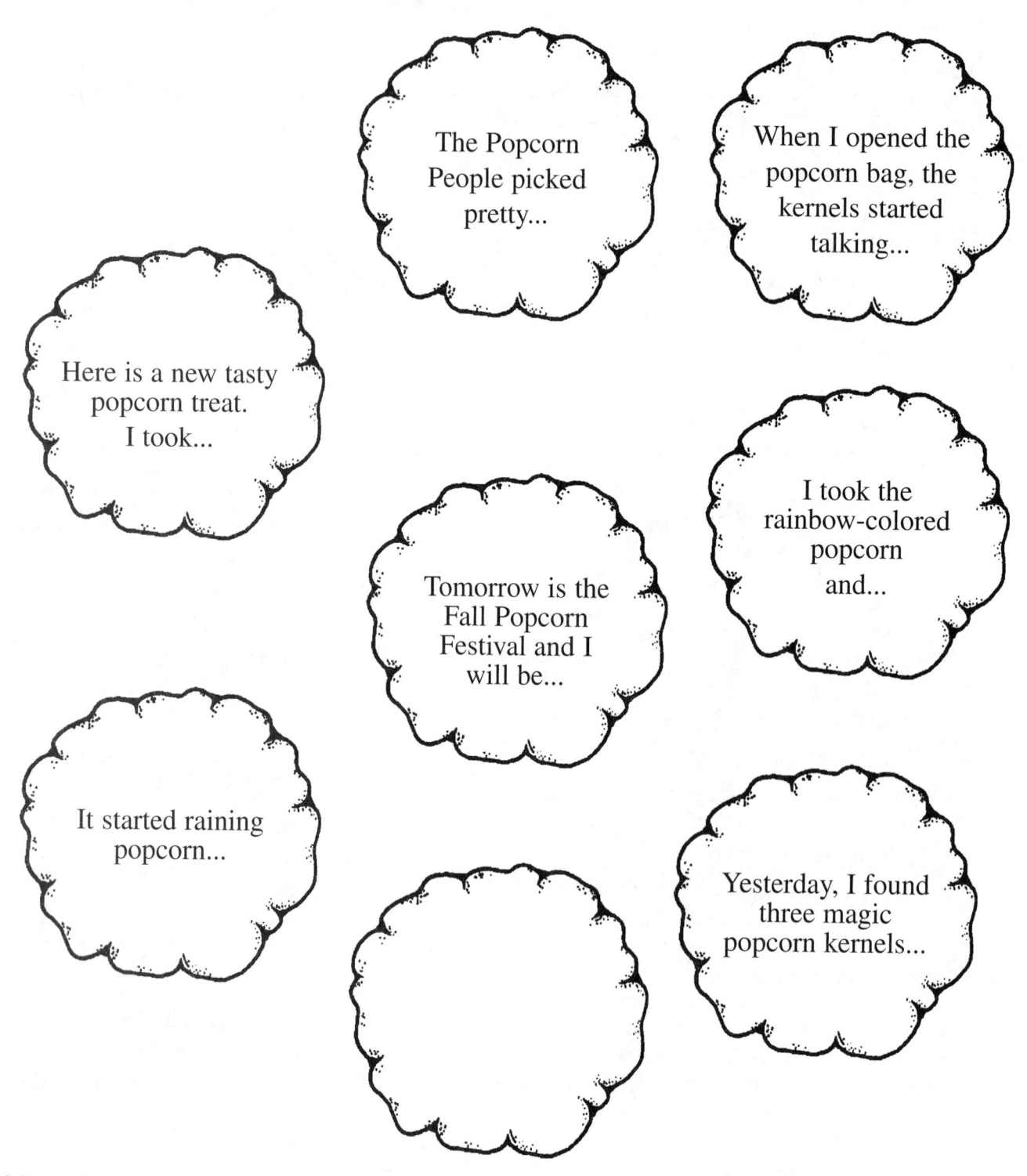

- The Popcorn People picked pretty...
- When I opened the popcorn bag, the kernels started talking...
- Here is a new tasty popcorn treat. I took...
- Tomorrow is the Fall Popcorn Festival and I will be...
- I took the rainbow-colored popcorn and...
- It started raining popcorn...
- Yesterday, I found three magic popcorn kernels...

Use the blank so you can write in your own story starter.

Popcorn Theme

Popcorn Math

Objective

The students will estimate how much popcorn will fit in a given space.

Materials

- a large amount of popped popcorn
- a large (approximately 2 x 3 feet, or smaller for younger children) cutout of any desired shape (perhaps an ear of corn or a bowl shape)
- "Popcorn Estimate" activity sheets, one per student

Procedure

1. Show the students the cutout shape and pass out the "Popcorn Estimate" activity sheets.

2. Have a discussion about what it means to estimate. Show them the popped popcorn and have them record their estimates for how many pieces they think will fit on the shape.

3. Working as a class, cover the cutout with the popped corn, until the area is entirely filled in. Once the class agrees the area is adequately covered, begin counting the popcorn. Brainstorm ways to count the corn, i.e., by putting them in groups of 5s or 10s.

4. Once the popcorn is counted, have the students record the actual amount of popcorn it took to fill in the shape. If appropriate, have the students figure the difference between their estimate and the actual amount.

Extension Ideas

- Similar to the lesson plan above, but to be done on a more individual basis or to be done as a follow up to the above lesson, have the students estimate and then discover how many popped pieces of popcorn will fit on a given line. Use the "Measuring with Popcorn" activity sheet.

- Make pie charts using the following statistics—Americans use 500,000,000 pounds of popcorn each year—30% is eaten at movies and other events, 10% is saved for seed and sold to other countries, and 60% is eaten at home. (Statistics found in Tomie dePaola's *The Popcorn Book*.)

- Graph the students' favorite way to eat popcorn—plain, with only salt, with only butter, with butter and salt.

- Estimate the amount of popcorn (either kernels or popped corn) in a given container. Actually count it out for the correct answer.

- Place a popcorn popper in the middle of an open space, with the lid off. Have each student pick a spot where they think a piece of popcorn will land. Allow each student to put a post-it™ note on that spot with their name on it. Pop some popcorn with the lid off and see how close the popcorn lands to their estimates!

Popcorn Theme

Name:_____

Popcorn Estimate

I think _____ pieces of popcorn will fit on the paper.

The actual number of pieces that fit on the paper are _____.

Name:_____

Popcorn Estimate

I think _____ pieces of popcorn will fit on the paper.

The actual number of pieces that fit on the paper are _____.

Popcorn Theme

Popcorn Science

Objective
The students will observe popcorn seeds expanding when soaked in water.

Materials
- "Popcorn Kernel Experiment" activity sheet, one per student
- popcorn kernels
- a jar or other see through container
- a paper plate

Procedure
1. Hand out the "Popcorn Kernel Experiment" activity sheet. Have the students observe the popcorn kernels being put in a jar (about an inch from the top) and then filling the jar with water almost all the way to the top. Place the paper plate on top of the jar. Older students may want to get in small groups and set up this experiment for themselves.

2. Have the students draw a picture of the experiment immediately after it is set up on their "Popcorn Kernel Experiment" activity sheets.

3. This experiment needs to sit for a few hours and then be observed for any changes.

4. When the seeds absorb the water in the jar, they should expand and push the paper plate off the top. Once this happens have the students complete the activity sheet and have a discussion on how seeds absorb water. This helps seeds push through soil and allows the seeds to have room to grow their shoots.

Extension Ideas
- This will take longer than one day, but the students can place popcorn kernels on wet towels in a pan, cover it with plastic wrap, poke some holes in the wrap, and observe the kernels for several days.
- Find pictures or real examples of different types of corn: sweet corn, dent corn (the kind we feed to animals), Indian corn, and popcorn.

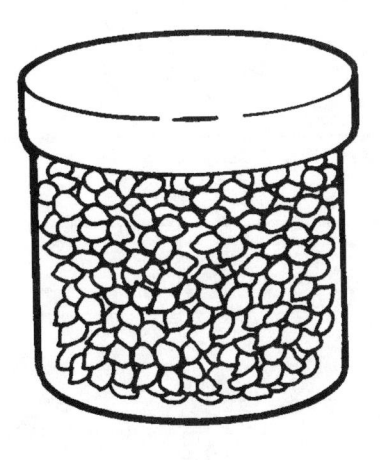

Popcorn Theme

Name:_____

Popcorn Kernel Experiment

Here is a drawing of the kernel experiment immediately after it was set up:

Here is a drawing of the kernel experiment after _____ hours:

Here is what happened and why:

_____

_____

_____

_____

_____

Popcorn Theme

Popcorn Social Studies

Objective

The students will learn to create a time line regarding popcorn history facts.

Materials

- *The Popcorn Book* by Tomie dePaola and/or information from the **Popcorn.org** site
- a chalkboard or a long piece of butcher paper on which to create a timeline
- "Popcorn History" activity sheet

Procedure

1. Read *The Popcorn Book* or share some of the interesting history facts off internet printouts. Focus on the 4 following facts:

   - In 1492 Christopher Columbus saw in the New World (the West Indies) Indians selling popcorn and wearing it as jewelry.
   - In 1621 the Native Americans brought popped corn in deerskin sacks to the first Thanksgiving.
   - In the 1700s the colonists served popcorn with cream on it for breakfast—it was one of the first cereals.
   - In 1885 the first popcorn machine was invented.

2. Using chalkboard or a long piece of butcher paper, draw a time line featuring the years 1492, 1621, 1700, and 1885. Have the students help place the popcorn history facts on the time line. Older students may want to create their own time lines.

3. Pass out the "Popcorn History" activity sheet and have the students complete the sheet as a follow-up activity.

Extension Ideas

- Discuss how Native Americans brought popcorn to the first Thanksgiving in deerskin pouches. Have the students make "deerskin" pouches out of felt and fill them with popcorn.

- Share with the students the different ways people popped popcorn before there were stoves, microwaves, or popcorn poppers. They either put the kernels in clay pots filled with hot sand, which heated the kernels until they popped, they threw the kernels directly on the hot fire and waited for them to pop, or they held the cob of popcorn over the fire and then ate the popped kernels directly off the cob. Have the students construct a whole class graph of what would have been their favorite way to pop corn back in those days.

- Find the cities on a map which are the biggest popcorn-eating cities—Milwaukee, Minneapolis, Chicago, and Seattle.

Popcorn Theme

Name:_____

Popcorn History

Use the word bank to complete the following sentences:

| breakfast | Thanksgiving | Christopher Columbus | machine |

1. 1492—_____ saw Native people in the New World wearing popcorn as jewelry.

2. 1621—Native Americans brought popped corn to the first _____.

3. 1700s—The colonists ate popcorn with cream and sugar on it for _____.

4. 1885—The first popcorn _____ was invented.

Popcorn Theme

Popcorn Art

Objective

The students will create a picture using popped corn and corn kernels.

Materials

- heavy weight paper
- popped popcorn
- popcorn kernels
- glue
- markers
- crayons
- colored pencils

Procedure

1. Discuss using popcorn and popcorn kernels to create a picture. For example, popped corn could be snowflakes, the eyes on a face, heads of flowers, etc. Popcorn kernels could be teeth on a face, raindrops, buds on a tree, etc. The age of the students will dictate the amount of assistance needed in brainstorming ideas.

2. Pass out the paper, popcorn, kernels, and any other art materials.

3. Have the students create pictures in which they incorporate the popcorn and kernels.

Extension Idea

- Make shakers using paper plates stapled together with popcorn kernels inside. The students may decorate the paper plates before assembling the shakers.

Popcorn Theme

Popcorn Movement

Objective

The students will engage in movement similar to that of a popcorn kernel.

Materials

- space for children to freely move and jump around
- music (if available) with a quiet, slow tempo as well as music with a fast beat

Procedure

1. Facilitate a discussion on how popcorn kernels remain still and quiet until they become hot enough to pop. Once a few kernels pop, the others begin to pop as well and they become noisy and move around a great deal.

2. Play the slow tempo music and have the children imitate un-popped kernels by remaining still. Perhaps they could crouch down on the ground and make themselves as small as possible.

3. Tell the students they are getting hotter and are close to popping. Now introduce the fast tempo music and have them begin "popping." This would entail jumping up and down and making their bodies larger.

Extension Ideas

- If the class made "shakers" during art time with popcorn kernels, they can play along with some music.

- Have the students jump rope and sing the following song:

    "Little Lu-Lu made some popcorn. How many kernels did she pop?" (And then have them count the number of jumps until they miss.)

Potato Theme

Setting the Stage
If possible, have each student bring in a potato from home. If this is not feasible, bring in as many potatoes as you are able to for activities and discussions.

Related Web Sites

Idaho Potatoes
This site has recipes and an area for kids with printable work sheets, with activities such as mazes and word searches. Included are recipes, nutrition information, clip art, tips, and offers.

Mashed Potato Fun for Kids
This site contains a variety of potato recipes, focusing on those that allow kids to have fun with their food. Recipes include Mashed Potato Ghosts and Rainbow Potatoes.

Potato Maze
This is an activity for growing a potato maze! Kids can plant a potato and make an obstacle course to show how the potato plant grows toward the light.

Potato Battery
This page has directions for constructing a potato battery.

Dole 5 A Day
In the Kids' area of this site, there is a lot of good information on the potato.

Related Literature

The Amazing Potato Book by Paulette Bourgeois
This book is filled with information and activities all revolving around potatoes!

Brave Potatoes by Toby Speed.
This is the story of potatoes who sneak out at the state fair to enjoy some adventures. The story is full of rhymes and wordplays.

The Enormous Potato by Aubrey Davis
A farmer needs to call in some help in extricating a large potato from the soil.

Jamie O'Rourke and the Big Potato: An Irish Folktale by Tomie dePaola
This is a retelling of an Irish tale, involving a lazy man, a big potato and a leprechaun.

Luck With Potatoes by Helen Ketteman
This tall tale concerns a farmer, some cows, and very large potatoes!

One Potato: A Counting Book of Potato Prints by Diana Pomeroy
This is a great counting book to use in a math lesson. The illustrations are done with potato prints. There are even directions for making potato prints!

Potato: A Tale of the Great Depression by Kate Lied
A depression-era family story is written by an eight-year-old girl.

Potatoes (What's for Lunch) by Claire Llewellyn
This is a simple, nonfiction book about potatoes.

Sweet Potato Pie (Step into Reading, Early) by Anne F. Rockwell
A grandmother's sweet potato pie is the focus of this rhyming book.

Potato Theme

Potato Language Arts

Objective
The students will create a fictional character and write a description of that character.

Materials
- "My Potato Head Character" activity sheet
- chart paper or blackboard

Procedure
1. Facilitate a discussion on what kind of information can be gathered to help describe a character in a book. Pick a well-known storybook character and have the students list attributes of that character. For example, "What do we know about Curious George?" The students may respond by saying, "He is a monkey, he is curious, he gets in trouble, he lives with The Man with the Yellow Hat, he used to live in a jungle," etc. It may be helpful to pick a character the students have recently been exposed to. If they have just finished listening to a chapter book, pick a character from that book.

2. Hand out the "My Potato Head Character" activity sheet and have the students compare the questions regarding their own created character. Allow them to be as creative as possible.

3. Older students may then go on to write a story starring the potato heads they created. Younger students may present their potato heads to the rest of the class, sharing their characteristics.

4. If desired, have this potato character serve as the basis for the creation in the art lesson.

Extension Ideas
- Write recipes, which contain potatoes.
- Read *Cloudy With a Chance of Meatballs* by Judi Barrett. Focus on the ending of how the hill of snow looks like mashed potatoes. Have the students think of other landscapes that resemble food. Introduce the term "simile." This activity may also be combined second extension idea of the art lesson.

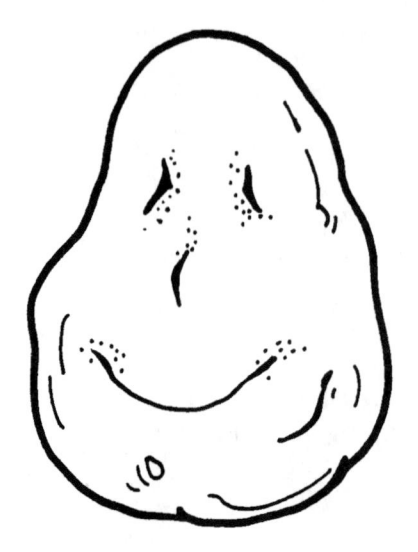

Potato Theme

Name:_____

My Potato Head Character

Answer the questions about your potato head.

1. What is your potato head's name?
   _____

2. Where does your potato head live?
   _____

3. How old is your potato head?
   _____

4. Does your potato head have any family?
   _____
   _____

5. What does your potato head like?
   _____
   _____

6. What does your potato head not like?
   _____
   _____

7. Who are your potato head's friends?
   _____
   _____

8. Is there anything else special about your potato head?
   _____
   _____

©Teacher Created Materials, Inc.   #3823 Internet Activities Through the Year

Potato Theme

Potato Math

Objective

The students will weigh and measure potatoes.

Materials

- potatoes (one per student, if brought from home, or as many as the teacher can provide)
- scales (one per three students, if available)
- rulers (one per three students)
- "Potato Measurement" activity sheet, one per group
- brown paper bags (one per three students)

Procedure

1. Discuss/review measuring and weighing objects.
2. Place the students in groups of three and pass out the "Potato Measurement" activity sheet.
3. Depending on the amount of supplies available, give each group a ruler, a scale, and one brown paper bag. If there are not enough scales available, set up a weighing area which the groups may take turns visiting.
4. Have the students assign the potatoes in their group a #1, #2, and a #3.
5. The students should complete the activity sheets, working as a group.
6. If the students are too young to do this activity in small groups, work together as a whole class, or have them take turns working with the teacher in small groups.

Extension Ideas

- Graph the students' favorite ways to eat potatoes—french fries, baked, potato chips, mashed, etc.
- Make patterns using potatoes cut in half and dipped in paint.
- Figure out the price per pound of sacks of potatoes.
- Carve shapes (triangle, circle, etc.) in potatoes and have the students print the shapes after dipping the potato in paint.
- Since every American eats about 126 lbs. of potatoes per year, have a lesson on what equals 126 lbs.
- Graph the students' favorite vegetable. (Potatoes rank as Americans' favorite vegetable, followed by head lettuce and then onions.)

Potato Theme

Name: _____

Potato Measurement

1. Potato #1 weighs _____.

   Potato #2 weighs _____.

   Potato #3 weighs _____.

   Which potato is the heaviest? _____

   Which potato is the lightest? _____

2. Weigh the following combinations of potatoes:

   Potato #1 and potato #2 weigh _____.

   Potato #1 and potato #2 and potato #3 weigh _____.

3. Potato #1 is _____ long.

   Potato #2 is _____ long.

   Potato #3 is _____ long.

   Which potato is the longest? _____

   Which potato is the shortest? _____

4. Measure the length of more than one potato:

   Potato #1 and potato #2 are _____ long.

   Potato #2 and potato #3 are _____ long.

©Teacher Created Materials, Inc.   #3823 *Internet Activities Through the Year*

Potato Theme

Potato Science

Objective

The students will identify the parts of a potato plant and classify foods which grow above ground and foods which grow underground.

Materials

- a book about potatoes or information from the following site: **Dole 5 A Day** (Click on "Fruit and Vegetable Encyclopedia" and select "potato." Then click on "How Potatoes are Grown and Harvested.")
- a variety of real vegetables (some which grow above ground and some which grow below), or pictures of vegetables (The pictures may be found on the "Above or Below?" activity sheet.)
- chart paper or blackboard
- "Above or Below?" activity sheet
- "Potato Plants" activity sheet (for older students)

Procedure

1. Read the chosen book or share the information from the **Dole 5 A Day** Web site about potato plants.

2. Discuss with the students how potatoes grow underground. People eat the "tuber" which is the actual potato. A tuber stores food for the rest of the plant.

3. Make two columns on the chart paper or blackboard. One column is for listing foods which grow above ground. The other column is for listing foods which grow below ground. Brainstorm with the students foods for each column. If real vegetables are available, show them to the class and ask them to classify in which column they belong. The students may complete the "Above or Below?" activity sheet while their lists are being made.

4. If desired, pass out the "Potato Plants" activity sheet and have the students complete it for reinforcement.

Extension Ideas

- Make a potato recipe.
- Set up a potato for sprouting.
- Use one of the following Web sites for experiments involving potatoes: **Potato Maze** or **Potato Battery**.

Potato Theme

Name:_____

Above or Below?

Write an **A** next to the foods which grow above ground and a **B** next to the foods which grow below ground.

potatoes 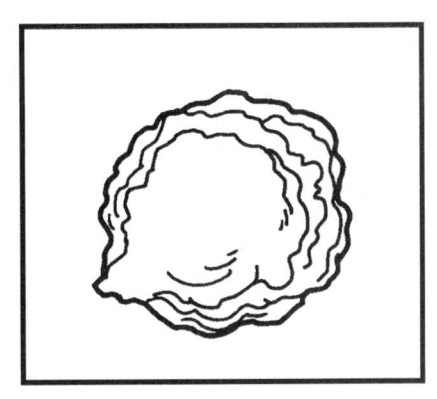 _____   lettuce  _____   radish _____

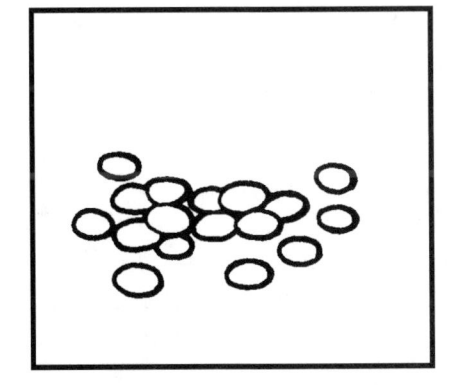

beans  _____   carrots  _____   tomato _____

onions 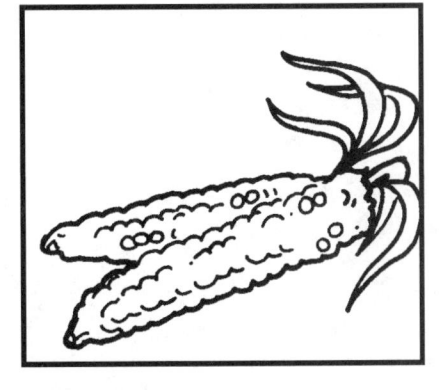 _____   corn  _____   broccoli _____

©Teacher Created Materials, Inc.   293   #3823 Internet Activities Through the Year

Potato Theme

Name:_____

Potato Plants

1. Draw and label the four parts of a potato plant: flowers, leaves, stems, and tubers.

```
┌─────────────────────────────────────────┐
│                                         │
│                                         │
│                                         │
│                                         │
│                                         │
│                                         │
└─────────────────────────────────────────┘
```

2. Which part of the plant is underground?

   _____

   _____

   _____

3. What does the tuber do for the plant?

   _____

   _____

   _____

   _____

Potato Theme

Potato Social Studies

Objective

The students will identify the components needed for selling goods.

Materials

- "Potato Stand" activity sheet, one per group
- a variety of art materials—paper, crayons, scissors, etc.

Procedure

1. Put the students in small groups of four or five. For younger students, work as a whole class to complete the lesson.

2. Challenge the students to create a "Potato Stand." The purpose of the stand is selling potatoes. What will the students need to set up this business? Pass out the "Potato Stand" activity sheet so the students may brainstorm and list their ideas.

3. Give the students access to the art supplies for creating any of the items they have identified. For example, a sign advertising their business, the potatoes for selling (could be cut from tan paper), the money for buying the potatoes from the farm, a container to serve as a cash register, etc.

4. When the students have completed their "Potato Stands" have them share their creations with the rest of the class.

5. Once all the groups have shared their work, discuss what they had in common, as well as any differences.

Extension Ideas

- Most of America's potatoes are grown in Idaho. Locate Idaho on a map. What are the states that surround Idaho? How would the students get to Idaho from their home?

- Locate potato recipes from around the world, for example, German Potato Pancakes. Locate Germany on a map or globe.

- Have a lesson on how potatoes get to market. Use the **Dole 5 A Day** Web site for assistance. (Click on the information regarding the potato in the "Reference Center.")

Potato Theme

Name:_____

Potato Stand

"Potatoes for Sale!"

List the items needed to set up a potato stand.

_____

_____

_____

_____

_____

_____

Potato Theme

Potato Art

Objective
The students will create a potato person using a potato and a variety of art supplies.

Materials
- one potato per student (If enough real potatoes are not available, have the students use a potato cut from construction paper.)
- a variety of art supplies—construction paper, fabric, cardboard, toothpicks, etc.

Procedure
1. Allow the students to create a face on their potatoes using any variety of art supplies provided. They may adhere the eyes, nose, etc. onto the potato by using glue, toothpicks, or push pins. They may also add arms, hats, feet, etc.
2. The finished potato heads may serve as the subject of the language arts lesson.

Extension Ideas
- Make potato prints. Use one of the following books as a starting point for ideas: *One Potato: A Counting Book of Potato Prints* or *Wildflower ABC: An Alphabet of Potato Prints*, both by Diana Pomeroy.
- Read *Cloudy With a Chance Of Meatballs* by Judi Barrett. At the end of the book there is a reference to a hill of snow looking like a mound of mashed potatoes. Have the students draw scenery using other foods as a basis. For example, trees may look like broccoli, etc.

Potato Theme

Potato Movement

Objective

The students will participate in potato games and develop their own game involving a potato.

Materials

- four to five potatoes
- music
- burlap sacks or pillow cases
- wide space allowing for movement

Procedure

1. Play two common potato games with the students. Use the potato and the music to play a game of hot potato. Use the sacks to have potato sack races.

2. Once the class has participated in the potato games, divide the students into small groups. Give each group a potato and a sack. Allow them time to create their own potato games.

3. Have the groups share their developed game with the rest of the class.

Extension Ideas

- Play "potato bowling." Use a potato as the "ball" and plastic soda bottles for the "pins."
- Have the students act out digging up potatoes, placing them in a wheelbarrow, and pushing them to an ending point.

Pumpkin Theme

Related Web Sites

The History of Thanksgiving
This site has basic information on the history of Thanksgiving. Included is a quiz, a story which includes the role of pumpkins, a word search puzzle, and links to other Thanksgiving pages.

The First Thanksgiving
This site has good information on the first Thanksgiving.

Pumpkin Recipes
MMMM good! Lots of great pumpkin recipes can be found here—from cookies, cheesecake, and muffins, to pumpkin-style chili and pumpkin stew.

Pumpkins and More
This site provides some basic pumpkin history, including early references to pumpkins, early use of pumpkins, and a history of the jack-o-lantern.

Pumpkin Nook
The Pumpkin Nook has all sorts of information about pumpkins—how to grow them, their life cycle, holiday information, recipes, and history. The Kid Stuff page has jokes and links to online activities on other sites.

Related Literature

The All-Around Pumpkin Book by Bargery Cuyler
This book tells how to plant a pumpkin patch and what to do with the pumpkins you have grown.

The Bear Detectives by Stan and Jan Berenstain
The Bear family searches for the missing pumpkin.

Big Pumpkin by Erica Silverman
This is the story of a witch's struggle to make a pumpkin pie from a gigantic pumpkin.

The Biggest Pumpkin Ever by Steven Knoll
A field mouse and a village mouse disagree on what to do with the best pumpkin ever.

It's a Fruit, It's a Vegetable, It's a Pumpkin by Allan Fowler
This is an easy book about the history of the pumpkin.

It's the Great Pumpkin, Charlie Brown by Charles M. Schulz
The whole Peanuts gang gets into the Halloween spirit in this pumpkin tale.

The Great Pumpkin Switch by Megan McDonald
Two boys accidentally cut their sister's prize pumpkin from its vine. They struggle to repair their mistake.

Jeb Scarecrow's Pumpkin Patch by Jana Dillon
A scarecrow works hard to protect his pumpkin patch from greedy crows.

Kid's Pumpkin Projects by Deanna F. Cook
This resource for teachers is full of all kinds of pumpkin projects.

The Kitten in the Pumpkin Patch by Richard Shaw
Jenny searches for a home for a little kitten found in the pumpkin patch.

Pumpkin Theme (cont.)

Related Literature (cont.)

The Magic Pumpkin by Bill Martin Jr. and John Archambault
Tells about the mysterious short life of a Jack-o'-Lantern.

Martin and the Pumpkin by Margaret Friskey
A boy carves a pumpkin for Halloween.

Peter's Pumpkin House by Colin and Moira Maclean
A story based on the tongue twister Peter, Peter, Pumpkin Eater.

Proud Pumpkin by Nora S. Unwin
A pumpkin brags that he will grow so big he will never be eaten.

The Pumpkin Blanket by Deborah Turney Zagwyn
A beautiful story of a girl, her blanket, and letting go.

Pumpkin Circle: The Story of a Garden by George Levenson
Beautiful photographs are the highlight of this story that emphasizes the circle of nature in a pumpkin garden.

The Pumpkin Patch by Elizabeth King
Great information and pictures on pumpkins can be found in this book.

It's Pumpkin Time by Zoe Hall
This wonderfully illustrated tale traces the pumpkin from the garden to the Halloween party.

From Pumpkin Time to Valentines by Susan Ohanian
This is a book of crafts and lessons which includes pumpkin topics.

The Story of Pumpkin by Frank Fiorello
This book identifies the parts of a pumpkin and traces it from a seed to a pumpkin. It includes a great chart showing the development of a pumpkin seed into a tiny pumpkin plant.

Pumpkin Theme

Pumpkin Language Arts

Objective

The students will recognize the letter sound "p," group words into categories, and explore the literary device alliteration.

Materials

- white board/chalkboard
- squares of drawing paper, cut 6" x 6"
- crayons or colored pencils
- a story about a pumpkin (A suggestion for the reading is *The Pumpkin Blanket* by Deborah Turney Zagwyn.)

Procedure

1. Introduce the word "pumpkin" by reading the story of your choosing about a pumpkin.
2. Brainstorm by asking the students to list food words that start with the letter P. (For example, pumpkin, pear, pizza, plum, etc.) Record their responses on the white board or chalkboard.
3. Ask the student to list people's names that start with "P" (Peter, Penny, Paige, Paul).
4. Ask them to list animals that start with the letter "P" (porcupine, platypus, porpoise, penguin).
5. Have the students choose one thing from each list.
6. They will be asked to combine the three things to make a named character that likes a particular food. For example, "Peter the penguin likes to eat pizza."
7. They will illustrate their character.
8. Combine all the squares to make your own class "Pumpkin Blanket." This activity can still be done without reading the suggested story. Choose any story you like about a pumpkin.

Extension Ideas

- Play the Pumpkin Get Acquainted Game on page 302 to help students learn more about their classmates.
- Use this story starter: "I looked into a pumpkin and saw. . . ."
- Have each child bring in a recipe using pumpkin. Combine all the recipes to make a pumpkin recipe book they can take home. You can make pumpkin bread to share with the class during this time.
- Read the tongue twister "Peter, Peter, Pumpkin eater." Have the students rewrite the first line only of the twister. Instead of "Peter," have them insert their own name. They should change the food they eat to match the beginning sound of their own name. Example: "Samuel, Samuel Sandwich eater." They could include an illustration with the line.

Pumpkin Theme

Pumpkin Get Acquainted Game

Directions: If you are finding that some children still do not know each other's names, play this get acquainted game. Duplicate and cut out the pumpkin boxes below for each student in the class. Mark every two pumpkins with the same number. (Make enough pumpkins so that a pair of students will have the same number written on their pumpkins.) Play some Halloween music or marching music and let the children walk around until the music stops. Have children find another child whose pumpkin has the same number and introduce themselves. Exchange pumpkins so that each student receives a new pumpkin and play again.

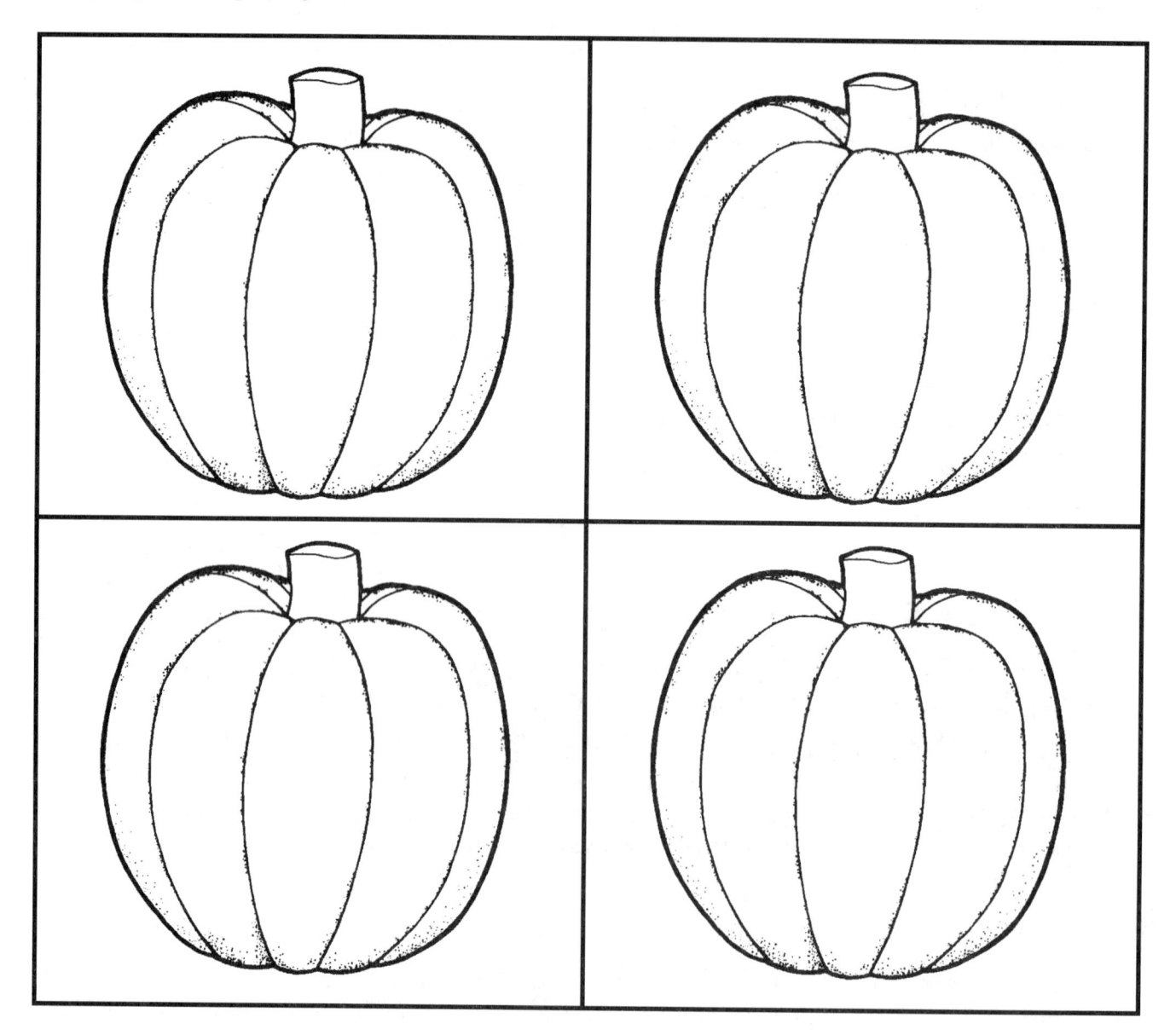

Variations: Number the pumpkins from 1–4 and let the children form groups. Ask students if they can name everyone in their group. Or, use the activity to help students find out each other's ages, favorite foods, interests, etc.

Instead of pumpkins, use cats, ghosts, or bats and play a musical record on a slow speed. (The strange sounds will create a Halloween atmosphere.)

#3823 Internet Activities Through the Year ©Teacher Created Materials, Inc.

Pumpkin Theme

Pumpkin Math

Objective

The students will practice estimation, working with weight and measurement, and counting in groups.

Materials

- one large pumpkin
- twine/string
- scale
- "Pumpkin Measurement in Inches" activity sheet or "Pumpkin Measurement in Unifix Cubes" activity sheet
- tape measures, rulers, or unifix cubes

Procedure

1. Begin by putting the students into pairs and passing out the "Pumpkin Measurement in Inches" activity sheet or the "Pumpkin Measurement in Unifix Cubes" activity sheet.

2. Each pair will then cut a length of twine they believe will most closely go around the circumference of the pumpkin. Have them measure their strings and record their estimates on their activity sheets. (Measurements could be done with tape measures or unifix cubes.)

3. Measure the circumference of the pumpkin with a string and cut it to the proper length.

4. Tape this string up on the wall and allow each pair to compare their estimated string to the actual string. Measure the actual string and allow the students to record the measurement on their activity sheets. Older students may want to figure the difference from the actual length.

5. Do the same process for the height of the pumpkin. (For this step, you may opt to not do the string. Just have the students estimate how tall they believe the pumpkin to be.)

6. Weigh each student on the scale and have them record their weight. It may be best to round their weight to the nearest 5 or 10 pounds to make the math easier. (If the students or you are not comfortable with dealing with body weight, pick a heavy item in the room such as a chair, desk, etc. to do the same activity with. If you opt to do this, simply cut off the bottom of the activity sheet.)

7. Have the students guess how many pumpkins would equal their weight (or the selected item's weight.) Example: My weight in pumpkins will be _____ pumpkins.

8. Actually weigh the pumpkin. Have the students figure how many pumpkins it would take to actually equal their (or the item's) weight.

   Example: I weigh the same as _____ pumpkins.

   If the pumpkin weighs 5 pounds the students would count in fives until they reach their weight. You may want to weigh your pumpkin before you buy it so you have a pumpkin that makes it easier for them to count by that number to reach their weight (five or ten pounds).

Pumpkin Theme

Name:_____

Pumpkin Measurement in Inches

I think the pumpkin is _____ inches around.

The pumpkin is actually _____ inches around.

My estimate was _____ than the actual measurement.
(Fill in the word <u>more</u> or <u>less</u>.)

I think the pumpkin is _____ inches tall.

The pumpkin is actually _____ inches tall.

How Many Pumpkins do I Weigh?

I weigh _____ pounds.

I think I weigh _____ of our class pumpkins.

I actually weigh _____ of our class pumpkins.

Name:_____

Pumpkin Measurement in Unifix Cubes

I think the pumpkin is _____ unifix cubes around.

The pumpkin is actually _____ unifix cubes around.

My estimate was _____ than the actual measurement.
(Fill in the word <u>more</u> or <u>less</u>.)

I think the pumpkin is _____ unifix cubes tall.

The pumpkin is actually _____ unifix cubes tall.

How Many Pumpkins do I Weigh?

I weigh _____ pounds.

I think I weigh _____ of our class pumpkins.

I actually weigh _____ of our class pumpkins.

Pumpkin Theme

Pumpkin Science

Objective

The students will dissect a pumpkin and record data regarding the parts of the pumpkin.

Materials

- "Pumpkin Dissection Guide" activity sheet
- scales
- five medium-sized pumpkins
- measuring tape
- *The Story of Pumpkin* by Frank Fiorello, or another book that discusses how pumpkins grow and the parts of a pumpkin
- metal spoons and vegetable peelers

Procedure

1. Read the book about growing pumpkins.

2. Divide the class into small groups sitting around tables or desks that are pushed together to form a table.

3. Each dissection team will receive one pumpkin (the top should rest on the pumpkin after having been cut off previously), several metal spoons, and one vegetable peeler (be sure it is not too sharp).

4. Lead the class through the steps on the "Pumpkin Dissection Guide."

5. Give each group or student one dissection guide to complete.

6. For younger children, the entire class may work together to fill out one dissection guide under the leadership of the teacher.

Extension Ideas

- Have the students plant a pumpkin seed and record its growth This activity will not be finished in one day.

- Compare the pumpkin to other fruits. Compare it to other vegetables. Decide if it is a fruit or vegetable. Suggested reading for this activity: *It's a Fruit, It's a Vegetable, It's a Pumpkin!* by Allan Fowler.

- Have the students trace a pumpkin seed's journey to becoming a ripe pumpkin.

Pumpkin Theme

Name:_____

Pumpkin Dissection Guide

1. Our pumpkin weighs _____ pounds.

2. Our pumpkin is _____ inches around.

3. Here is one of our pumpkin's seeds (glue seed below).

4. One word to describe the seed is _____.

5. Here is a piece of pumpkin skin (glue skin below).

6. One word to describe the skin is _____.

7. Here is a piece of pumpkin flesh (glue flesh below).

8. One word to describe the flesh is _____.

9. Our pumpkin had _____ seeds inside.

Pumpkin Theme

Pumpkin Social Studies

Objective

The students will learn about the first Thanksgiving. They will experience the sharing that took place between the Native Americans and the pilgrims.

Materials

- strips of orange construction paper 1" wide and at least 11" long
- pumpkin bread recipe (One can be found at **Pumpkin Recipes Galore**.)
- a story about the first Thanksgiving (The following links could be helpful: **Thanksgiving History and Traditions, America's First Thanksgiving, Pumpkins and More, Pumpkin Nook History**.)

Procedure

1. Tell the story of the first Thanksgiving relating how the pilgrims used pumpkins and how Native Americans used pumpkins. Use the following link: **Pumpkins And More**.
2. Divide your class into two groups: pilgrims and Native Americans. (Today would be a good day to have a parent helper you can depend on.)
3. The Native American group will make mats for the class to sit on. Each student will make two—one for themselves and one to share with a pilgrim classmate. These will be made using the precut orange paper strips.
4. Demonstrate how to weave them into a mat. If this is too complicated for your students they can paste strips onto a piece of paper to make the process easier.
5. The pilgrim group will make the bread dough. Divide the pilgrims into workable groups. Decide how many loaves of bread you need for each student to have a small piece of pumpkin bread.
6. While the bread is baking, retell the Thanksgiving story.
7. Instruct the Native American students to present their extra pumpkin mat to a pilgrim student.
8. Then have them sit on the ground in a circle all together.
9. Enjoy the bread! If it is not possible to do any baking at your school, make the bread ahead of time. The sharing lesson could be conveyed by having the pilgrim group prepare the bread by cutting it and placing it on a paper plate they have decorated.

Extension Ideas

- Trace the pumpkin from the pumpkin farm to the grocery store.
- List all the uses we have for pumpkins.
- Compare the two pumpkin holidays: Thanksgiving and Halloween. List how they are alike and how they are different. Use a Venn diagram to make this comparison.

Pumpkin Theme

Pumpkin Art

Objective
The students will create artwork using a mosaic technique.

Materials
- pumpkin seeds dyed a variety of colors (Do this ahead of time so the seeds will be dry. Use vinegar, water, and food coloring)
- heavy art paper
- glue
- pencils

Procedure
1. Show a partial mosaic you have started ahead of time. Explain to the students how a pencil drawing guides the placement of seeds.
2. Using a pencil, the students should make an outline of the pattern or picture they want to create.
3. The students then apply the colored seeds to create their own original mosaic.

Extension Ideas
- Have each student paint a small pumpkin using tempera paint.
- Using green string for vines and yellow tissue paper, the students could make a pumpkin vine with blooms.
- Experiment with color mixing using (primary colors only) tempera or watercolor paint. Try to make green (vine color) and orange (pumpkin color).

Pumpkin Theme

Pumpkin Movement

Objective
Students will participate in relay team races while manipulating an obstacle course.

Materials
- one small pumpkin
- one broom
- one orange cone
- marking tape

Procedure
1. Separate the students into relay teams.
2. The students will race by pushing the pumpkin with the broomstick.
3. Mark a starting line with tape. Place an orange cone a reasonable distance from the starting line marked with the tape. Instruct the students to go to the cone, around the cone, and return to the starting line while pushing the pumpkin with the broom.
4. Each student in the relay team must do the same.
5. The first team to complete the rotation of the relay is the winning team.

Extension Ideas
- Have a pumpkin walk similar to a cakewalk.
- Have the students act out the life of a pumpkin seed. First small and in the ground, then the sprout, grow long vines, bloom, and grow into a large round pumpkin filled with more seeds. This idea would be excellent for a Kindergarten class that does not enjoy intense competition for athletic lessons. This could be set to music to combine a movement and music lesson.

Rain Theme

Related Web Sites

Encarta Encyclopedia
This is the *Encarta* entry for "rain."

Make-Stuff.Com
Find here the instructions for making a rain stick.

FamilyEducation.Com
Find out how rain works and explore some activities related to rain.

Rain or Shine
Get a weather forecast for any city in the world.

FEMA for Kids—Thunderstorms
This section of the FEMA site offers information and activities on thunderstorms.

FEMA for Kids—Floods
This section of the FEMA site offers information and activities pertaining to floods.

BrainPop Weather
Find at this site great information, short movies, and quizzes on the water cycle and thunderstorms.

Dan's Wild Weather Page—Precipitation
This section of the Wild Weather page focuses on precipitation with definitions, activities, and links to other sites.

Web Weather for Kids
Weather-related experiments can be found here.

Related Literature

Bringing the Rain to Kapiti Plain : A Nandi Tale by Verna Aardema
This is a lovely rhyming book with cumulative text.

Flash, Crash, Rumble and Roll by Franklyn Mansfield Branley
This book contains great information on thunder, lightning, and how sound travels. It also has safety tips for what to do in a thunderstorm, as well as activities at the end.

Jungle Jamboree by Kimberly Knutson
Children spend a rainy day building a "jungle" out of couch cushions and blankets. They then go outside and romp in the puddles of the rainstorm.

Pete Spier's Rain by Peter Spier
A brother and sister have a fun adventure on a rainy day in this wordless picture book.

Rain by Manya Stojic
This is a simple, vibrant picture book which incorporates the five senses in detecting a coming rainstorm.

The Rain Came Down by David Shannon
This story tells the happenings in a neighborhood through a funny series of events in a rainstorm!

The Rainstick: A Fable by Sandra Chisholm Robinson
This is the West African tale of a boy looking for rain. Included at the end of the story are directions for making a rain stick. Great book to use in combination with an art lesson.

Rain Theme

Rain Language Arts

Objective
The students will put words in alphabetical order.

Materials
- pieces of paper cut in the shape of raindrops (These only need to be big enough for the students to write one word on them.)
- any fiction or nonfiction book about rain, such as *Come On, Rain!* by Karen Hesse, *Rain* by Robert Kalan, *Rain* by Andres Llamas Ruiz, *A Rainy Theme* by Sandra Markle, or *Listen to the Rain* by Bill Martin Jr. and John Archambault. (See the Rain Theme Page for more suggestions.)
- tape
- "Rain Words" activity sheet (for older students)

Procedure
1. Read the chosen book to the students. The purpose of the book is to set the tone and help the students start thinking of words which are associated with rain.

2. Give each student a raindrop-shaped paper.

3. Have the students write one word on the raindrop which is associated with rain. They may use what they remember from the story as one of their words, or think of a word on their own. Younger students may need some help in thinking of words. Some examples may be wet, boots, umbrella, sprinkle, etc.

4. Once the students have written a word on their raindrops, work as a class to put the raindrop words in alphabetical order. Tape the raindrops on the wall in the correct order, as if they are falling from the ceiling. (The words at the beginning of the alphabet will be closest to the ceiling, and the words at the end of the alphabet will be closest to the floor.)

5. For reinforcement, older students may complete the "Rain Words" activity sheet.

Extension Ideas
- Have a lesson on position words, such as on, in, over, under, etc. All these words can be related to where rain fell.

- Have a phonics lesson on the "-ai" sound.

- The students may write real or fictional stories for what they like to do on rainy days. Use some of the books on the Rain Theme page for starting points.

- Use the language arts lesson for Cloud Theme and have the students write weather reports.

- The students may brainstorm words which depict sounds of rain or thunderstorms. For example, pitter-patter, drip, crash, rumble, etc. Introduce the term *onomatopoeia*. The **Onomatopoeia** Web site may be helpful. Think of other words which depict sound.

Name:_____

Rain Words

Write the following words in ABC order.

wet   puddle   umbrella   splash   boots

April   clouds   hat   mud   flower

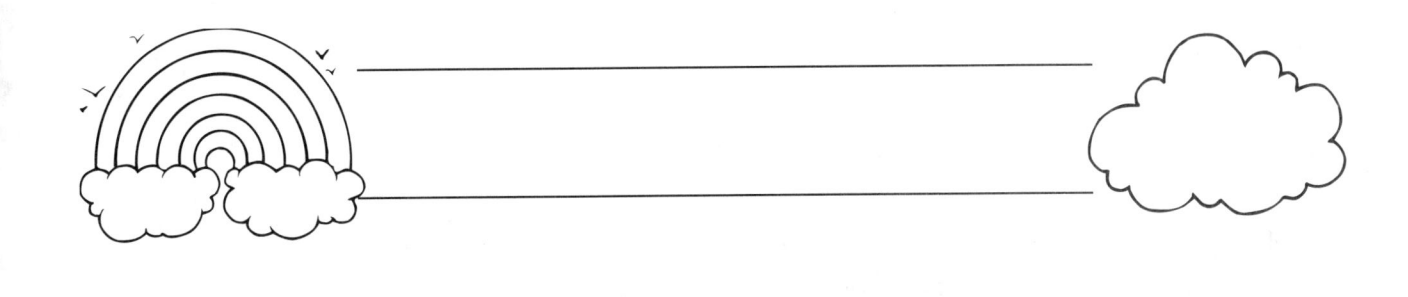

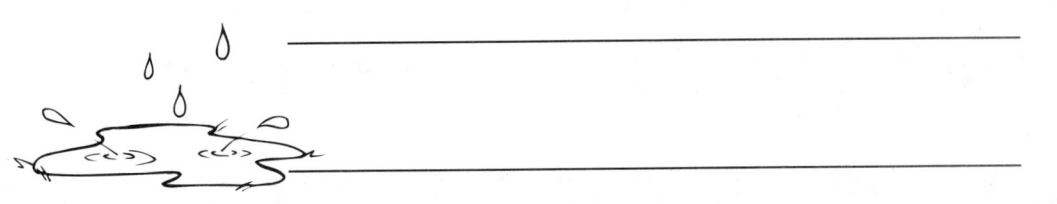

_____

_____

_____

_____

_____

_____

_____

_____

_____

_____

Rain Theme

Rain Math

Objective
The students will measure different amounts of water.

Materials
- information from the **Normal Monthly Precipitations** Web site or information on average rainfalls from different regions
- clear containers
- water
- rulers
- "Measuring Rainfall" activity sheet

Procedure
1. Set up ten (or more, if desired) "stations" in advance. Using the **Normal Monthly Precipitations** Web site, pick a summer month in which the precipitation amount will be rain and not snow. Next pick the ten cities which are going to be represented. (Try to have a varied range of measurements.) Then fill ten containers with water to the amount which equals each of the cities you have picked (round to the nearest half-inch.) Set up the ten stations by having a container of water, a card with the name of the city, and a ruler at each station.

2. Divide the students into pairs. Discuss with the students what is represented at each station. The amounts are averages which have been measured for a 30-year period. (Some years there may be more rain, some years less, but on the average this is the amount that falls for the given month.) Give instructions on how to measure the water.

3. Pass out the "Measuring Rainfall" activity sheet and have the students travel through the stations, measuring the amounts of water and recording it on their papers.

4. See the social studies lesson for continuing procedures.

Extension Ideas
1. Have the students arrange the average rainfalls from least to greatest.

2. Have a lesson on how averages are figured (average rainfall.) This would be most appropriate for older students.

3. Have the students make a rain gauge and record rainfall over a given period of time. One of the following Web sites may be helpful: **The Weathered Look** or **Weather and Climate Lesson**.

4. Go outside with buckets of water and measuring cups. Have the students create puddles of different sizes using the measuring cups. How big is a two-cup puddle? (Measure its diameter.) How big is a five-cup puddle?

5. Write story problems which involve rainfall. For example, it rained two inches on Thursday and one inch on Friday. How many inches did it rain altogether?

Rain Theme

Name:_____

Measuring Rainfall

Write the name of the city and the amount of average rainfall.

City	Average Rainfall
_____	_____
_____	_____
_____	_____
_____	_____
_____	_____
_____	_____
_____	_____
_____	_____

Which city had the greatest average rainfall?

_____

Which city had the least average rainfall?

_____

Rain Theme

Rain Science

Objective

The students will identify the different phases of the water cycle. (This lesson is similar to the Snow Theme science lesson.)

Materials

- ice
- a metal pan
- a source of steam (If possible use a pan of boiling water. If this is not possible, use very hot tap water in a glass container that has been run under the hot water.)
- information from one of the following sites: **BrainPop, The Water Cycle at Work**, or **Water Science for Schools** (Books which contain information on the water cycle, such as *Down Comes the Rain* by Franklyn M. Branley, can also be used.)
- "It's Raining in My Classroom!" activity sheet

Procedure

1. Share information with the students about the water cycle. Use one of the aforementioned Web sites or read the book. Be sure to touch on the three main points of evaporation, condensation, and precipitation.

2. Explain to the students that you are going to create "rain" in the classroom. Set up the experiment by putting ice in the metal pan and holding it over the source of steam (either the boiling water or the hot tap water.) If you are using hot tap water, set the pan directly on top of the glass container. The steam will condense on the bottom of the pan, and when the condensation becomes heavy enough, it will fall from the pan.

3. Discuss with the students how each part of the experiment represents a phase of the water cycle in nature. The steam is the evaporation of water from lakes, streams, the ground, etc. The pan with the ice represents the cold atmosphere where water droplets condense and form clouds. The water falling from the bottom of the pan is the precipitation.

4. Pass out the "It's Raining in My Classroom!" activity sheet and have the students complete the sheet for reinforcement.

Extension Ideas

- Have a lesson on how rain affects other things in nature. Brainstorm how plants, animals, and humans all need water in order to survive. What effects are there from droughts as well as floods?
- Discuss different types of rainstorms. What causes thunder and lightning? *Flash, Crash, Rumble, and Roll* by Franklyn M. Branley is a good book to use for information.
- Have a meteorologist come into the classroom and discuss his/her job. How does he/she predict rain?
- Compare the scenery, plants, and animals found in a rainforest with those found in a desert.
- Have a lesson on evaporation. Place a small container of water in a sunny place in the classroom and have the students observe the level of water over a period of time.

Rain Theme

Name:_____

It's Raining in My Classroom!

Draw a picture of the experiment. Label your picture using these three words: evaporation, condensation, precipitation.

Rain Theme

Rain Social Studies

Objective

The students will locate different cities/states on a map and use cardinal directions for describing the location of the city/state.

Materials

- a list of the cities and their average rainfalls used in the math lesson
- a map of the United States (or the region used in the math lesson)

Procedure

1. Once the Math Lesson has been completed, give each pair of students a card with the name of a city and its average rainfall written on it which was used in the math lesson.

2. Discuss the map that will be used in the lesson. Where is the students' home city/state? Which way is North, South, East, and West?

3. Have each pair of students approach the map and locate the city (or just the state) for each card. Is the city/state North, South, East, or West from where the students live?

Extension Ideas

- Locate rainforests on a world map. Use the following sites for information and maps on rainforests: **Rainforest Live** or **Children's Tropical Rainforests**.

- Locate regions on a map which are prone to flooding and regions which are prone to droughts. Use the following sites for information on floods and draughts: **FEMA For Kids** and **Forces of Nature**. How do floods and draughts affect people, animals, and agriculture?

- Have a lesson on monsoons and locate where they occur on a world map. There are monsoons in India, Thailand, Mexico, as well as Arizona! Use the following sites for help: **The Arizona Monsoon**, **Forces of Nature**, and **The Mexican Monsoon**.

Rain Art

Objective
The students will create rainy day pictures using a crayon resist technique.

Materials
- paper
- crayons
- watercolor paints

Procedure
1. Have the students make a crayon drawing of a rainy day scene. Instruct them to color in the picture quite hard and to not draw in any rain falling (the falling rain will be done in water color.)

2. Once the students have completed the crayon portion of their art work, they may then add in the "rain" with the water color paint. Black and white mixed together will make a gray rain, or they may choose to use blues for the rain. Encourage the students to experiment putting "rain" on the crayon parts of their pictures, as well as the plain parts. They may want to add puddles and rainbows as well.

Extension Ideas
- Have the students create figures of themselves out of clay. Give each student an umbrella (one of the small drink umbrellas) to put in the hand of their figure.

- Create a whole class mural. The students should draw pictures of themselves on a "rainy day" mural. They should then create an umbrella out of any variety of art material to be placed in the hand of their picture. Art materials may include: baking cups, torn paper, pieces of fabric, pipe cleaners, etc.

- Give each student two large pieces of paper cut in the shape of rain boots. Have the students decorate their rain boots in whatever materials they desire.

- Give each student a large piece of paper in the shape of an umbrella. Using a wide variety of materials, have the students decorate their umbrellas.

Rain Theme

Rain Movement

Objective

The students will use parts of their bodies to create the sounds of a rainstorm.

Materials

- a wide open space to sit in a circle

Procedure

1. Brainstorm with the students the different sounds which can be heard during a rainstorm.

2. Have the students sit in a circle on the floor. Start by having them all rub their hands against their thighs gently. This will sound like a gentle rain first beginning. They should then pat their hands against their thighs very slowly. Everyone should increase the speed of the pats to simulate the rain falling faster and harder. Then everyone should slow down at the same pace to simulate the rainstorm moving away and getting quieter.

3. Brainstorm with the class how to make claps and rumbles of thunder using their bodies as well.

Extension Idea

- Go outside and draw "puddles" with chalk on a paved area. Have the students jump in the puddles or from puddle to puddle.

Rainbow Theme

Setting the Stage

Have the students wear their favorite rainbow color to school, as well as bring in an object of their favorite color!

Related Web Sites

About Rainbows

There is good information on rainbows to be found here, but it is most appropriate for teacher reference. Included is information on colors, arcs, and different kinds of rainbows. Links to rainbow photographs can also be found.

Encarta Encyclopedia—Rainbow

This is the Encarta entry for rainbow. Basic information is included.

Rainbow Lab

This page, subtitled "The Mathematics of Rainbows," is another site for teacher reference. The lab includes objectives, information on how light travels, reflection and refraction, exploration, and analysis.

How Stuff Works

This page answers the question, "What causes a rainbow?" It is most appropriate for teacher reference.

The Rainbow Maker

This is a site promoting an artist who creates giant rainbows. He uses large scale pumps and sunlight to create natural rainbows all over the world. Information on his exhibits is included as well as information on the history of rainbows and making rainbows.

Rainbows

This is a photographer's site which features beautiful rainbow photographs. Many beautiful images can be found here.

RainbowLand

Here is a story of rainbow colors in which the ending is left out for the students to complete. Also found here are pages to print and color and an online mix-and-match activity.

Hooray for the Rainbow!

This site has lesson ideas involving a rainbow's colors, along with a rainbow song, riddles, games, and a list of books for a rainbow unit.

Related Literature

Eugie's Rainbow by Debbie Powell Smith
In this story, a caterpillar finds himself on an adventure in a rainbow.

The Rainbow Bridge by Audrey Wood
A Native American legend describes people crossing a "rainbow bridge" to a new mainland.

Rainbow Crow: A Lenape Tale by Nancy Van Laan
This Native American Legend describes how the crow lost his colors.

The Rainbow Fish by Marcus Pfister
This is the well known story of a fish sharing his brilliant rainbow-colored scales.

Rainbow Theme

Rainbow Language Arts

Objective

The students will speak and write about a favorite object, while distinguishing between fiction and nonfiction.

Materials

- Each student should have an object from home which represents his/her favorite color.
- paper and writing utensils

Procedure

1. Allow the students to speak in front of the class about their favorite-colored object. If the class is too large, have them break into pairs and tell their partner about the object.

2. Once everyone has had a chance to speak, have the students write about their object. Discuss the difference between fiction and nonfiction writing.

3. Have the students choose what type of writing they would like to do about their object. They may write a nonfiction piece in which they describe the object, explain how they acquired it, etc. Those who choose to write a fictional piece may be given the story starter, "My blue (or the appropriate color) (object) went looking for a rainbow. . . ." Younger students may work together to write a fictional story incorporating all of the objects brought into school. The teacher may record this story on chart paper.

Extension Ideas

- Read some additional fiction and nonfiction stories such as *A Rainbow of My Own* by Don Freeman (fiction), *Planting a Rainbow* by Lois Ehlert (fiction), or *Raindrops and Rainbows* by Rose Wyle (nonfiction).

- To expand on the above lesson, review some statements that are facts about rainbows and those that are fiction. This will help to reinforce the concept of fiction vs. nonfiction.

- Have a lesson on compound words using "Rainbow" as the starting point.

- Complete the story starter, "I want to find a _____ at the end of a rainbow."

- Read the book, *The Rough-Face Girl* by Rafe Martin. Within this Native American Legend book, there are allusions made to the rainbow. Compare and contrast this book to the story of Cinderella.

- Learn to sign the colors using the **American Sign Language** Browser Web site.

Rainbow Theme

Rainbow Math

Objective
The students will create and interpret a graph of their favorite colors.

Materials
- a large piece of butcher paper divided into seven columns for graphing
- index cards, or pieces of paper to fill in the graph
- crayons, markers, or colored pencils
- "Favorite Color" activity sheet
- graph paper, if desired.

Procedure
1. Distribute the index cards (or small square pieces of paper). Have the students pick which rainbow color is their favorite—red, orange, yellow, green, blue, indigo, or violet. They should then color the index card their favorite color.
2. Have the students place their card in the appropriate column on the chart paper graph.
3. If desired, have the students copy the graph onto graph paper of their own.
4. Discuss and interpret the graph. Ask questions such as, "Which color has the most votes?," "Which has the least?" The depth of the questions will depend on the age level of the students.
5. Pass out the "Favorite Color" activity sheet, if appropriate. Problems number 6 and 7 will need the blanks filled in once the graph is complete.

Extension Ideas
- If the students have worn their favorite colors to school on this day, make a human (real) graph.
- Have the students write math problems in which the answer is seven (due to the seven colors in the rainbow).
- Assign each color a number—red = 1, orange = 2, yellow = 3, green = 4, blue = 5, indigo = 6 and violet = 7. Have the students do math problems in this "color secret code." For example, using their crayons, a red box + an orange box = a yellow box. The problems may be more complicated depending on the age level.

Rainbow Theme

Name:_____

Our Favorite Colors

1. Which color has the most votes?

   _____

2. Which color has the least votes?

   _____

3. How many votes do red and orange have altogether?

   _____

4. How many votes do yellow and green have altogether?

   _____

5. How many votes do blue, indigo, and violet have altogether?

   _____

6. How many more votes does _____ have than _____?

   _____

7. How many more votes does _____ have than _____?

   _____

Rainbow Theme

Rainbow Science

Objective

The students will describe how rainbows form.

Materials

- if it's a sunny day—a glass filled with water, a sunny window, white paper, or prisms (if available)
- a book about how rainbows form, such as *All the Colors of the Rainbow* by Allan Fowler—or use one of the following Web sites for information: **What Causes A Rainbow?**, or **About Rainbows**.
- "How a Rainbow Forms" activity sheet

Procedure

1. Ask the students what they know about rainbows forming. When do we see them? Why do they occur? Have the students make a hypothesis about why rainbows occur.

2. Discuss the 7 colors that make up a rainbow—ROY G. BIV.

3. If it's a sunny day, fill a glass with water and place it in a sunny window. A rainbow may be picked up on a white sheet of paper angled below the glass. This may be done as a teacher demonstration, or small groups of students may be given their own glass to experiment with, depending on the age. Sometimes a mirror angled in the water can help to create a rainbow as well. Another option would be using prisms if they are available. Then the students may experiment with the prisms in the sunlight. Remind the students that the prisms are taking the place of raindrops in nature.

4. If it's not a sunny day, skip right to this step and read the aforementioned Web sites. They offer good information which can be altered to the students' ability of understanding.

5. Once the information has been presented, ask the students if their hypotheses were correct.

6. Have the students complete the "How a Rainbow Forms" activity sheet.

Extension Ideas

- If possible, go outside on a sunny day, use a hose, and create rainbows. The sun should be at your back when spraying the water.
- Have a more in-depth lesson on rain and the water cycle.
- Have a lesson on the light spectrum.
- Have a lesson on light refraction (the bending of light).

Rainbow Theme

Name:_____

How Rainbows Form

1. Rainbows form when _____

   _____.

2. Here is a diagram of how rainbows form.

Rainbow Theme

Rainbow Social Studies

Objective
The students will explore Sir Isaac Newton as the scientist who discovered the spectrum of light and create a time line of scientific discoveries and inventions.

Materials

- a book, such as *The Rainbow and You* by E.C. Krupp, or a Web site with information on Isaac Newton, such as: **Fact Monster: Sir Issac Newton** or **Newton Short Stories** (scroll down to the bottom of the page where it gives a story on Isaac Newton and light)
- the **History of Science and Technology: A Timeline** Web site. Decide ahead of time which inventions/discoveries will be included in a class-created time line.

Procedure

1. Read the book or share information off a Web site regarding Isaac Newton as an important scientist in our history. Specifically discuss how he discovered that white light is composed of all the colors in the spectrum. He did this by using a prism and sunlight.

2. Discuss how many important discoveries and inventions occurred throughout history. Isaac Newton discovered the spectrum in 1666.

3. Work as a class to create a time line featuring other important discoveries. Use the **History of Science and Technology: A Timeline** Web site for reference. The detail of the time line will depend on the age of the children. For example, younger children may just need four to five points on their timeline:

    - 1500s—a scientist discovered that the planets revolve around the sun
    - 1600s—Isaac Newton discovered the spectrum of light
    - 1700s—the hot air balloon was invented
    - 1800s—the steam boat was invented
    - 1900s—the first airplane took flight

    Older students may include more dates on their time line. For younger students this will be a more general lesson on what a timeline is and what it represents.

Extension Ideas

- Have a lesson on Hawaii, where rainbows occur more often than other parts of the country, due to its climate.

- Discuss rainbows and how they play a part in various folklore. A good variety of these are discussed in the book *The Rainbow and You* by E.C. Krupp.

Rainbow Theme

Rainbow Art

Objective

The students will mix the primary colors to create the colors in a rainbow.

Materials

- red, yellow, and blue paint
- paintbrushes
- paper
- trays or containers for mixing paint

Procedure

1. Have a discussion on how all the seven colors in the rainbow can be created from the three primary colors—red, blue, yellow.

2. Allow each student to have access to the primary colors of paint, a paintbrush, and water. Have the students explore mixing the colors to create the other four colors needed to complete the rainbow.

3. Once the colors are mixed, the students may paint a rainbow of their own.

Extension Ideas

- Create a whole class rainbow using any variety of mediums—torn tissue paper, sponge painting, etc. Make the rainbow large enough to be displayed in the classroom or hallway.

- Since rainbows in nature are transparent, have the students work with watercolors to paint transparent-looking rainbows.

Rainbow Theme

Rainbow Movement

Objective

The students will engage in a treasure hunt to find a "pot of gold."

Materials

- index cards with teacher-given hints on where the treasure can be found, placed to conduct a treasure hunt.
- a large area to conduct the treasure hunt.
- aA picture of gold treasure, or real rewards for the students at the end of the hunt (For example, a new shiny penny for each student, a gold wrapped chocolate candy, a gold sticker, etc.)

Procedure

1. Discuss with the students the folklore of a "pot of gold" at the end of a rainbow. Tell them they are going to go on their own treasure hunt for a "pot of gold."

2. Working as a class, have the students read (or read to them) the first clue of where the treasure is. Be as creative as possible and gear the clues toward the age of the students. For example, "go to the place where we throw our waste" (meaning the classroom trash can). The treasure hunt may lead them outside, to other areas of the school, whatever is possible.

Extension Ideas

- Have the students form their bodies into an arch shape.
- Pass out pieces of rainbow-colored crepe paper or fabric. Have the students dance to music trailing their rainbow colors behind them.
- Make a human demonstration of how a rainbow forms. Have some students cluster together posing as the sun, another group of students should form a line by holding hands, representing a ray of sunlight, and another group of students should pose across the room as a group of raindrops. Have the ray of sunlight move in a straight line to the raindrops then pretend to bounce off of the rain and bend their direction back out towards the sun. If possible, have seven students form the ray of sunlight. Each of these students should have a piece of construction paper representing a different color of the rainbow glued to a piece of white paper. When they enter the raindrop area, they should display the white side of the paper. When they bounce and "refract" back out toward the sun, they should flip the paper to the color side. At that time, the line of students should separate hands and form a line into rainbow order—ROYGBIV.

Rock Theme

Related Web Sites

Rock Collecting Around the USA
This site provides links to different rock collecting sites, organized by state.

Mineral Information Institute
This site has lots of information on minerals, including a separate teacher section with free lesson plans, student pages, and more. Also included is homework help for students with maps, photos, and minerals.

Ask-A-Geologist
E-mail a question to a geologist. Geologists answer earth science questions about volcanoes, earthquakes, mountains, rocks, maps, ground water, lakes, or rivers.

Canadian Rockhound
Good rock information can be found here. Included is information about the differences between rocks and minerals, identifying minerals, fossils, and more.

Women in Mining
This site provides information to educate students about the importance of minerals. There are activities, games, and links to an area specifically for teachers.

Busy Teacher's Web Site
This page provides a number of geology links, including information on landscapes, geologic time, and virtual field trips.

Cape Cod Rocks
This site is a museum on the Internet. Great pictures and information on all types of rocks can be found here, with collections of fossils and popular rocks.

Rockhounds
This is a must-see site with activities, lesson plans, and basic information on the rock cycles.

Geology Project
This is an elementary classroom's project on their journey to the center of the earth. Students focus on the earth, volcanoes, plate tectonics, and how rocks and minerals are formed.

Related Literature

The Best Book of Fossils, Rocks, and Minerals by Chris Pellant
This is a good, basic book on geology..

Eyewitness: Rocks and Minerals by R.F. Symes
This is a large book, good for reference.

Geology Rocks!: 50 Hands-On Activities to Explore the Earth by Cindy Blobaum
This book is full of activities to explore geology!

A Gift From the Sea by Kate Banks
A boy finds a rock and the book goes back in time to tell the story of the rock.

If You Find a Rock by Peggy Christian
Discover how to find rocks and the different ways they can be used..

On My Beach There are Many Pebbles by Leo Lionni
This is a story about appreciating all the things that can be found on a beach.

Rock Theme

Rock Language Arts

Objective

The students will classify fiction and nonfiction writings. They will also write descriptive accounts or fictional stories about the finding of their rocks.

Materials

- the rocks the students brought in to school
- paper and writing utensils
- at least six to ten books on rocks, some fiction and some nonfiction
- the book *Everybody Needs a Rock* by Byrd Baylor, if available

Procedure

1. Have a discussion on fiction vs. nonfiction. Show the books and give descriptions of what the books contain. Have the students decide whether the books are fiction or nonfiction.

2. Read *Everybody Needs a Rock*, if available.

3. The students should choose which type of story they would like to write ahead of time. They may either write the true story of how they found their rocks, or a fictional story on the finding of their rocks. They may then share these stories with the rest of the class. Have the class determine which writings are fiction and which are nonfiction.

4. Younger students may draw pictures of themselves finding their rocks and write a few words describing the rock or how it was found. Their pictures may illustrate a fiction or nonfiction story of finding their rock.

Extension Ideas

- See the Extension Ideas section of the science lesson (page 336). Have students use their pet rocks for a science experiment.

- Read *Sylvester and the Magic Pebble* by William Steig. Have the students write what they would wish for if they found a magic pebble. This may be combined with an art lesson in which they decorate a small rock or cutout of a rock, name it their "magic pebble" and write their wish to accompany their artwork.

- Read *Stone Soup* by Marcia Brown. Have the students write recipes for their own stone soup.

- Have the students personify the rocks they have brought in to school. They may name them, give them birthdays, and write what a typical day entails for their rocks. Discuss the term personification and find examples of it in literature. Use the "My Pet Rock" activity sheet.

- Do the language arts lesson at the beginning of the day. Have a lesson on questions, including question words and question marks. Have each student write or dictate a question about what they would like to learn about rocks. For example, "Where do rocks come from?"

Rock Theme

Name:_____

My Pet Rock

Answer the questions about your rock.

1. What is your rock's name?
   _____

2. Where does your rock live?
   _____

3. How old is your rock?
   _____

4. Does your rock have any family?
   _____
   _____

5. What does your rock like? _____
   _____

6. What does your rock not like? _____
   _____
   _____

7. Who are your rock's friends? _____
   _____
   _____

8. Is there anything else special about your rock? _____
   _____
   _____

Rock Theme

Rock Math

Objective

The students will weigh and measure their rocks.

Materials

- rocks brought in from home
- scales
- balance scales
- measuring tapes or rulers
- "My Rock" activity sheet or "Rock Length" activity sheet (for younger students)
- If desired, set the room up in centers for the students to move through. For example, set up two weight centers with scales, balance scales, and a variety of objects to be compared to the weight of their rocks. Also set up two measuring centers with rulers, measuring tapes, and a variety of objects to compare the length to their rocks. Each student need only visit one weight center and one measuring center.

Procedure

1. Review measuring and weighing objects as needed.

2. Pass out the "My Rock" activity sheets and allow the students to go to one weight center and one measuring center to complete the activity sheet. On the activity sheets, a balance scale should be used for questions 2, 3, and 4 on the weight section.

3. If the students are too young to complete the activity sheet individually, use one rock and do a demonstration of weight and measurement. Then allow the students to take turns exploring the weight of their rocks on the scales. The rest of the class can be measuring their rocks during this time, or simply finding objects in the classroom that are shorter or longer than their rock. Have the students draw pictures on the "Rock Length" activity sheet.

Extension Ideas

- In expanding on the above lesson, have the students weigh and measure more than one rock. For example, Bobby and Sara's rocks together weigh this much. Jimmy and Laura's rocks are this long when placed together. They can also compare the weight of different rocks on the balance scale. They may also do addition and subtraction problems with the weights of their rocks. As a finale see how much all the rocks in the class weigh together.

- Have the students order all the rocks according to size.

- Have the students make up story problems about rocks. For example, "There are three rocks sitting on a table and one of them rolls off. How many are left?"

©Teacher Created Materials, Inc.

Rock Theme

Name:_____

My Rock

Weight Center

1. My rock weighs _____.

2. My rock weighs more than _____.

3. My rock weighs less than _____.

4. My rock weighs about the same as _____.

Measuring Center

1. My rock is _____ long.

2. My rock is longer than _____.

3. My rock is shorter than _____.

4. My rock is _____ tall.

Rock Theme

Name:_____

My Rock

Objects Shorter Than My Rock	Objects Longer Than My Rock

Rock Theme

Rock Science

Objective
The students will list the three different types of rocks, explain where rocks come from, and identify objects in their environment which are made from rock.

Materials
- a book about rocks, such as *The Magic School Bus Inside the Earth* by Joanna Cole, or information from the **Rock Hounds** Web site
- chart paper or chalkboard
- "What is a Rock?" activity sheet
- a collection of different types of rock, if available, or pictures of different rocks may be used from the Web site mentioned above

Procedure
1. Ask the students to think of items in their environment which are made out of rocks. Typically they will only be able to name a few, if any. List these on the chart paper or blackboard. Next ask them if they know where rocks come from.

2. Read the book or share the information at the Web site. Focus on the facts of how the earth is made of rock and how the three different types of rocks are formed. Sedimentary—settled dust and sand which have been pressed together over time, turning into rock. Metamorphic—one kind of rock has been changed by heat and pressure, turning into a new kind of rock. Igneous rocks—also called fire rocks are formed from melted rock, such as lava, which have cooled. Link the following words together to help the students remember what the three types mean: sedimentary—settle, metamorphic—change, igneous—fire. If real examples of some of these rocks are available, share them. If not, allow the children to view pictures of these different types of rocks in books or on the aforementioned Web site.

3. Also share information on items in our environment which are made from rock. The *Magic School Bus Inside the Earth* contains information on this topic as well as the **Rock Hounds** Web site.

4. Once the book and/or information have been shared, ask the students to add to their list of items made from rock. Include items such as; concrete: chalk, chalkboards, statues, bricks, roads, etc. If possible, go outside and look around for objects made from rock.

5. Pass out the "What is a Rock?" activity sheet. Depending on the age of the class, either complete the activity sheet together or have the students do it independently. Younger students may draw pictures of items made from rock at the bottom of the sheet.

Extension Ideas
- Students can use their pet rocks from the language arts lesson for a science experiment. Have students complete the Pet Rock Experiment activity sheet on page 338.
- Have the students classify their rocks they brought in according to different attributes, such as color, texture, size, etc. This would be most appropriate for younger students. They may determine the characteristics for classification on their own.
- Have the students write observation sheets on their rocks. For example, its color, texture, size, distinguishing features, etc. They may draw a picture to accompany their description. Display the rocks and descriptions in a "Rock Museum."
- Have a lesson on fossils. Use one of the following links for reference: **Fossils and Fossil Collection** or **PaleoZoo**.

Rock Theme

Name:_____

What is a Rock?

1. Match the type of rock with the word that means how it was formed.

   | Change | Settle | Fire |

   Sedimentary _____

   Metamorphic _____

   Igenous _____

2. Where do rocks come from? _____

   _____

   _____

3. List some items in our environment which are made from rock.

   _____

   _____

   _____

Rock Theme

Pet Rock Experiment

Draw a picture of your rock here:

Where did you find your rock?

_____

Check the correct boxes.

My rock is:

☐ SHINY   ☐ SPARKLY   ☐ HARD   ☐ BIG   ☐ ROUGH

☐ DULL   ☐ NOT SPARKLY   ☐ SOFT   ☐ LITTLE   ☐ SMOOTH

Now conduct your experiment. Predict what you think the answers will be and write them down in the first row. After the experiment, write down the results. Compare.

	LENGTH Measure with a ruler.	**WEIGHT** Measure with a scale.	**HARDNESS** Which will scratch your rock?*	**ACID** Does your Rock Bubble when vinegar is dropped on it?**	**FLOATS** Does your rock float or sink?***
PREDICTION					
RESULTS					

Hardness Numbers

* Hardness scale: Fingernail can scratch rock. 2   A soft rock

Penny can scratch rock 3   ↕

Nail can scratch rock 4   A hard rock

** If there are bubbles appearing on your rock, it has lime (or calcium carbonate) in it. This mineral is found in limestone and marble.

*** Rocks that float usually have come out of a volcano. Was the area where you live ever a volcano?

Rock Theme

Rock Social Studies

Objective

The students will locate Mt. Rushmore on a map and be exposed to the history of the monument.

Materials

- a link to the **South Dakota: Mount Rushmore** Web site.
- a book, if available, about Mt. Rushmore, such as *Curious George and the Hot Air Balloon* by Margaret Rey (for younger students) or *Mount Rushmore (Building America)* by Craig A. Hoherty (for older students)
- a map of the United States

Procedure

1. Discuss with the students how mountains are formed from rock. The amount of depth will depend on the age of the students. If appropriate discuss plate tectonics and how the earth's plates have pushed against one another forming the mountains.

2. Introduce the students to one of the famous landmarks in the United States, Mt. Rushmore. Read the chosen book and/or view the above mentioned Web site with the students. Allow them to see pictures of the carvings, etc. Discuss the history and the creation of the monument.

3. Display a map of the United States. Have the students locate South Dakota on the map. Where is South Dakota in relation to the students' home? North, South, East, West? How would the students travel to South Dakota?

4. If time allows, continue the lesson with locating other mountains on the map. Allow each pair of students to pick one of the mountains from the "Mountains in the United States" activity sheet (have the paper cut up and the pieces placed in a container) and locate its home state on the map. The **America's Roof Guide to the Highest Points** Web site may be helpful if more mountains are needed.

Extension Ideas

- Conduct a similar lesson to the above one on the Grand Canyon. **The Encarta Encyclopedia: Grand Canyon** site may be helpful.
- Locate other famous monuments, which are made of rock. For example, the Washington Monument, the Lincoln Memorial, and El Morro (Inscription Rock). Use the **National Park Service** Web site to help with finding other monuments made of rock.
- Have a lesson on how many early tools were made of rock, such as arrowheads.
- Have a local geologist come in and speak about his/her job.

Rock Theme

Mountains in the United States

Granite Peak, Montana

Mt. McKinley, Alaska

Mount Magazine, Arkansas

Mount Whitney, California

Mount Elbert, Colorado

Bear Mountain, Connecticut

Mauna Kea, Hawaii

Borah Peak, Idaho

Black Mountain, Kentucky

Driskill Mountain, Louisiana

Mount Greylock, Massachusetts

Mount Arvon, Michigan

Mt. Rainier, Washington

Rock Art

Objective

The students will paint rocks.

Materials

- rocks (either brought in by the students or provided by the teacher)
- paint and paint brushes

Procedure

1. Have the students use their imaginations and paint on rocks they have brought in from home or found around the school.
2. Display the painted rocks in a "Rock Art Museum."

Extension Ideas

- Create "Rock Collecting Boxes" out of a variety of containers. Shoeboxes, egg carton, etc. The students may decorate these containers to keep their rock collections inside.
- Combine this lesson with the language arts lesson's first Extension Idea. Have each student paint a small rock (or paper cut out of a rock) which will be their "Magic Pebble." After reading *Sylvester and the Magic Pebble* by William Steig, the students will write about the pebble they have designed and write what their wish would be on a magic pebble.

Rock Theme

Rock Movement

Objective

The students will participate in a game of "turn to rock."

Materials

- music
- a wide open space allowing for movement

Procedure

1. Explain to the students that there will be music playing. They should dance and move about while the music is playing. Once the music stops (done by the teacher), they should "turn to rock" by freezing their movement.

Extension Ideas

- Play hopscotch, using a small rock as the marker.
- Play hot potato with a rock.

Snow Theme

Related Web Sites

Snow Crystals
This site has lots of information on snowflakes and snow crystals. Included are actual photographs of snow crystals, information on "designer" snow crystals, and snow crystal FAQs.

All About Snow
This site sponsored by the National Snow and Ice Data Center has a Q&A section, Snow Facts, a Glossary, and a Snow Gallery.

Kids Snow Page
Developed by a homeschooling family, this page includes good information and activities. Included are Snow Science, Activities, Art, Literature, Food, Links, and directions for growing a snowflake in a jar.

Dragonfly Web Pages
This Web site contains a section on Ice and Snow appropriate for kids. It has information on Antarctica, ice and snow facts, directions for making snowflakes, and a list of books on ice and snow.

ChidFun.Com
This page from ChildFun.com contains a variety of craft ideas relating to snow, including snowmen, snowflakes, and snow scenes.

Related Literature

Brave Irene by William Steig
A little girl needs to deliver a special package in a snowstorm.

Flannel Kisses by Linda Crotta Brennan
This is a rhyming book about the adventures of a snowy day.

I am Snow by Jean Marzollo
This easy reader is about snow.

The Jacket I Wear in the Snow by Shirley Netizel
This book builds on a simple phrase with repetitive language. A fun read-aloud.

Snip, Snip...Snow! by Nancy Poydar
A little girl anticipates the first snowfall. She and her class create paper snowflakes only to discover a real snowfall has begun!

Snow Crystals by W.A. Bentley
A good reference book on snow crystals, this book includes photographs of actual snowflakes.

Snow is Falling by Franklyn M. Branley
This is a simple nonfiction book about snow and how it affects nature.

Sugar Snow (My First Little House Books) by Laura Ingalls Wilder
Laura learns that a late Spring snowfall will help the trees produce more sap for maple syrup.

When it Starts to Snow by Phillis Gershator
A series of animals answer the question of what they do when it snows.

White Snow Bright Snow by Alvin Tresselt
This is the classic story of a late winter snow.

Snow Theme

Snow Language Arts

Objective
The students will write about their adventures on a snowy day.

Materials
- two or three books about adventures on snowy days (Some examples would be *The Snowy Theme* by Ezra Jack Keats, *Emmett's Snowball* by Ned Miller, *Flannel Kisses* by Linda Crotta Brennan, *The Wild Toboggan Ride* by Suzan Reid, *Snow Dance* by Lezlie Evans, or *The Snowman* by Raymond Briggs.)
- paper and writing utensils

Procedure
1. Read the chosen books to the class. Have a discussion on the differences between the stories as well as how they were alike.
2. Have the students write their own stories (fiction or nonfiction) about their adventures on a snowy day.
3. If time permits, have the students share their writing with the rest of the class.

Extension Ideas
- Have the students write directions for making a creation in the snow, such as a snowball, snowman, snow angel, etc.
- Have a lesson on metaphors, using "blanket of snow" as a starting point.
- Conduct a lesson on compound words, using snowball and snowman as a starting point. Give each child a white circle made of paper (a snowball) with half of a compound word written on it. They will then need to find the classmate who has the other half of the compound word written on their "snowball."

Snow Theme

Snow Math

(This lesson is to be combined with the Snow Social Studies lesson.)

Objective

The students will measure different heights and arrange them in ascending order.

Materials

- measuring tapes or rulers
- pieces of string
- information from the **Average Snowfalls** Web site

Procedure

1. Decide ahead of time which of the cities and which month will be used from the **Average Snowfalls** site. Pick as many cities as appropriate for your class. There may be one city per student, pair of students, or a few cities for the entire class to do together.

2. Give each student, or pair of students, a piece of paper with a city and the average snowfall written on it. Have the students measure a piece of string to the length of the average snowfall and tape the name of their city and the inches of snow onto the string.

3. Convene as a class and work to arrange the strings in ascending order. Tape the pieces of string to the wall (with the bottom of the string touching the floor) to clearly illustrate the snow averages.

4. As a further expansion, ask questions such as "Which city has the greatest/least average snowfall?" or "What is the snowfall for city A and city B combined?," etc.

Extension Ideas

- If it has recently snowed in your region of the world, try the "Measure Snow" activity on page 346.
- Graph the students' favorite snowy day activity—sledding, making a snowman, making a snow angel, etc.
- Have a lesson on the number six, since snow crystals have six sides.

Snow Theme

Measure Snow

Try this activity if it has snowed recently in your region of the world. If you live in a warmer climate, try using crushed ice instead!

Materials

clear 8 oz. measuring cups; balances or utility scales

Directions

1. Go outside and measure 1 cup of snow. Bring it inside.
2. How much does it weigh?

   It weighs _____.
3. Set it on a table to melt.
4. How much water is in the cup?

   One cup of snow equals _____ cups of water.
5. Weigh the cup of water (melted snow).

   It weighs _____.
6. Did the weight change when it melted?

Challenge

Try to find out if a loose cupful of snow weighs the same as a tightly packed cupful of snow.

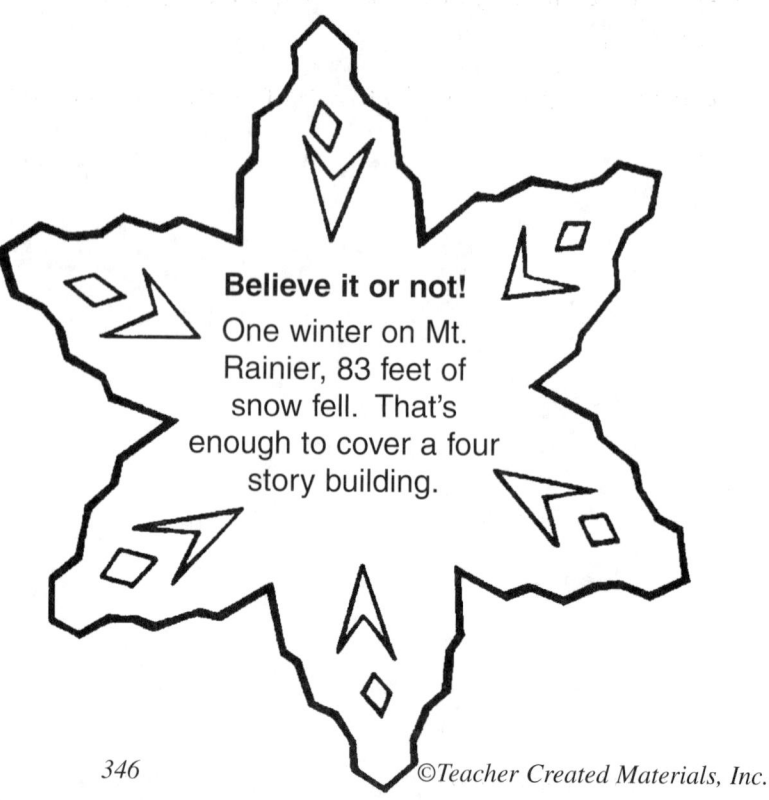

Believe it or not! One winter on Mt. Rainier, 83 feet of snow fell. That's enough to cover a four story building.

Snow Theme

Snow Science

Objective
The students will draw and label a picture of the water cycle.

Materials
- books or Web sites containing information on the water cycle (The following Web sites may be helpful: **Water Science for Schools** and **Kidzone**.)
- "Why Does it Snow?" water cycle activity sheet

Procedure
1. Ask the students if they know why it snows. Write down their responses.
2. Lead the discussion to the water cycle and read the chosen book or share the information from one of the aforementioned Web sites.
3. Pass out the "Why Does it Snow?" activity sheet and have the students complete the sheet.

Extension Ideas
- If it's snowing on this day, go outside and look at snowflakes through magnifying glasses. This activity works best if the snowflakes are caught on a dark object, such as black construction paper.
- Have a temperature lesson, emphasizing the average temperatures for different seasons. Discuss the proper clothing for different temperatures as well as the freezing point. Divide a sheet of paper into four squares. Have the students write the average temperature for each season and draw a picture of themselves wearing the proper clothing.
- Have a lesson on animal tracks which can be made in the snow. Reference the Pig Science lesson for ideas.
- Create a water cycle in the classroom using the **National Wildlife Federation** Web site.

Snow Theme

Name:_____

Why does it snow?

The water cycle!

Draw a picture of the water cycle. Label your picture using these three words: evaporation, condensation, precipitation.

Snow Theme

Snow Social Studies

(This lesson is to be combined with the Snow Math lesson.)

Objective

The students will locate different cities on a map.

Materials

- information from the **Average Snowfalls** Web site

- pieces of paper with the name of a city/state and the average snowfall written on it for the decided-upon month, one piece per student or pair of students (These pieces of paper should be in a container from which the students may draw. Try to pick a variety of cities, representing both large and small average snowfalls.)

- a large map of the United States

- three different colors of small post-it™ notes or pieces of construction paper—white, light blue, and green, for example (The size of the paper will depend on the size of the map being used. For a typical large classroom map, use a piece of paper approximately ½" square. If the map is on a bulletin board, use color-coded push pins instead of paper.)

- tape

Procedure

1. As in the math lesson, have the students pick a piece of paper containing a city/state and its average snowfall.

2. Decide as a class what the key for the map will be as far as colors of paper (or pushpins) representing the average snowfalls. For example, cities with an average snowfall of 5" or less = green paper, 5–10" = light blue paper, and 10" or greater = white paper.

3. Have the students take turns reading the name of their city and the average snowfall. Work together as a class to locate the cities on the large map. The students will then select the proper color paper and attach it to the map on their city's location.

4. Once each student has had a turn, interpret the map. What parts of the country seem to have the greater average snowfalls? Which parts have the least?

Extension Ideas

- Use **The Snow Book** Web site to look further into United States' snowfall patterns.

- Find the average snowfall for the students' home city.

- Find the record snowfall for the students' home city. What year was it? Make a time line showing other events in relation to the record snowfall.

Snow Theme

Snow Art

Objective
The students will create snow scenes.

Materials
- dark colored construction paper, such as black or dark blue
- white chalk, paint, colored pencils, or crayons

Procedure
1. Pass out the paper. Have the students choose which form of medium they would like to use—the chalk, paint, pencils or crayons. They may also pick a combination of the mediums.
2. Allow the students time to create a snow scene using the medium they have chosen.
3. As a variation, have the students create a large mural snow scene. Put up a large piece of dark butcher paper. Have the students work together to create the scene using the mediums of their choice.

Extension Ideas
- Make snow flakes by cutting out folded white paper.
- Have the students create snowmen out of a variety of art materials—paper, fabric, buttons, craft sticks, etc.
- Make a large "hill of snow" using butcher paper and hang it on the wall. Have the students craft a figure of themselves sledding or skiing down the hill. They may use paper, fabric, craft sticks, etc. Once everyone has completed their figure, attach them to your classroom "hill of snow."
- Have the students use cotton balls to create snowy scenes.

Snow Theme

Snow Movement

Objective

The students will imitate different activities which are normally done in the snow.

Materials

- A large open area allowing for movement
- Different types of music—slow, soft music as well as fast-paced music

Procedure

1. Brainstorm with the students all the different activities which can be done in the snow—making a snowman, catching snowflakes on your tongue, snowball fights, sledding, skiing, etc.

2. Play the slow, soft music and have the students act out different "quiet" snow activities, such as catching snowflakes on the tongue or making a snow angel.

3. Play the fast-paced music and have the students act out the "noisier" snow activities, such as sledding, skiing, or having a snowball fight.

Extension Idea

- If there is snow on the ground, go outside and play in it!

©Teacher Created Materials, Inc. #3823 Internet Activities Through the Year

Spider Theme

Related Web Sites

The Young Entomologist Society
This site has information on spiders as well as other kinds of insects. It includes a Minibeast Museum, Teacher's Tower, Garden Gazebo, Youth Center, Research Library, and more.

Discovery.Com—Spiders!
This site has lots of good information and excellent photographs from a spider expedition. The "Up Close With Spiders" page allows you to learn the location and function of a spider's body parts.

Arachnology for Kids
This page has a list of links to other spider Web sites for kids. It includes general spider links as well as links to lesson plans and activities for *Charlotte's Web*.

Southwest Educational Development Laboratory—Spiders
This is a fantastic resource for lesson plans on spiders. Lesson titles include Spiders! Scary or Nice?, Spiders Have Special Characteristics, Spiders Catch Prey, The Spider's Life Cycle, Spiders Have Natural Enemies, Spiders Live Everywhere, and Now We Know Spiders! There are also links to other spider resources on the Internet.

I Love Spiders
This is a unit plan to be used with the book *I Love Spiders* by John Parker. There are art ideas with pictures included, spider songs, poetry, and links to other sites.

Science Learning Network
This page has information on how to make a "spider glider."

Bonus.Com
This link leads to a page with basic information on spiders and their webs. It includes information on the different types of spider webs, web experiments, and a 3-D view of the mouth of a spider.

Related Literature

The Adventures of Spider: West African Folktales by Joyce Cooper Arkhurst
The Anasi stories in this book are good for lessons on folktales.

Anasi Goes Fishing by Eric Kimmel
Anansi the spider is tricked by a turtle.

Are You a Spider? by Judy Allen and Tudor Humphries
This simple book is written to highlight the basic characteristics of spiders.

Be Nice to Spiders by Margaret Bloom Graham
What happens to the zoo when they clean out all the spider webs? This classic book teaches the good that spiders do.

The Very Busy Spider by Eric Carle
This is an engaging story with repetitive text for young children.

I Wonder What It's Like to Be a Spider by Erin M. Hovane
This story has good factual information and photographs.

The Magic School Bus Spins a Web by Joanna Cole
Ms. Frizzle's class learns all about spiders!

Miss Spider Book Series by David Kirk
This series is best suited for younger children.

Spider Theme

Spider Language Arts

Objective

The students will write a story focusing on the elements of setting, characters, and plot.

Materials

- three paper plates with spinners—made with paper plates, paper fasteners, and tag board arrows for spinners
- paper and writing utensils
- "Spinning a Tale" activity sheet (for older students)
- a story containing a spider (optional)

Procedure

1. Make the spinners ahead of time. One of the spinners should have settings for stories on it, another should contain characters, and the last should have general plots on it.
   - Examples of characters: spider, fly, and horse; or spider, the child, a giant
   - Examples of settings: a farm, a child's house, a forest
   - Examples of plots: meeting for the first time, finding a magic rock, sharing a toy

2. Have a discussion on the elements of a story—setting, characters, and plot. If desired, read a story containing a spider and identify the different elements.

3. Allow each student to have a turn spinning the 3 spinners. Use the term "spinning a tale." For younger students, work as a class to spin the spinners and make a whole-class story, which can be recorded on chart paper.

4. Older students may record their elements on the "Spinning a Tale" activity sheet.

5. Based on the elements the students have spun, they should then write a story.

6. Younger students may draw pictures of the story once the teacher has recorded the story on chart paper.

Extension Ideas

- Start reading *Charlotte's Web* by E.B. White.
- Read a book containing a spider and make a story web of what happened in the book.
- Read any of the *Anansi the Spider* books and discuss legends and oral tradition.

Spider Theme

Name: _____

Spinning a Tale

Setting: _____

_____

Characters: _____

_____

Plot: _____

_____

_____

Spider Theme

Spider Math

Objective

The students will use manipulatives to complete addition and subtraction problems involving the number eight.

Materials

- small pieces of clay or Play Dough™ (Each student or pair of students should have enough to make a 1–2" ball.)
- eight toothpicks per student or pair of students
- "Spider Leg Math" activity sheet

Procedure

1. Give each student, or pair of students, a piece of clay and eight toothpicks.
2. Discuss how spiders have eight legs.
3. Have the students roll their clay into bodies for the spiders. They may want to roll two pieces—one for the head and one for the body.
4. The toothpicks will serve as the legs. The teacher may give the students age-appropriate math problems. The students should then use the legs to figure out the answers. For example, "Your spiders only have 4 legs, then they grow 4 more. How many do they have altogether?" "Your spiders have 8 legs, 2 fell off. How many are left?" Older students may work with adding three numbers together, or even multiplying by eight by joining their spiders with other students'.
5. The "Spider Leg Math" activity sheet may be used to record some of the problems the students are given, or for recording their own problems.

Extension Idea

- Have a measurement lesson in which comparisons are made between spiders which can be as small as pencil points, all the way up to tarantulas which can have a 10" leg span. The students may also use 10" spans to measure distances. This would be a good lesson in counting by tens.

Spider Theme

Name: _____

Spider Leg Math

Write math problems which include the number 8.

1. _____

   _____

   _____

2. _____

   _____

   _____

3. _____

   _____

   _____

4. _____

   _____

   _____

5. _____

   _____

   _____

6. _____

   _____

   _____

7. _____

   _____

   _____

8. _____

   _____

   _____

Spider Theme

Spider Science

Objective

The students will record facts about spiders.

Materials

- a collection of nonfiction books and Web sites on spiders such as *Spiders* by Gail Gibbons, *Spiders Are Not Insects (Rookie Read-About Science)* by Allan Fowler, *Spider's Lunch: All About Garden Spiders* by Joanna Cole, *Tarantulas* by Louise Martin, and *Do All Spiders Spin Webs?* by Melvin and Gilda Berger (See the Related Literature and Related Web Sites on the Spider Theme page for more ideas.)

- eight strips of paper per student, pair of students, or the whole class to record the spider facts (Whether they work individually, in pairs, or as a class will depend on the level of the students.)

- two circles of paper per student, pair of students, or whole class to form the body and head of the spider

Procedure

1. Depending on the age of the students and the amount of resources available, either read and share facts from the books and Web sites, or allow them to gather information on their own.

2. Direct the students to gather eight facts about spiders, either individually, in pairs, or as a whole class. Four of the facts should come from books and four of the facts should come from Web sites.

3. The students should record the facts on the strips of paper (to act as spider legs). Younger students may dictate facts to the teacher to be recorded on one spider created by the whole class.

4. Once the facts are recorded, the students may assemble their spiders by attaching the legs, heads, and bodies with either glue or tape.

5. If time allows, have the students share their spider facts with the rest of the class.

Extension Ideas

- Have the students observe real spiders. These may either be brought in from home, collected outside on the school grounds, or brought in by the teacher.

- Have a lesson on predators, prey, and the food chain.

- List how spiders are good for the environment.

- Have a lesson on names for young animals, such as spider—spiderling, pig—piglet, cow—calf, etc.

- Compare arachnids to insects.

- Have a lesson on all the different types of spider webs.

- Allow the students to pick a type of spider and do some research on that type.

Spider Theme

Spider Social Studies

Objective

The students will identify different types of homes and transportation.

Materials

- a book about spiders, such as *Spiders* by Gail Gibbons, which contains information on types of webs and "ballooning," a form of transportation young spiders use to move to new homes

- if desired, a link to one of the following sites which contains ballooning information: **The Wild Side**, or **Up, Up and Away**, or **Bonus.com**, which contains some basic information on different types of spider webs

- "Spiders, People, Homes, and Transportation" activity sheet

Procedure

1. Read the chosen book or share information from a Web site on different types of spider webs and ballooning.

2. Relate this to people and different types of homes and transportation. Ask the students to brainstorm different types of homes for people. Record their responses on chart paper or the chalkboard. For example, houses, apartments, houseboats, igloos, etc.

3. Discuss how people use different types of transportation to reach their homes, cars, buses, boats, planes, trains, etc. Again, record responses on the chart paper or chalkboard.

4. For reinforcement, have the students complete the "Spiders, People, Homes, and Transportation" activity sheet. Younger students may draw pictures in the appropriate boxes and older students may make lists.

Extension Ideas

- Discuss how some people are afraid of spiders and have a lesson on fears.

- Spiders lived before the dinosaur—create a time line.

- Have a lesson on oral tradition, using the *Anansi the Spider* stories as an example.

Name:_____

Spiders, People, Homes, and Transportation

Spider Homes	People Homes
Spider Transportation	**People Transportation**

Spider Theme

Spider Art

Objective

The students will create spider webs and spiders using a variety of materials.

Materials

- black construction paper
- glue
- white yarn or string
- construction paper, pipe cleaners, or any variety of materials to create a spider

Procedure

1. Have the students create a spider web by using glue and white yarn or string on black (or any other dark-colored) construction paper. (If this process is too difficult for younger students, have them draw a web on black construction paper using a white crayon or chalk.) With older students discuss the different types of webs, such as a funnel web, a triangle web, and an orb web.

2. While the web is drying, have the students create a spider out of any of the offered materials.

3. When both pieces are dry, have the students glue their spider into the web.

Extension Ideas

- As a variation on the above lesson, working together as a class, create a large spider web out of yarn or string on a dark piece of butcher paper. The students may then create their own spiders to place in the web.

- Paint paper plates black and put notches around the perimeter. The students may then wrap white yarn or string around the plate (securing the yarn in the notches) to create a web.

- Use the following Web site to create spider gliders: **Science Learning Network**.

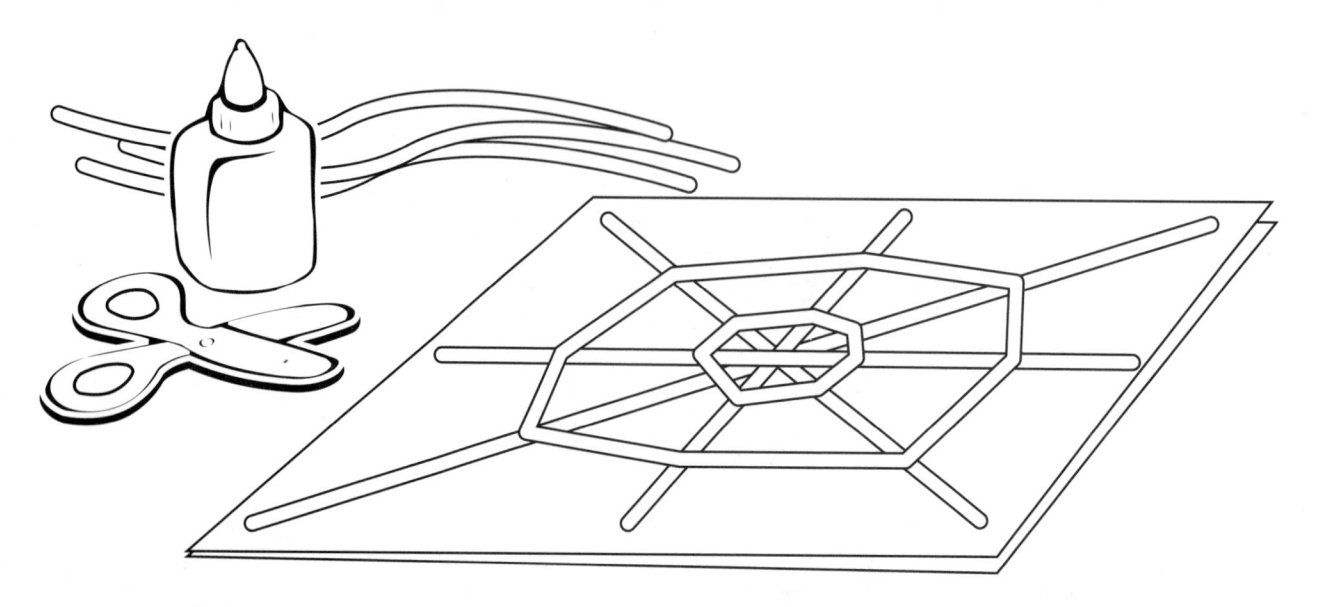

Spider Theme

Spider Movement

Objective
The students will move to music.

Materials
- a wide open space allowing for movement
- if available, a recording of the "Tarantella" (Spider Dance) (There are many different recordings available—from Chopin to Gottschalk. Conduct a search in the **Amazon.com** Music Store on the Tarantella.)
- if a Taratnella recording is not available, any fast-paced classical music piece

Procedure
1. Explain to the students the story/legend behind the Tarantella dance. There was once a boy in Italy named Tony who was bitten by a poisonous Tarantula. His mother acted quickly and had the village musician play a fast-paced tune. Tony was made to dance until he fell covered with perspiration. He did not die and it is believed that perspiring during the fast-paced dance flushed the poisons from his body.
2. Play the selected piece of music and have the students dance quickly about the room and "collapse" from exhaustion at the end of the music.

Extension Ideas
- Play a game in which some students are spiders and other are flies. Have the spiders try and "capture" the flies.
- Make a large spider web by having all the students position themselves in a circle. Using a ball of yarn or string, have the students "spin a web" around themselves, experimenting with different designs and techniques.

Star Theme

Related Web Sites

The Constellations and Their Stars
This is a good reference site for different constellations. It includes photos, Frequently Asked Questions, constellations listed alphabetically and by month, and stars listed alphabetically and by bright star catalog number. It is most appropriate for teacher reference.

Astronomy.Com
This online magazine includes a section for kids, as well as a teacher section. It includes news, featured stories, and a picture of the day.

StarChild
This page from StarChild.com has content about stars written for children. It includes information about different kinds of stars and an audio recording of a song about stars.

Stars
This site has sophisticated information and is most appropriate for teacher reference. Good pictures of different constellations can be found here.

The Constellations
The Constellations has information on the mythology behind all 88 constellations with pictures outlining the actual formations.

Astronomy for Kids
This is a great site for simple pictures and descriptions of the constellations, plus information on the stars. Go to the Virtual Telescope to see planets and constellations.

Match the Constellation
This online matching game is an easy one for kids. They drag and drop to match the constellations with their names.

Related Literature

The Stars by Patrick Moore
This is a basic book of stars and constellations.

Where's the Big Dipper? by Sidney Rosen
Learn the history of constellations and how to find them on your own.

The Magic School Bus Sees Stars (Scholastic)
Ms. Frizzle and her class journey into space to learn all about stars.

Constellations: A True Book by Paul P. Sipiera
More for teachers than for students, this is best used as a reference book.

Stars and Galaxies: Looking Beyond the Solar System by Miquel Perez
This is an informational book on stars.

There are 508 Stars in the Sky by Marky Allen
Two girls sit in the backyard and count the stars.

Sky is Full of Stars by Franklyn Branley
Good information on the sky and its stars.

The Sun: Our Very Own Star by Jeanne Bendick
A basic book on the star we call our sun.

Star Theme

Star Language Arts

Objective
The students will write a story about a star constellation they have developed in the Star Art lesson.

Materials
- a book containing information on the constellations and how people have given them names (*Our Stars* by Anne Rockwell or *Stars* by Jennifer Dussling are good choices. If these books are not available use **The Constellation Web Page** for information on the mythology of constellations. Or for easier-to-view constellations with simple names, use the **Virtual Telescope** Web site.
- the constellation the students have developed in the art lesson (If these lessons are not to be combined, allow the students to draw their own constellation on a piece of black paper with white crayon.)
- paper and writing utensils

Procedure
1. Read the chosen book or review some of the constellations and their names with the students at one of the above mentioned sites.
2. Discuss how constellations are groupings for stars, which have been given a name. Some of these constellations have stories behind their names.
3. The students should write a story about the constellations they have developed. What's the name of it? What is the story behind the constellation? The depth of the writings will depend on the age of the students.
4. Allow the students to share their constellation and it's accompanying story with the class. Display these around the classroom or in the hallway.

Extension Ideas
- Read a book containing a legend about how the stars got in the sky, such as *How the Stars Fell into the Sky: A Navajo Legend* by Jerrie Oughton or *Coyote Places the Stars* by Harriet Peck Taylor. Have a lesson on what a legend is and if appropriate, have the students write their own fictional stories for how the stars were placed in the sky.
- Have the students complete the story starter, "One night I saw a shooting star and wished for. . . ."
- Have a phonics lesson on the "st-" blend.

Star Theme

Star Math

Objective
The students will count by fives.

Materials
- star shapes
- pencils

Procedure
1. Show the students a picture of a star shape. Discuss how the star has five points.
2. Pass out the star shapes. (Decide ahead of time how many stars each child receives—younger children may need two stars to practice counting by 10s. Older students may be given more stars to practice counting higher by fives, or even doing some multiplication problems.)
3. Have the students write the numbers 1–5 on each of their star points (each point should be labeled with one number). If they have more than one star, they should label each of them 1–5, except if the decision has been made to work with 10s. If so, have the students label their two stars with the numbers 1–10.
4. The students will now be able to practice counting by fives or tens. How many star points do three students have? How many are there in the whole class? With older students lessons may be done with multiplication. To find the answer of how many points three stars have, use the problem 3 x 5 = 15.

Extension Ideas
- Make color patterns with small foil star stickers.
- Have a geometry lesson on how two triangles can be used to make a 6-pointed star.
- Challenge the students to design a game in which they use a large star with each point labeled with a number 1–5 and a die.
- Fill a piece of paper with hand-drawn stars, or star stickers. Have the students estimate how many stars are on the paper. Then count the stars and see how close the estimates are!

Star Theme

Star Science

Objective

The students will list facts about stars.

Materials

- a nonfiction book about stars or information from the **AstroKids** Web site.
- chart paper or chalkboard
- "Star Shape" activity sheet, one per student
- black butcher paper

Procedure

1. Ask the students what they know about stars. List their responses on the chart paper or chalkboard.
2. Read the chosen nonfiction book or share information from the above Web site.
3. Ask the students anything new they have learned about stars and list those on the paper as well.
4. For reinforcement pass out the "Star Shape" activity sheet and have each student list a star fact on the paper. Attach these star facts to a blank piece of butcher paper in a random design, or in the form of a constellation.

Extension Idea

- Have an in-depth lesson on the sun, Earth's closest star.

Star Theme

Star Shape

Star Theme

Star Social Studies

Objective

The students will follow directions for locating items in a given area.

Materials

- information from the **Stellar Scenes: Ursa Minor** Web site
- index cards posted in the classroom, labeling the directions North, South, East, and West
- maps labeled with North, South, East, and West or information from the **Maps.com Cardinal Directions** Web site.
- "Cardinal Directions" activity sheet (for older students)

Procedure

1. Have a discussion with the students on how people have used stars to guide their way. In particular the North Star has been used to help people traveling north. Share the above link with the students illustrating Polaris (the north star) and where it is in the Little Dipper.

2. Point out to the students where the labels have been placed in the classroom, showing the cardinal directions North, South, East, and West.

3. Relate for the students how these directions are used on maps. Share an example of a map, which has cardinal directions on it. The **Maps.com Cardinal Directions** site would be helpful.

4. Play a game with the students in which they stand up and have to follow oral directions for moving about the classroom. For example, "Take two steps north," "Take three steps east," etc.

5. Older students may complete the "Cardinal Directions" activity sheet.

6. Younger students may continue to play the game in pairs. They may each take turns giving directions to each other to reach a destination in the classroom.

Extension Ideas

- Read *Follow the Drinking Gourd* by Jeanette Winter. This is a story of how slaves would follow the "Drinking Gourd" (big dipper) to reach freedom in the north. Have a lesson on slavery.

- Discuss the use of stars on the American Flag and what they stand for.

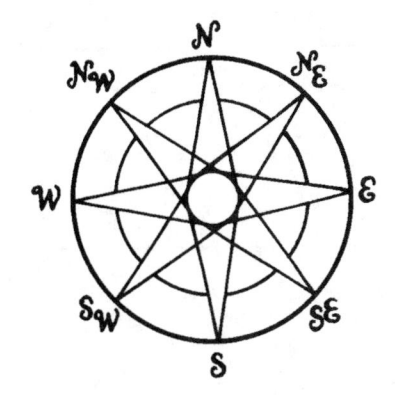

Star Theme

Name:_____

Cardinal Directions

Here are directions from the _____ to

the _____.

1. _____

2. _____

3. _____

4. _____

5. _____

6. _____

7. _____

Star Theme

Star Art

Objective
The students will design a constellation of stars.

Materials
- black construction paper
- white paint, white crayons, or white chalk
- information from the **Astronomy for Kids** Web site, which has pictures of some simple constellations.

Procedure
1. Share the link listed above so the students can have some visuals of different constellations.
2. Discuss with the students how they will be designing their own constellation by using a series of dots.
3. Pass out the materials and allow the students to design their own constellation on the black paper. If desired, proceed to the Language Arts Lesson to combine the two objectives.

Extension Ideas
- As a variation of the above lesson, have the students poke holes through black construction paper to create constellations. These may then be placed on an overhead projector to display their constellations or mounted on white or yellow paper for the "stars" to shine through.
- Work as a whole class on a large piece of black butcher paper to create a night sky using white paint, chalk, or crayons.
- Allow the students to put silver or yellow glitter on star shapes and hang them from the ceiling.

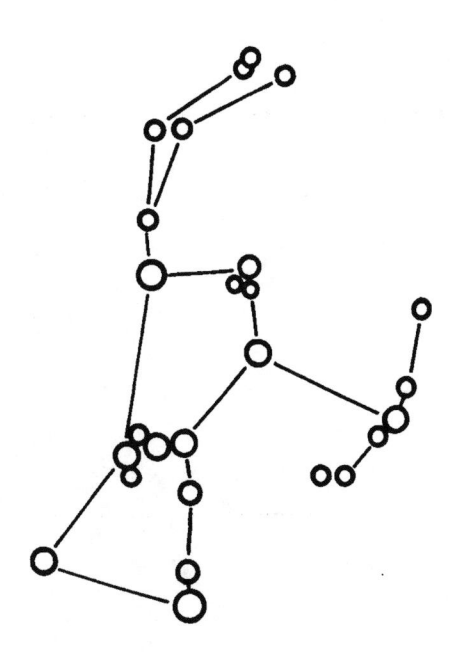

Star Theme

Star Movement

Objective

The students will move as shooting stars.

Materials

- a large open space allowing for movement
- classical music

Procedure

1. Have a discussion with the students about shooting stars and how they fall quickly across the sky.
2. Play some classical music and have the students imitate shooting stars moving across the sky.

Extension Ideas

- Have the students arrange themselves into some common constellations such as the big dipper.
- Go outside and chalk star shapes on the pavement. Have the students hop from star to star.

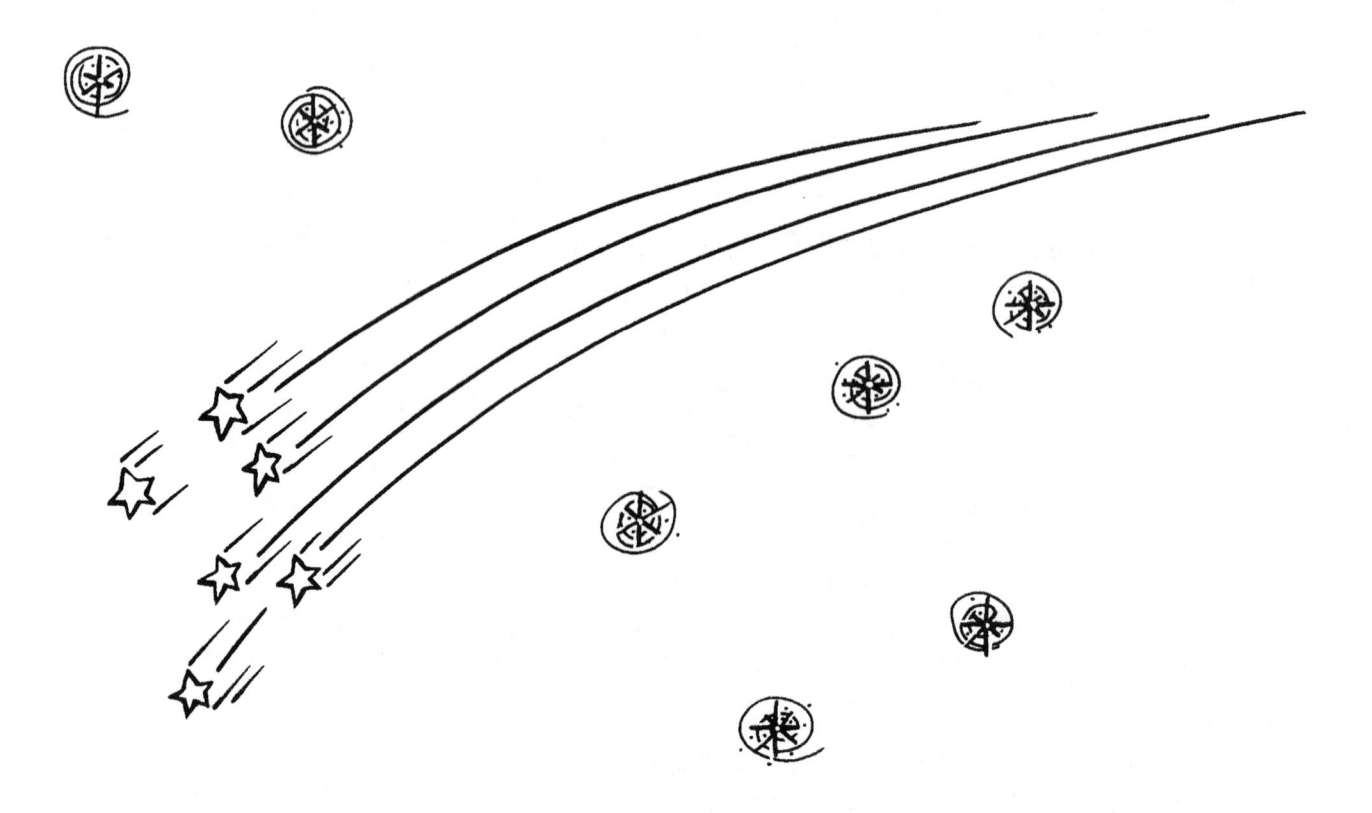

Tooth Theme

Related Web Sites

ADHA Kids' Stuff
The American Dental Hygienists Association has answers to commonly asked questions, games, and lots of information. Included are links and facts for kids.

Crestsmiles
This site from Crest toothpaste has information and online activities for children on proper oral care. Included are games and professional resources.

The Wisdom Tooth
The Wisdom Tooth has information on teeth and proper dental hygiene. Included are topics such as Wisdom Teeth, Brushing Tips and Flossing Tips, and Oral Heath Concerns.

The Magic School Bus—Brushing Up
This page has games and information about teeth, such as "Brushing Up" and "Arnold's Great Tooth Exploration."

Colgate's No Cavity Clubhouse
This site has more games and information on teeth. Included is a brushing chart to print and complete, a story book to read and color online, games to play, and facts to learn.

Related Literature

Franklin and the Tooth Fairy by Paulette Bourgeois
Franklin the Turtle learns it's alright to be different, since he doesn't have any teeth!

How Many Teeth by Paul Showers
This simple book has information and rhymes on teeth. Most appropriate for kindergarten.

I Know Why I Brush My Teeth by Kate Rowan
A mother and son have a discussion on why it's important to brush teeth—good information presented in a fun way.

Madlenka by Peter Sis
When a little girl discovers her tooth wiggles, she simply must tell everyone. In the process, she has a trip around the world which helps her figure out where she fits in. A good book to use for a social studies lesson.

Nice Try, Tooth Fairy by Mary W. Olson
When Mary asks the tooth fairy to give her tooth back, the fairy makes mistakes and brings her various animal teeth.

Open Wide Tooth School Inside by Laurie Keller
This delightful book has terrific information about teeth presented in a humorous way. Most appropriate for older children in order to get the humor.

Throw Your Tooth on the Roof: Tooth Traditions from Around the World by Selby B. Beeler
Learn traditions from around the world for teeth which have fallen out—another good book for a social studies lesson.

Tooth Decay and Cavities by Dr. Alvin Silverstein, et. al.
This nonfiction book is filled with real photographs and answers to lots of questions regarding teeth.

Tooth Truth: Fun Facts & Projects by Jennifer Storey Gillis
This activity book has plenty of hands-on ideas for tooth-related projects.

Tooth Theme

Tooth Language Arts

Objective
The students will write instructions for the proper way to brush their teeth.

Materials
- a book (or a discussion) about the proper way to brush teeth
- "How an Alien Should Brush His Teeth" activity sheet
- "Toothbrush Pattern," "Tooth Pattern," and "Mouth Pattern"

Procedure
1. Read the chosen book or have an open discussion about how to brush teeth. Use the Toothbrush, Tooth, and Mouth patterns as visual aids. Tell the student that an alien from another planet has landed (who happens to have teeth) and he needs a lesson in how to brush them properly.

2. Brainstorm with the students the steps that would need to be written down so the alien would know how to brush his teeth. For example, turning on the water, putting the toothpaste on the brush, using a circular motion on all teeth for at least two minutes, rinsing with water, etc.

3. Pass out the activity sheets and have the children write the steps for proper brushing. The age of the students will dictate whether they do this independently or copy the steps off the class list which was made on the chalkboard or chart paper.

Extension Ideas
- Have students make the "Happy Teeth" big book on pages 377 through 382.

- Write letters to the tooth fairy.

- Give the story starter "One night the tooth fairy woke me up and asked me to fill in for her for the rest of the night…" or "One day I heard voices coming from the inside of my head. Boy, was I surprised when I realized my teeth were talking to me!"

- Discuss what it it like to lose a tooth and what students think the tooth fairy might do with the teeth she collects. Some good books to read for this discussion are *Andrew's Loose Tooth* by Robert Munsch, *Arthur's Tooth* by Marc Brown, *Tooth Fairy* by Audrey Wood, and *What Do the Fairies Do With All Those Teeth?* by Michel Luppens.

- Have the students write accounts of how they lost one of their teeth (or make up an exciting way they would like to lose a tooth). Have the style of writing mimic that of a newspaper article. Read some short newspaper articles to relay the style of news report writing. They must think of a headline, i.e., "Boy Loses Tooth in Carmel Apple!"

- Do a phonics lesson on the "oo" sound.

Tooth Theme

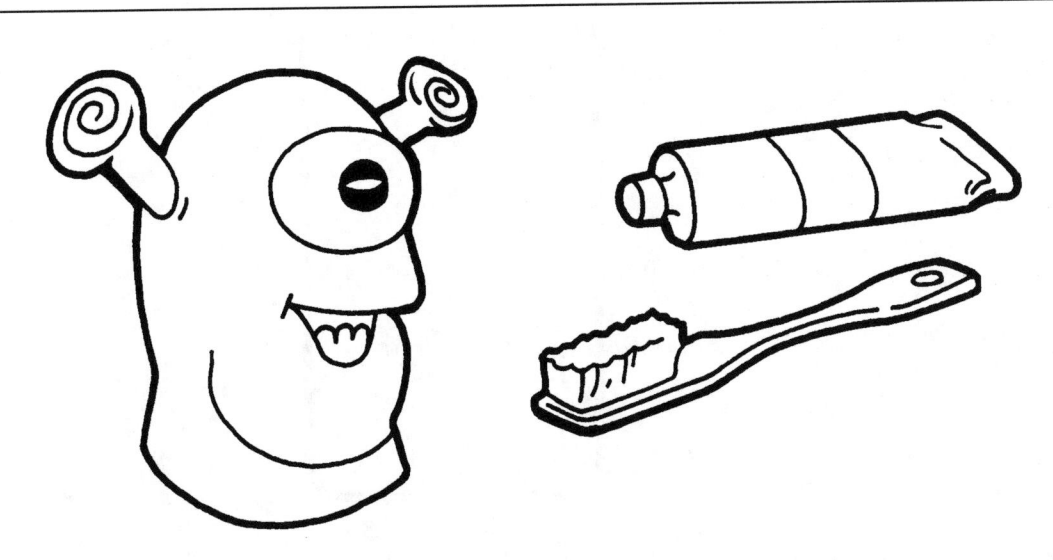

Name: _____

How an Alien Should Brush His Teeth

1. _____
   _____
   _____

2. _____
   _____
   _____

3. _____
   _____

©Teacher Created Materials, Inc. #3823 Internet Activities Through the Year

Tooth Theme

Toothbrush Pattern

Tooth Theme

Tooth Pattern

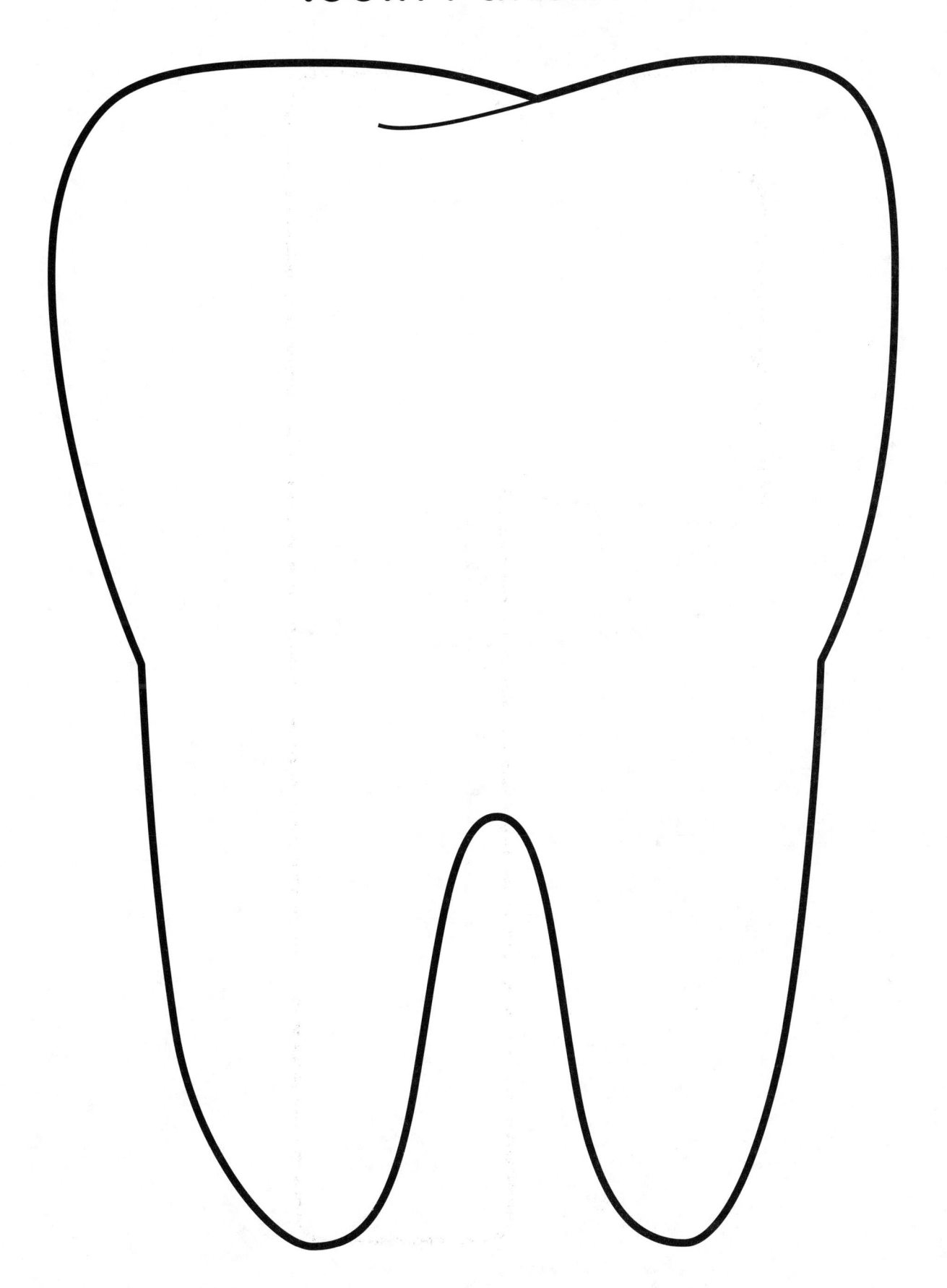

©*Teacher Created Materials, Inc.* #3823 *Internet Activities Through the Year*

Tooth Theme

Mouth Pattern

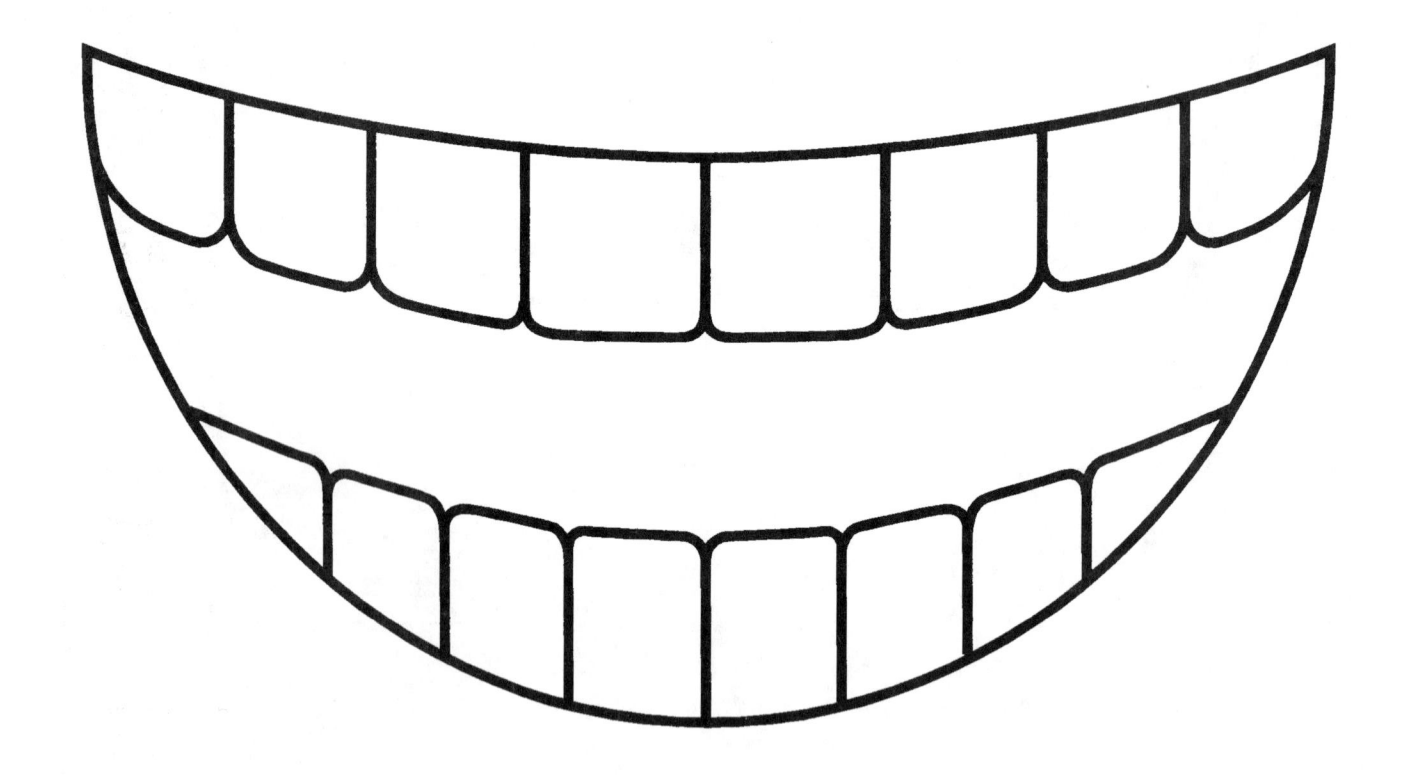

#3823 Internet Activities Through the Year 376 ©Teacher Created Materials, Inc.

Tooth Theme

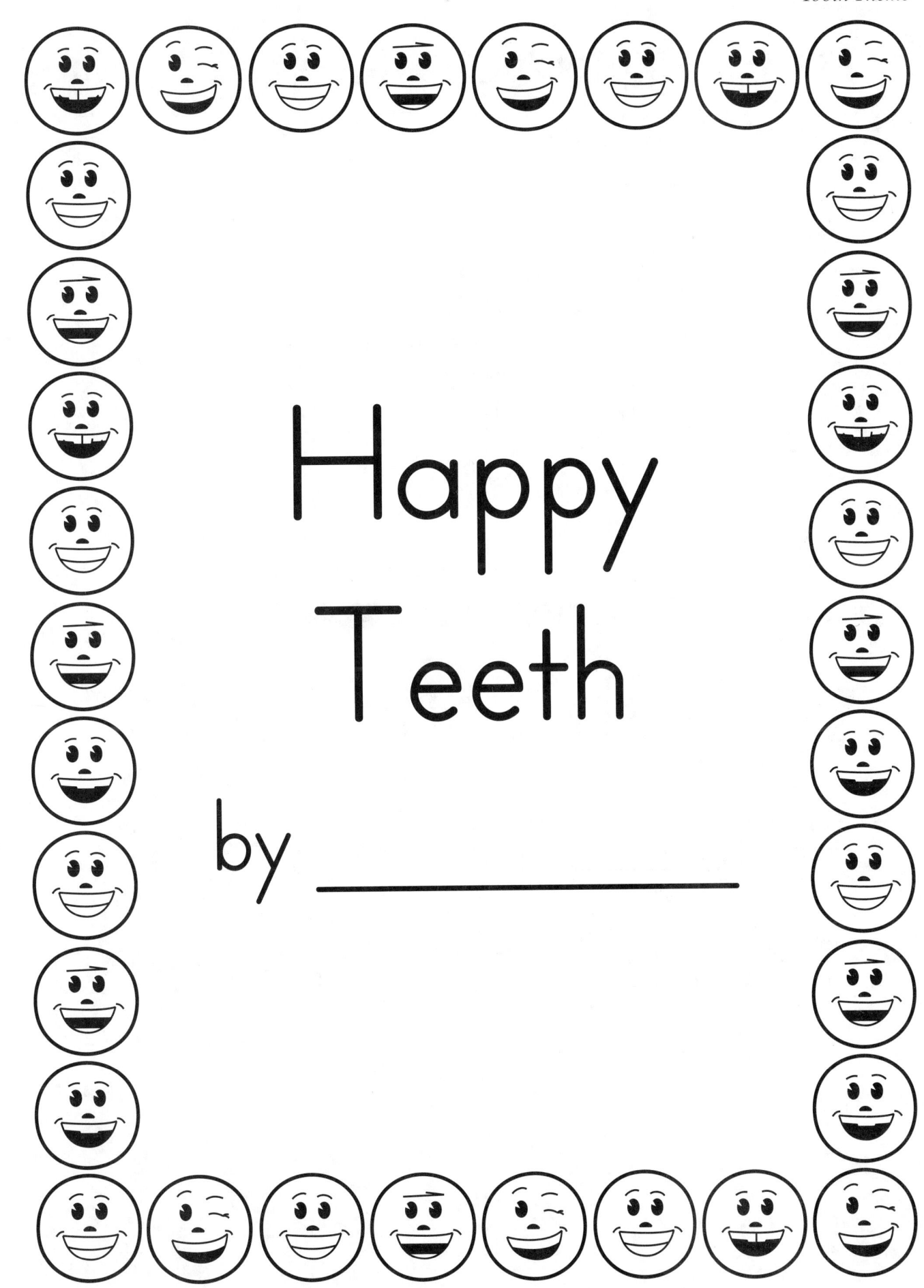

Happy Teeth

by _____

©Teacher Created Materials, Inc.   377   #3823 Internet Activities Through the Year

Tooth Theme

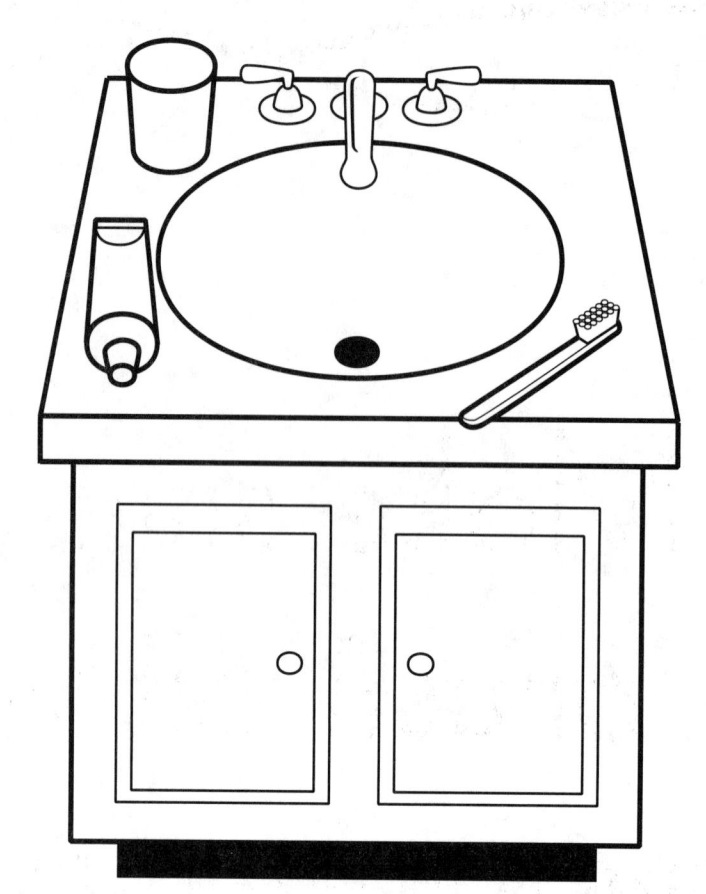

Brush your teeth when you wake up and see the morning sun.

page 1

Tooth Theme

Make sure you brush all your teeth—every single one.

page 2

Tooth Theme

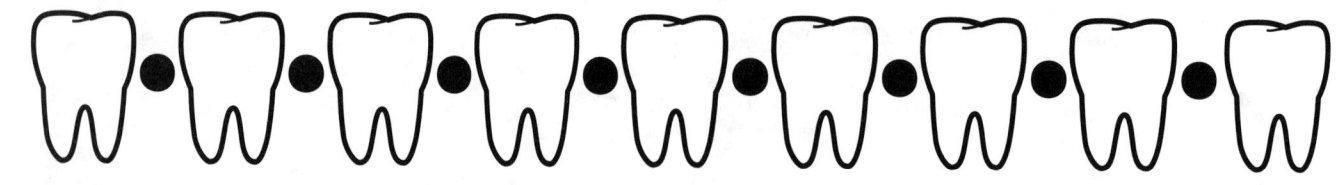

Having teeth with cavities is never any fun.

Tooth Theme

Eat healthful food at every meal and when the day is done

page 4

Tooth Theme

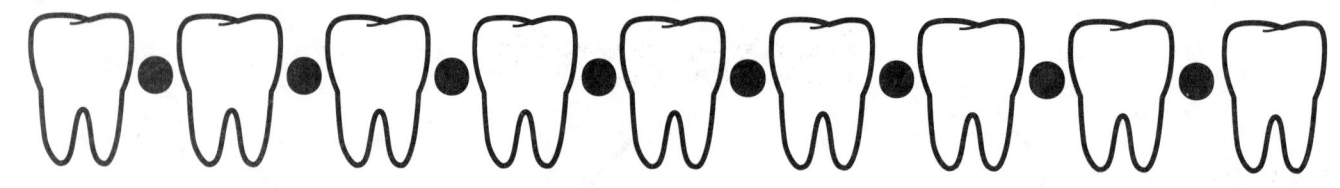

You will have healthy teeth and very happy gums.

page 5

Tooth Theme

Tooth Math

Objective
The students will add how many teeth they have as an entire class.

Materials
- popcorn kernels, beans, or some other small item to be used as a representation for teeth
- "How Many Teeth?" activity sheet. (This activity sheet has been formatted to be cut in half to save on paper.)

Procedure
1. Hand out the activity sheet and have the students make a good estimate for how many teeth they think are in their class as a whole. The students should record this estimate on their paper.
2. Have all the students, using their tongues, count how many teeth are in their mouth.
3. They should then count out that number of kernels, beans, (or whatever item is being used) onto their desks.
4. Ask the students the best way to now count all these "teeth." Guide them to putting the items into piles of tens. They will have to work as a class to combine their leftover items with other students' items to continue making tens.
5. Once these are all laid out, count up the number of teeth in the class.
6. Have the students figure out how far off their guess was.

Extension Ideas
- Make a whole-class graph of the students' favorite toothpaste flavor or favorite tooth-healthy snack.
- Graph how many teeth the students have lost.
- Solve story problems containing the topic of teeth.
- Work with money under the topic of coins left by the tooth fairy. For example, how much money will a child have if he loses three teeth and the tooth fairy leaves a dime for each tooth.
- Read the book *A Quarter From the Tooth Fairy (Hello Math Reader, Level 3)* by Caren Holtzman. This is a great lesson on the different combinations of coins that equal 25 cents.

©Teacher Created Materials, Inc.   383   #3823 Internet Activities Through the Year

Tooth Theme

Name:_____

How Many Teeth?

I think there are _____ teeth in my class.

There are really _____ teeth in my class.

I was off by _____ teeth.

Name:_____

How Many Teeth?

I think there are _____ teeth in my class.

There are really _____ teeth in my class.

I was off by _____ teeth.

Tooth Theme

Tooth Science

Objective
The students will observe the effects soda has on an egg shell and relate it to the effects on teeth.

Materials
- a hard-boiled egg
- a container with dark soda in it
- "Egg and Soda Prediction" activity sheet

Procedure
1. Show the students the egg and the container of dark soda.
2. Have the students fill out the "Egg and Soda Prediction" activity sheet for what they think will happen to the egg when it sits in the soda.
3. Let it sit for a few hours and then take the egg out and discuss what has happened to the shell.
4. Explain to the students that an egg shell is similar to a tooth and can absorb sugars and become discolored.
5. Have the students complete their activity sheet with what actually happened and whether their prediction was correct.

Extension Ideas
- Do some research on different animals and the types of teeth they have based on their diet.
- Discuss the different parts of a tooth: root, crown, enamel, dentin, pulp, cementum.
- Discuss tooth-healthy snacks.

Tooth Theme

Name: _____

Egg and Soda Prediction

Draw a picture of the egg before it is placed in the soda.

```
┌─────────────────────────────────────────────┐
│                                             │
│                                             │
│                                             │
│                                             │
│                                             │
└─────────────────────────────────────────────┘
```

What do you think the egg will look like after it sits in the soda?

_____

_____

_____

What does the egg actually look like once it is taken out of the soda?

_____

_____

_____

Why?

_____

_____

_____

Tooth Theme

Tooth Social Studies

Objective
The students will learn some history facts about George Washington and his false teeth.

Materials
- "George Washington's Teeth" activity sheet
- a book or story about George Washington, if available.

Procedure
1. Ask the children what they know about George Washington.
2. Read the story or have a discussion about who George Washington was.
3. Tell the students that George Washington eventually lost all of his teeth except for one. Many people believe that he had dentures made out of wood. This is a myth. George Washington's teeth were made from filed down elephant ivory, hippopotamus tusks, and cow teeth. These dentures had lots of sharp screws, hooks, and springs. Because of this, he had difficulty smiling.
4. Pass out the activity sheet and have the children complete it individually, or as a class.

Extension Ideas
- Learn about different types of animals and their teeth. Locate those animals' homes on maps.
- Have a dentist or dental hygienist come in and talk about what his/her job entails.

Tooth Theme

Name:_____

George Washington and His Teeth

1. George Washington was the _____ president of the United States.

2. He had lots of problems with his _____.

3. He lost all of his teeth except for _____.

4. His false teeth were made of (circle all of the correct answers):

   elephant ivory   wood

   stones   hippopotamus tusks

   cow teeth   dog teeth

Tooth Theme

Tooth Art

Objective
The students will design a label for their created brand of toothpaste.

Materials
- pictures or actual boxes from various brands of toothpaste
- cutouts of sturdy paper in either the rectangle shape of a toothpaste box or the shape of a toothpaste tube (You may want to make these shapes much larger than an actual toothpaste box/tube, especially for younger children.)
- paint, markers, crayons, colored pencils, etc.

Procedure
1. Show the students the various boxes/pictures of toothpaste packaging. Talk about how the companies want the packaging to be appealing so people will buy the product.
2. Either as a class or individually, the students can think up a name for their brand of toothpaste.
3. Have them design the packaging for the toothpaste using the mediums provided.

Extension Ideas
- Paint with toothbrushes.
- Make and decorate pouches out of felt, for storing lost teeth. If felt is not available, design/decorate envelopes for keeping lost teeth. The students may want to take them home to place teeth under their pillows for the tooth fairy.
- Design wings for the tooth fairy. This can be done with any variety of materials—water colors, glitter, left-over craft supplies (such as button, pieces of fabric, etc.).

Tooth Theme

Tooth Movement

Objective
The students will act out flossing a set of teeth.

Materials
- a large area allowing for movement
- jump ropes or long pieces of string to serve as "dental floss"

Procedure
1. Assign some of the students tooth names—incisors, molars, premolars, and canines.
2. Have them assemble themselves in the proper order of these teeth.
3. Have the remaining students pair up and each hold one end of a jump rope. These students can then act out flossing in between the teeth.

Extension Ideas
- Sung to the tune of "Here We Go 'Round the Mulberry Bush," have the students sing "This is the Way We Brush our Teeth" and act it out.
- Discuss how other things besides people have "teeth" such as combs. Using combs and wax paper, make "comb kazoos."

Turkey Theme

Related Web Sites

Encarta Encyclopedia
This is the Encarta entry for "turkey," with basic information about turkeys.

Thanksgiving on the Net
This site has information on the first Thanksgiving and Turkeys. Included are coloring pictures and crafts. Topics include The Story of Thanksgiving, America's Thanksgiving, The Thanksgiving Turkey, Thanksgiving Proclamation, National Theme of Mourning (focuses on injustices to Native Americans), Goodies, Thanksgiving Crafts, and Holiday Home Decorations.

Scholastic—The First Thanksgiving
This trusted source provides a wealth of information with interactive activities on the Pilgrims, the Mayflower, and life in Plymouth Plantation. Play the Cyber Challenge to become an expert.

All About Turkeys for Kids
This site has turkey information geared towards kids. It also includes activity sheets, clip art, teacher pages, and links to activities.

An American Thanksgiving
This page has history and games for kids and families. Download and color Thanksgiving pictures.

Craft Exchange
This page from KidsDomain.com has Thanksgiving crafts such as Thanksgiving geese, place mats, and pilgrim hats and clothes.

Birding.Com
This page has basic information on the wild turkey, including a sound clip of a turkey call.

The Natural History Museum's Bird Site
This site has information on birds, including anatomy and physiology and adaptations.

Sounds of the World's Animals
This page has a turkey call and translations of the call into other languages.

Meet the Wild Turkey
This page has information on the turkey population in Connecticut, but also includes general information on the wild turkey, as well as a word scramble activity.

Related Literature

Gracias, The Thanksgiving Turkey by Joy Cowley
A boy befriends the turkey his father has sent to be Thanksgiving dinner. How does chicken for Thanksgiving sound?

It's Thanksgiving by Jack Prelutsky
This is a collection of Thanksgiving poems.

Thanksgiving Theme by Gail Gibbons
This book has information on the history and traditions of the Thanksgiving holiday.

A Thanksgiving Turkey by Julian Scheer
This is the story of a boy and his grandfather hunting for a Thanksgiving turkey. When they find the turkey, can they bring themselves to shoot it?

Turkeys, Pilgrims, and Indian Corn: The Story of Thanksgiving Symbols by Edna Barth
These symbols of Thanksgiving are the focus of this nonfiction book.

Turkey Theme

Turkey Language Arts

Objective
The students will write a menu.

Materials
- the book *A Turkey for Thanksgiving* by Eve Bunting (If this book is not available, choose another book about a turkey trying to escape being served for Thanksgiving dinner.)
- "Menu" activity sheets or large pieces of paper to create a menu
- examples of menus or the **Bob's Big Boy Menu** Web site

Procedure
1. Read the chosen book or have a discussion on foods served at Thanksgiving dinner. Pose the dilemma to the students that they are turkeys who want to create a new Thanksgiving Menu which does not feature turkey. Allow them to be as creative as possible and include some of their favorite foods.
2. Share the examples of menus. Discuss the different categories of foods—starters/appetizers, entrees, desserts, etc.
3. Have the students work individually, in pairs, or in small groups to create their own menu for their turkey-free Thanksgiving meal. They may complete their menus on large pieces of construction paper folded in half. The fronts can be decorated with the name of the restaurant and illustrations. The inside should contain the written menu.
4. As an option, have the students complete the "Menu" activity sheet.

Extension Ideas
- As a variation on the above lesson, have the students create a menu, which features a wide variety of turkey dishes. For example, turkey pizza, turkey soup, etc.
- Have the students write a description of their best hiding place for a turkey in November!
- Have the students complete a writing in which they persuade people to eat foods other than turkey on Thanksgiving.
- Have a lesson on syllables, using "tur-key" as a starting point.
- Have a phonics lesson on the "–ur" sound.
- Have the students read animal sounds and match them to the correct animal.
- Read *The Turkey Girl: A Zuni Cinderella* by Penny Pollock and compare it to the classic story of Cinderella.

Turkey Theme

Name:_____

Menu

(Featuring a Turkey-Free Meal)

Appetizers

_____
_____
_____
_____

Main Course

_____
_____
_____
_____

Desserts

_____
_____
_____
_____

Turkey Theme

Turkey Math

Objective

The students will create patterns.

Materials

- feathers as manipulatives—these can either be colored feathers from a craft store, construction paper feathers, or crayons so the students may color their own feathers.
- long strips of paper (the size of sentence strips)

Procedure

1. Discuss color patterns with the students. Explain how to label patterns using letters.

2. Hand out the paper and the feathers (if available). Give the students patterns they need to create using their feathers (or to be drawn with crayons). For example, ask the students to create a pattern using the format A-B-A-B-A-B. Continue to give the students oral directions to complete the patterns.

3. Have the students create their own color patterns using the feathers to be glued on the paper strips, or using their crayons to draw feather shapes. They should label their pattern using letters.

Extension Ideas

- As an alternative to the above lesson, have the students complete feather story problems using the feathers as manipulatives. For example, "A turkey had five feathers, he lost two, how many does he have left?"

- Practice counting by twos. Use turkey feet as a guide. For example, "If there are three turkeys, how many turkey feet are there?"

- Use turkey tracks as a unit of measure. Distribute the "Turkey Track" activity sheet and have the students count how many steps a turkey takes to get across your desk?" The turkey tracks may be cut out in strips and taped together to form a turkey track measuring tape. Discuss with the students how it will be easier to do their measuring if they mark off every fifth or tenth track. Then they may count by fives or tens to do their measuring.

Turkey Theme

Turkey Tracks

Cut out the strips and tape them together to form a Turkey Track Measuring Tape.

Turkey Theme

Turkey Science

Objective
The students will identify the characteristics of birds for classification and identify facts about turkeys.

Materials
- a book or Web site which defines the characteristics of birds (The **Encarta Encyclopedia: Bird** Web site may be helpful.)
- specific information on the turkey (from a book such as *All About Turkeys* by Jim Arnosky or one of the following Web sites: **All About Turkeys for Kids** or **Meet the Turkey**)
- "Turkey Talk" activity sheet
- chalkboard or chart paper
- craft feathers or feathers cut from construction paper (one per student)

Procedure
1. Discuss the different ways animals can be classified: mammals, reptiles, insects, fish, birds, etc. Ask the students where the turkey belongs in the classifications.
2. Ask the students to attempt a definition of bird. Write their responses, whether they are correct or not, on chart paper or the on the chalkboard.
3. Share the book or Web site which classifies birds as warm-blooded animals with wings, feathers, a backbone, and a beak, which hatch from eggs. Go back over the responses of the students to determine if their statements were correct. For example, the students may have said, "All birds fly." Point out that not all birds can fly, such as the penguin and domesticated turkeys (wild turkeys can fly).
4. Hand out the "Turkey Talk" activity sheet. Have the students complete the answer to question #1. (Younger students may draw pictures or complete the activity sheet as a whole class on chart paper).
5. Have the students read the remaining questions (or the teacher read the questions) before sharing the information from the Web sites and in the book.
6. Pass out the "feathers." Direct the students to raise their feathers in the air every time they hear an answer to one of the questions from the activity sheet.
7. Read the book or share the information on turkeys. The students should raise their feathers in the air as they hear answers to the activity sheet questions. Allow time for the students to record the answers as they are found.

Extension Ideas
- Conduct a lesson on bird beaks and/or feet and how they are adapted to fit the bird's needs. The **Natural History Museum of Los Angeles: Birds** Web site may be helpful. (Click on the Adaptations link.) This lesson could also expand to include comparing turkey feet to other kinds of animals' feet, i.e. webbed feet, paws, etc.
- Read the book *All About Turkeys* by Jim Arnosky. Have the students write turkey facts on feather shapes and create a classroom turkey fact book.
- A baby turkey is called a poult. Use the **Zooish Baby Animal Names** Web site to learn more baby animal names.

Turkey Theme

Name _____

Turkey Talk

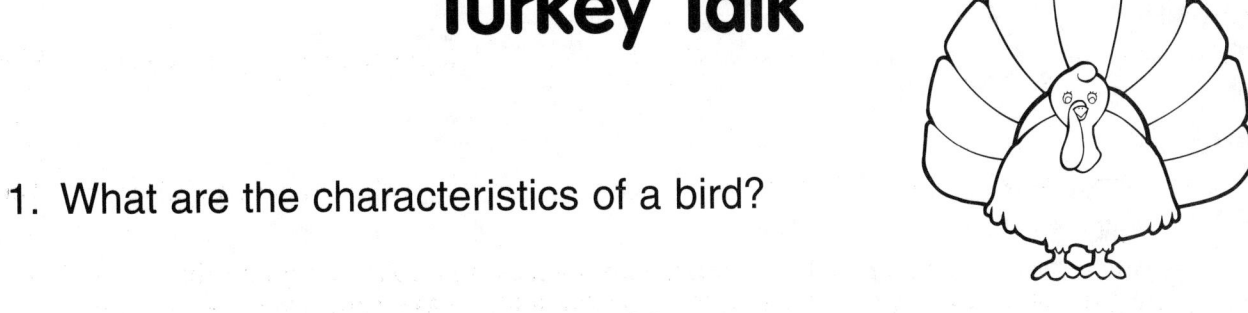

1. What are the characteristics of a bird?

   _____
   _____
   _____

2. Can a wild turkey fly?

   _____

3. What do turkeys like to eat?

   _____

4. What is a baby turkey called?

   _____

5. What is a female turkey called?

   _____

6. What is a male turkey called?

   _____

Turkey Theme

Turkey Social Studies

Objective

The students will participate in the voting process.

Materials

- books and Web sites containing information on Benjamin Franklin and the bald eagle as the national bird (Make sure one of the sources contains the information on Benjamin Franklin and his desire for the turkey to be the National Bird.)

    Web site suggestions:

    Encarta Encyclopedia: Turkey, The World of Benjamin Franklin, Ben Franklin—The Eagle and the Turkey, The Bald Eagle, or **An American Emblem.**

    Book suggestions:

    Meet Benjamin Franklin (Step Up Biographies) by Maggie Scarf or *A Picture Book of Benjamin Franklin* by David A. Adler.

- pieces of paper to serve as ballots

- a piece of chart paper or the chalkboard

Procedure

1. Ask the students to name the national bird. Show examples of the bald eagle and where it appears, as on coins.

2. Share the information from one of the web sites on the eagle and how Benjamin Franklin was opposed to the eagle as the national bird. He felt the turkey should be the national bird.

3. If desired, read a book or share Web site information on Benjamin Franklin and who he was.

4. Discuss the voting process and how Americans and government officials vote on issues.

5. Have the students cast votes on whether they would like the eagle to remain the national bird, or whether they agree with Benjamin Franklin and want the turkey to be the national bird.

6. Tally the votes!

Extension Ideas

- Conduct a lesson on the first Thanksgiving.

- Discuss the history of writing implements and how turkey quills were used in conjunction with ink. The **Encarta/msn—Writing Implements** Web site has useful information.

- Visit the **Sounds of the World's Animals** Web site for a lesson on how to say "gobble-gobble" in a variety of languages. Locate the various countries on a map or globe.

Turkey Theme

Turkey Art

Objective

The students will create turkeys.

Materials

- a wide variety of art materials—construction paper, craft feathers, paint, crayons, markers, etc.
- *A Plump and Perky Turkey* by Teresa Bateman, if available

Procedure

1. If the book is available, read the story to the students. (The story centers on a group of townspeople creating turkeys out of a variety of materials.)
2. Offer a wide variety of materials and allow the students to be as creative as possible in creating a turkey.
3. Younger students may need some suggestions such as tracing their hands to create a turkey, painting a turkey by dipping a feather into paint and using it like a paintbrush, or gluing feathers in place on a drawn turkey.
4. When the turkeys are complete, allow the students time to share how they created their turkey.

Extension Ideas

- As a variation on the above lesson, provide a greater variety of materials allowing the students to create a three-dimensional turkey.
- Have the students drop small amounts of food coloring onto coffee filters cut in half. Once these dry, they can serve as the fan of feathers for a turkey. Have the students glue the filter onto construction paper and complete the turkey body with crayons, markers, or colored pencils.

Turkey Theme

Turkey Movement

Objective

The students will move to music.

Materials

- a recording of "Turkey in the Straw"
- a large open area allowing for movement

Procedure

1. Play the recording of "Turkey in the Straw" and allow the students time to dance.

Extension Ideas

- Have a turkey trot. The students may design the race themselves, whether it's a relay, an individual race, or an obstacle course.

- Put the students in pairs and give them each a craft feather. Challenge the students to attempt to keep the feather afloat for as long as possible. They may blow on it or use an object to fan the feather.